Canons in Conflict

Canons in Conflict

NEGOTIATING TEXTS IN TRUE AND FALSE PROPHECY

James E. Brenneman

New York   Oxford
OXFORD UNIVERSITY PRESS
1997

Oxford University Press

Oxford   New York
Athens   Auckland   Bangkok   Bogota   Bombay   Buenos Aires
Calcutta   Cape Town   Dar es Salaam   Delhi   Florence   Hong Kong
Istanbul   Karachi   Kuala Lumpur   Madras   Madrid   Melbourne
Mexico City   Nairobi   Paris   Singapore   Taipei   Tokyo   Toronto

and associated companies in
Berlin   Ibadan

Copyright © 1997 by James E. Brenneman

Published by Oxford University Press, Inc.
198 Madison Avenue, New York, New York 10016

Oxford is a registered trademark of Oxford University Press

Library of Congress Cataloging-in-Publication Data
Brenneman, James E., 1954–
Canons in conflict : negotiating texts in true and false prophecy
/ James E. Brenneman.
    p.   cm.
Includes bibliographical references and index.
ISBN 0–19–510909–0
1. Bible—Canon.   2. Canon (Literature).   3. Prophecy.   4. Bible—
Prophecies.   5. Bible—Hermeneutics.   6. Bible—Evidences,
authority, etc.   I. Title.
BS465.B74   1997
220.1′2—dc20   96–27946

9 8 7 6 5 4 3 2 1

Printed in the United States of America
on acid-free paper

To Terri Jo Plank Brenneman

Preface

In 1994, Harold Bloom, in his popular book *The Western Canon,* declared war on enemy literary critics. He reduced them to a "School of Resentment" bent on overthrowing "*the* Canon" (emphasis added). Bloom is right to engage in battle against would-be destroyers of the Western canon. Lamentably, he does so using the sole weapon remaining to canon-makers on the bow of modernism's sinking frigate. Bloom's weapon of choice, what he calls the "irreducible autonomy of the aesthetic" in canonical literature, is fast becoming obsolete.

Bloom echoes a growing debate in biblical studies about *the* canon of sacred scripture. In secular literary circles, the war centers primarily on defining the limits of the literary canon and discussion about how those limits are determined. The battle in biblical circles is waged more narrowly over inherent meanings of texts already deemed canonical by their inclusion in the sacred canon. The battle fought among biblical critics can no longer be so sharply circumscribed. The conflicts over true and false prophecy, right and wrong exegesis, authentic and inauthentic hands, assured and mistaken historical reconstructions, correct and incorrect interpretation are, in the end, conflicts over power and authority. They are conflicts over canon.

In a postmodern contest for canonical shape or function, postmodern weapons are needed. Those who aim to win the battle for the canon must do so on new terms. Arguing for some aesthetic essence, some irreducible kernel *in the text* that asserts its own canonicity over the reader, may well provide the enemies of canonical authority of any and every kind the sword by which an elegy for the (biblical or Western) canon is assured. The key to winning the canonical war hinges on the question of ethics. Canon critics (literary and biblical) who prophesy that "eventually all this moralizing will subside" (so Bloom) or subsume all moralizing under an aesthetically pleasing "theologizing hermeneutic" (so James Sanders) have not yet fully appreciated the mortal blow the emergent postmodern age has wrought on all that is and was (pre-)modern.

This is a book about preserving and defending canons, sacred and otherwise. This endeavor does not grow out of a "politics of resentment," though it does contain a healthy suspicion of misappropriated power and coercive authority. Such suspicion need not and should not be grounds for canonical anarchy, though it might offer new ways of perceiving canons of authority, sacred or not. My aim is to synthesize work done in both literary and biblical studies in canonical criticism and canon formation. The foil for such a study falls on questions raised by conflicting biblical passages, in this case intentionally on the warring "plowshare" oracles of Isaiah 2:2–4 (Mic. 4:1–4) against Joel 4:9–12 (Eng. 3:9–12). Each prophet imagines a very different end to history. Can Joel and Isaiah both be true prophets when each blatantly defies the other in a rhetorical battle that has had real sociopolitical fallout over the years? To answer the question posed by these contradictory oracles is to raise other fundamental questions of meaning and authority: questions of canon.

One could try to defend the idea that reality has a basic unity and thus try to concoct arguments for how Joel and Isaiah (Micah) are both right in their own ways within this larger framework. Or one could defend, as I do, that Joel and Isaiah simply mirror the radical contradiction of reality. Judging from what we know about reality, empirically and otherwise, contradiction lies at the core of most epistemological descriptions, and rightly so. We know what we know only in contradiction, literally *in contra dictus,* in counterspeech. Indeed, such an inherently conflictual (relational) reality has epistemological and sociopolitical advantages, though fraught with danger. These dangers form the seedbed out of which decisions are made for and against prophets, poets, politicians, and their texts. So the responsible reader must necessarily choose between the imaginative construals offered by Joel and Isaiah (Micah). One cannot responsibly choose neither. Which prophet is true, which is false? The reader may want to know how I decide that question.

Explanatory constructs that have relied on the determinacy of texts, authorial intention, and other foundations are no longer adequate for deciding such canonical questions. Too much is at stake. Instead, arguing from a modified reader-response perspective, I defend the *principal* role of the interpretative community in meaning production. In contrast to an "autonomous aesthetic," I defend the canonical autonomy of the interpretative community, thus situating discussions of canon within the overall paradigm shift from modernity to postmodernity and all that such a maneuver implies for determining norms for living. Crises of authority in society, the academy, and elsewhere during the past three decades make the task more formidable but need not require a return to foundations toppled in the debate. The task does require responsible efforts to establish new canons of authority for a new world.

Inquiry into the "truth" or "falsehood" of biblical prophecy provides a manageable test case regarding canons and their formation. True and false prophecy arguments differ only in degree, not in kind, from canons in conflict more generally. A review of the standard story of research on true and false prophecy opens the way for an apology on the ethical force of canonical criticism as the best method for negotiating conflicting readings in the Bible.

As this manuscript goes to press, the trial of two suspects accused of the terrorist bombing of the Alfred P. Murrah Federal Building in Oklahoma City is anticipated by an anxious citizenry. We still mourn the loss of 168 fellow citizens to self-declared "patriots" whose imaginative construals of reality included apocalyptic scenarios of judgment on their enemies. Just three years to the day of the Oklahoma City bombing, we also faced off the Branch Davidians, whose prophet led them into a fiery apocalypse of another kind. Beyond our borders, the slaying of Israel's Prime Minister Yitzhak Rabin by a zealous interpreter of Torah remains a fresh wound in the lives of Jews worldwide. Christians in Northern Ireland and Rwanda terrorize each other in the name of the same God. The violent rhetoric of "true believers" has become violent action. The sad irony is that all of us read the same or nearly the same canon of sacred scripture. In this context, the politics of canon defended here cannot be ignored. Is it now time to declare once and for all that the authority of the Bible as canon derives primarily from its *performance* as a "democracy of words"? Is it now time to declare once and for all that the ethic of the biblical canon suggests a model of nonviolent praxis whose only weapon is persuasion? If so, such a model offers a hopeful step toward negotiating larger questions of canon and canon formation in all areas of life, including religion, literature, education, society, and culture.

Any book such as this is a communal exercise, and I wish to acknowledge that community of influence. If it is true, and I believe it is, that "the model of the believing community . . . is that of a pilgrim folk en route through the ambiguities of present reality to the threshold of truth" (Sanders), then I count it a privilege to have walked sometimes behind, but mostly alongside, a host of pilgrim folk on that quest to the threshold of truth.

I gratefully acknowledge all my teachers past and present who never claimed to have found truth but who never gave up searching after it. There are a few I must name. To Stanley Shenk and C. Norman Kraus, who guided me through some early and harried theological struggles to become a believing skeptic, I offer my thanks. I extend thanks to Millard Lind and Willard Swartley, who first critically walked me through the biblical "texts of terror" in a seminar devoted to violence and peace in sacred scripture. To Rolf Knierim, for his passion in the classroom and vigorous challenge to my budding canonical-critical inclinations, I am likewise grateful. To J. William Whedbee and Tammi Schneider, I extend appreciation for their careful reading and guidance during the writing of my dissertation, which is developed more completely here. I am especially indebted and grateful to James A. Sanders, whose writings, observations, and conversations have influenced me beyond measure. For his "constitutive support" and "prophetic critique," for his reading of reality and the Bible through the lenses of canonical criticism, I am deeply appreciative. I have donned those lenses with honor.

Another group of "pilgrim folk" I wish to acknowledge are my long-time friends John Wierick, Neal Nybo, and Stanley Green. Their friendship and prayers over the years kept me going through those all-too-regular bouts of despair when I could not see the light at the end of the research tunnel. I also offer thanks to Mark Nation, friend and walking bibliography, who continues to provide me with a reading list of immense pleasure, and to Stanley Hauerwas, who read early drafts and responded with much support and helpful critique. To Wonil Kim, a friend in opposition, who read this manuscript and battled against it in not a few places, I offer thanks for disagreeing.

To my family of origin, I give thanks for life itself, for my first Bible stories, for an inquisitive restlessness, and for early spiritual direction. To my Pasadena Mennonite Church family, I owe an immeasurable debt of gratitude for the year-long sabbatical that freed me to study and write. They are my primary canonical community, to whom I am pleased to be finally accountable.

To my editors at Oxford University Press, Cynthia Read and Paula Wald, and to my copyeditor, Danielle Alexander, I give thanks for seeing this book through the publication process. I have the comfort of having poured out my thoughts, "chaff and grain together knowing that a faithful hand [would] take and sift them, and then, with the breath of kindness, blow the rest away" (Eliot). Thank you for helping to blow away some of the chaff.

To Terri Plank Brenneman, psychologist, wife, and pilgrim lover, I give my greatest thanks for twenty-three years on the journey together and the many to come. I can't imagine life without her sacrifice and encouragement and a few "all-nighters" editing, proofreading, and typing parts of this manuscript. May she reap a whirlwind of blessings for her steadfast love, which, like Yahweh's, seems to endure forever. To her, I dedicate this book.

And finally, I admit with William Butler Yeats that for those people, including me, who may hope that "they are in their writings" even a bit "most wise," it is probably closer to the truth that they "own nothing but their blind, stupefied hearts." Though I am indebted to others for countless kindnesses at almost every page turn and places in between, any mistakes, errors in discernment, or failure in judgment are my own. "The LORD knows, but Israel shall know" (Josh. 22:22).

Pasadena, California   J. E. B.
February 1997

Contents

Abbreviations   xv

Introduction: Engaging the Battle   3

PART I   CONTRADICTION, COMMUNITY, AND CANON

1   Contradiction and Intertextuality   13
    Prophet against Prophet   13
    Contradiction: The Nature of Reality and
        Canonical Process   16
    Intertextuality and Canonical Hermeneutics   17
    Conclusions: Canon and Chaos   25

2   Reader Response and Community of Interpretation   28
    The Bible as Story   28
    Reader-Response Criticism   29
    The Community of Interpretation   38
    Conclusions: The Readers' Canon   43

3   The Fall and Rise of Canons   52
    The Fall of the Canon: The Problem of Canon   52
    The Rise of Canons and Their Canonical Communities   64
    Conclusions: God and Canon Power   74

PART II   NEGOTIATING READINGS IN TRUE AND
FALSE PROPHECY

4   True and False Prophecy in Canonical Criticism   83
    The Unfolding Story of Research in True and False Prophecy   84
    The Ethos of Mythos and the Politics of Canon   93
    Conclusions: Truth in Canon Politics   106

5   Swords into Plowshares into Swords   111
    Negotiating Readings: Rationale and Method   111
    Tradition-*Gestalt* and the Reader   114
    The Tradition-*Gestalt* of the Plowshare Passages   114
    Canon as Function: Diachronic Readings of the
        Plowshare Passages   118
    Canon as Context: Synchronic Reading of the Plowshare Passages   132
    Conclusions: Canon Hermeneutics   133

6   A Final Reading: Which Prophet? Whose Truth?   136
    Postscript: Instead of a Conclusion   137
    "Here I Stand": Under the Authority of the Community   140

Notes   149

Bibliography   197

Index   219

Abbreviations

The following abbreviations are used throughout this book.

AB	Anchor Bible
ABD	*Anchor Bible Dictionary,* ed. David Noel Freedman (New York: Doubleday, 1992)
BAR	*Biblical Archaeology Review*
B.C.E.	Before the Common Era
Bib	*Biblica*
BJRL	*Bulletin of the John Rylands University Library of Manchester*
BKAZ	Biblischer Kommentar Altes Testament
BTB	*Biblical Theology Bulletin*
BZAW	Beihefte zur ZAW
CBQ	*Catholic Biblical Quarterly*
C.E.	Common Era
CI	*Critical Inquiry*
CTM	*Concordia Theological Monthly*
DBSup	*Dictionnaire de la Bible, Supplement*
EvT	*Evangelische Theologie*
GTJ	*Grace Theological Journal*
GBS	Guides to Biblical Scholarship
HBT	*Horizons in Biblical Theology*
HSAT	Die Heilige Schrift des Alten Testaments
HSM	Harvard Semitic Monographs
HUCA	*Hebrew Union College Annual*
IBT	Interpreting Biblical Texts

ICC	International Critical Commentary
IDB	*Interpreter's Dictionary of the Bible,* ed. George A. Buttrick (Nashville: Abingdon, 1962)
IDBSup	*Interpreter's Dictionary of the Bible, Supplementary Volume*
IMS	Institute of Mennonite Studies
Int	*Interpretation*
JBL	*Journal of Biblical Literature*
JSOT	*Journal for the Study of the Old Testament*
JSOTSup	*Journal of the Society of the Old Testament—Supplement Series*
JSS	*Journal of Semitic Studies*
KAT	Kommentar zum Alten Testament
KHCAT	Kurzer Hand-Commentar zum Alten Testament
LXX	Septuagint
MLA	Modern Language Association
Ms	Manuscript
MT	Masoretic Text
NCBC	New Century Bible Commentary
NICOT	New International Commentary of the Old Testament
NIV	New International Version
NLH	*New Literary History*
NorTT	*Norsk teologisk Tidskrift*
NRSV	New Revised Standard Version
NT	*New Testament*
NTS	*New Testament Studies*
OBT	Overtures in Biblical Theology
OT	Old Testament
OTE	*Old Testament Essays*
OTL	Old Testament Library
OTS	*Oudtestamentische Studien*
OTWSA	Die Oudtestamentische Werkgemeenskap in Suid-Afrika
Pers	*Perspectives in Religious Studies*
PMLA	*Publications of the Modern Language Association of America*
RB	*Revue Biblique*
REB	Revised English Bible
SABH	Studies in American Biblical Hermeneutics
SAT	Die Schriften des Alten Testaments
SBL	Society of Biblical Literature
ST	*Studia Theologica*
STL	Studia Theologica Ludensia
S.v.	*sub verbo* ("under the word") used to refer to articles within dictionaries and encyclopedia

TBu	Theologische Buecherei
ThLZ	*Theologische Literaturzeitung*
TMs	typewritten manuscript
TToday	*Theology Today*
USQR	*Union Seminary Quarterly Review*
VT	*Vetus Testamentum*
VTSup	*Supplement to Vetus Testamentum*
WBC	Word Biblical Commentary
ZAW	*Zeitschrift für die alttestamentliche Wissenschaft*
ZBK	Zürcher Bibelkommentar
ZThK	*Zeitschrift für Theologie und Kirche*

Canons in Conflict

Introduction: Engaging the Battle

"Prepare war, stir up the warriors!" Apt words by the prophet Joel (4:9 [Eng. 3:9]) for an invitation to battle. With these words, I invite the reader to descend the linguistic ladder with me into a rhetorical war of sorts, down into society's formalized chaos, where all wars are finally won or lost. Joel's invitation to war, which is really Yahweh's invitation, provokes our most visceral fears about wars fought under the banner of God, especially if that god is not the god of our worship. Even more frightening, perhaps, is the mysterious, ambivalent, truth-bearing, deceit-laden power of words when broadcast by an all-too-human prophet claiming to speak for God.

In *Prophecy and Politics,* Grace Halsell traces the preachments of a dozen television evangelists spanning the last decade, all proclaiming that this generation will be the one in which the Battle of Armageddon will be fought, ushering in the messianic reign of Christ on a nuclear cloud.[1] The terror of being invited into the chaos of any war—however nobly fought, however just the cause, however theologically assured the outcome—lies in the very real possibility that the prophet uttering the invitation may be false. The prophet's words, after all, can mesmerize, beguile, rationalize, and finally lead us into a battle none of us has ever won or can ever hope to win: the battle with death itself. The fear is real.

Language is power and wields its own warring images. Plato, who stands in a long line of rhetoricians, frequently used metaphors of war to describe debates among his philosopher friends and enemies. He saw such war as civil, though by no means trivial. Is it any wonder that the sword is often closely allied to the spirit and word of God, a symbol of both physical extermination and psychic decision? The Middle Ages found this provocative imagery fodder for its crusading spirit. Vaclav Havel, the playwright, philosopher, and president of the Czech Republic, home of the "Velvet Revolution," also speaks of language and war in the same breath. He pictures "the word as arrow," "mightier than ten military divisions."[2] Images of war as rhetorical stratagem are aroused by the biblical tradition itself, which uses military metaphors to describe the efficacy of the spoken word, especially when spoken by God or one of God's prophets.[3]

The language of war has resurfaced with vigor in political debate across this country. Each side flings inflammatory missiles against the opponent in what has been described as a "cultural war" or a "war for the heart and soul of America." The battle is being fought rhetorically in town hall meetings and with legal arguments before the Supreme Court. Unfortunately, the battles of discourse brandishing real fire power have spilled over into our streets, classrooms, and neighborhoods, illustrating the truth of Nietzsche's aphorism, "Words are deeds." Indeed, actions do follow images. Already in the fifth century B.C.E., the Greek philosopher Democritus uttered the prophetic oracle that "word is a shadow of deed."

The imagery of war is especially appropriate to this study for more than its obvious masterful use by the biblical prophets Isaiah (Micah) and Joel. In general, this is a study of canon(s) in conflict wherein each prophet appeals to references of authority with dramatic sociopolitical repercussions. More specifically, the study of true and false prophecy within the biblical canon raises the same questions raging in our own lives about guiding norms. More specifically still, this is a study of one biblical tradition in mortal conflict with another. The struggle among conflicting canons, whether biblical, social, literary, educational, or otherwise, is nearly the same as the struggle of true prophets against false prophets, the difference being more in degree of specificity than in kind. In this work, I offer a model that I believe is relevant beyond the narrow concerns of biblical readers. The model has significance for readers across disciplines who seek clarity on the questions of authority, norms, and canons to organize claims to truth.

This book is divided in two parts. Part I is an attempt to synthesize work done in recent years by literary and biblical scholars on whose battlefields wars are still being fought over questions about the meaning of texts, the use of power in determining those meanings, who arbitrates between conflicting texts, and how texts are to be valued. The mutual problem of both fields of inquiry is authority as expressed by the term "canon."

Part I highlights the work of James A. Sanders as it relates to counterparts in literary criticism. Sanders's founding accomplishments in the arena of canon criticism are well known in biblical studies. For two decades since his programmatic work *Torah and Canon*,[4] a growing interest in the study of canon has simultaneously (re)surfaced in the literary field. The extent of the growing influence of Sanders's works on the question of canon in literary circles can best be detected in the comments of literary critic Jan Gorak:

> When he emphasizes the experience of exile at the heart of the Jewish canon, Sanders conforms to the pattern of modern experience reported by Kafka or a Raymond Williams. When he aligns canon with "the community's historic memory which is the locus of its identity," he suggests its consonance with the deep hope for continuity in the midst of change that secular authorities from Matthew Arnold to Frank Kermode have associated with culture. When Sanders interprets canon as transmitting the eschatological fears and hopes of a particular community, he speaks of Scripture in terms that Northrop Frye and Walter Benjamin use to discuss the apocalyptic potential of art and mythology. Sanders' emphasis on its diversity not only validates the biblical canon for a plural society, but renders it a potentially useful instrument for literary and cultural critics as well.[5]

Sanders readily acknowledges that he has been influenced by literary critics as well. Part I is an attempt to make explicit and connect what has been taking place independently in the two fields, especially in the realm of canon and canon formation.

Chapter 1 begins a guided descent into chaos. Jonathan Z. Smith describes social descent into chaos as "a ritual reversal of collective anomie," an exercise demanded of every society that hopes to re-create old images or recoin phrases from the past in order to form new construals of a new earth, a new society, a new person.[6] The very concept "canon" must undergo just this transformation. The reigning paradigm across disciplines appeals to inherent meanings in texts or kernels of truth in history or irreducible essences in reality as the foundation stones for building up truth claim upon truth claim to construct stable canons. Such foundations must be razed to expose the true nature of texts, history, and reality as nonfoundational.

The stability of canon that is essential to meaningful life must be articulated anew in the language of a postmodern sensibility. Such a confession comes as the necessary correlate to a scientific worldview that insists on quantum mechanics and relativity while acting as if positivistic universalizing truth claims govern. Modern science has not lived up to its own contradictory claims. In this chapter the canon construction site will be cleared, including the myth that *unmediated* truth claims of any would-be prophets, biblical or otherwise, are accessible.

The radical plurality of language and the radical ambiguity of history, which are defended in this first chapter, substantiate the fact that the play of difference—even contradiction—must become central to any epistemological description. Contradiction is not something to be avoided but is necessary and laudable. The counterpart to such a conflictual and contradictory reality is by definition relational and communitarian in ethos. Life is known in relationship, in twos and threes, never singularly. An old midrash on the first letter of the Torah, *b-* not *a-* (Gen. 1:1), suggested that God created the world beginning with two (*b-*) and not one (*a-*) for good reason. God alone is One (Deut. 6:4). The truth of this confession is more than mere theological cleverness; it is an ontological reality increasingly apparent to the postmodern mind. Given the intertextual nature of language, texts, people, and reality, including authoritative canons, the chapter closes by asking the question, Does not the biblical canon's inherent pluralism deconstruct its own canonicity?

Chapter 2 begins the journey back up and out of the labyrinth of radical pluralism, reorienting the reader by moving away from explanatory constructs that have relied on the determinacy of texts, authorial intention, and other foundations. Instead, I argue from a reader-response perspective for the *principal* role of the interpretative community in meaning production. A new image of the community's role *over* Scripture is constructed that borrows some older terms and juxtaposes them in a slightly new but consequential manner. The "canonical autonomy of the interpretative community" is thus defended. For Christians who fear a charge of heresy for usurping the biblical canon's authority *over* them, this confession merely describes what in truth is the way every believer lives in relationship to his and her scriptural canon. Claims of biblical authority have always been communal claims at heart. Acknowledgment of this truth need not undermine traditional views of the Bible's authority at all. However, such claims must be defended from a communitarian revelatory stance over against purely "objectivist" revelatory claims. Such commitments when fully described and defended are for the postmodern believer evangelical claims with missiological import. For other readers, they are hermeneutic and epistemological "facts."

Given the necessity of community-determined meanings in the quest for claims to truth and canon formation, chapter 3 opens with a salvo. The interpretative community must account for its context and why it reads as it does. This chapter situates discussions of canon within the overall paradigm shift from modernity to postmodernity and addresses all that such a maneuver implies for determining norms for living.

To describe the fall of a singular canon, biblical and otherwise, evokes a crisis. We must struggle to reclaim canonical authority in this potentially anarchic situation. The age-old question of what is meant by canonical authority is asked and answered anew, taking into account the advantages offered by a pluralistic frame of reference. In this chapter, I will argue that a chastened, monotheizing worldview, mirrored in the centuries-long development of the biblical canon itself, offers the best paradigm for living in the postmodern age. That the biblical canon deconstructs its own canonicity is key to its ongoing survival and offers a pragmatic sociopolitical model for life.

Although the canon is its own self-correcting apparatus, as a mirror of the One God, it also holds the potential for endorsing exclusive totalitarian claims to power.

Effort is given, then, to reversing the standard account of canon formation as being simply the product of such a totalitarian masculine majority. This chapter suggests a different view of canon: as the power of the powerless. Some literary critics include in literary canons works that stand opposed to power, indeed, whose literary force negates power criteria. Some biblical critics show the sheer vulnerability of the believing community during those periods of intense canonical formation of Scripture. These literary and biblical views are merged to substantiate the canon of the powerless. Tracing the reasons for the emergence of Israel's Torah (and Prophets) in exile, I argue that the canon of Scripture as a book of words became the paradigm for judging all forms of coercive power usually associated with canon formation. Indeed, its very form and function as canon dominate its own violent content. The battlefield of differences within the biblical canon demonstrates in form and function a nonlethal, noncoercive communitarian negotiating stance in which the only weapon is word against word, and the only battle, persuasion.

Part II restrains the discussion of conflicting canons and their canon-making communities to the question of true and false prophecy in Scripture. The proposals of part I are tested more narrowly by engaging the conflict of Isaiah and Joel, two so-called true prophets by virtue of their canonicity who nevertheless construct opposite visions of how the "day of Yahweh" will truly come about.

Specifically, chapter 4 recounts the "standard story" of the search for criteria when trying to decide the question of "truth" and "falsehood" in prophecy. The standard account drags the reader back down toward the abyss of interpretative chaos, not up and out. In part, the criteria so often proposed do not take into account the reader's own context. This is as true for deciding the question of true and false prophecy as it is for determining canonical authority in the first place. An alternative proposal is offered that correlates the text with its reader in its many "original" and subsequent contexts. Reliance on content alone to provide the criteria for distinguishing a true prophet from a false one must give way to clarifying how a text functions in its context, whatever its content. As we argue that a text's content is made relative to its use, the debate about truth and falsehood must shift to account for the ethical force of a story (ethos) *over* its content as story (mythos). What follows, finally, is an apology for a politics of canon that proposes that the biblical canon's authority derives from its *performance* as a "democracy of words" (arguments). Specific political gains are spelled out to account for why a nonviolent ethic of canon is not only necessary but also epistemologically advantageous. These very real political gains are derived from negotiating texts in true and false prophecy on the question of violence in biblical theology (Isaiah versus Joel). This method precisely demonstrates how the biblical canon becomes for its readers a model for nonviolent praxis. The form and function of conflicting prophetic utterances as juxtaposed in the sacred canon form a self-correcting mechanism that finally disciplines Scripture's own violent content. Such a paradigm in a day of terrorist threats, suicide bombings, and ethnic cleansing in the name of whatever god cannot be gainsaid.

Chapter 5 provides a specific test case for the study of conflicting prophetic utterances by using the method of canonical criticism, now reread to include the politics of canon. What makes a prophet true or false? Can a true prophet speak lies or a false prophet the truth? Were prophets ever completely assured of their own claims? Or do their very efforts at persuasion and declarations of legitimacy using all the tools available to them suggest that they were less sure of themselves than it at first appears? Can true or false prophets, regardless of their title, motivation, or call, be assured of permanent status, no matter what the historical hour in which they are read? That is, might a true canonical prophet be false today?

The plowshare passages provide provocative images useful to peacemakers and warmongers alike. Either party in the very real political context might appeal to one or the other version of the plowshare passages at any given time. Each appeal might rightly claim biblical precedent, defending itself with all the requisite authority of the Bible as canon. Isaiah's vision of universal peace (Isa. 2:2–4/Mic. 4:1–4) contradicts Joel's deliberate reworking of the vision to inspire universal war (Joel 4:9–12 [Eng. 3:9–12]). In this chapter, both visions are read across time and space (diachronically), accounting for the ethical performance of each reading in its historical context. Then both accounts are read in literary context (synchronically), their juxtaposition within the canon providing the reader some interpretative sight not apparent in reading the plowshare passages through time and space. In both reading experiences (diachronic and synchronic), the reader is challenged, as were all previous readers, to advocate for one prophet against another. This legacy of conviction on the part of readers within and beyond the boundaries of canon is modeled on the biblical canon itself. I argue that such a naming of one prophet "false" and the other "true" is required not only by biblical precedent but also by responsible politics, religious or otherwise. The ethical demand of the canon as life-paradigm requires nothing less than declaring one prophet true and the other false, even as one is compelled to choose under the watchful eye of an equally canonical, and often radically opposing, reading. At the close of this millennium, the question that must be asked and answered is this: Can it be canonically sustained that one of the two construals of history's denouement, whether Joel's or Isaiah's, must now be deemed false prophecy, the other true? If actions follow images, and they do, then the answer to that question is more than rhetorical. It holds the spiritual and political power of becoming a self-fulfilling prophecy for judgment or blessing.

Chapter 6 serves as much as a postscript as a conclusion. As a conclusion, it provides the reader with a review of the major deductions and inferences of this study. The book as a whole attempts to model the art of persuasion so necessary in reaching ethically sound exegetical and interpretative judgments regarding true and false claims made within Scripture itself. If the reader can agree with the testimony of each chapter, it is hoped that the reader might be persuaded by the cumulative force of the story told. Further, I would hope the reader would be convinced that the explanatory model suggested here is the better one among alternative others.

As a postscript, chapter 6 provides a personal and explicit account of my assumptions. If the reader cannot wait to know the outcome of my argument, he or she may wish to jump now to the end of the narrative to better understand all that precedes. Of course, a good story is made better by the slow unfolding of plot. Here, too, the plot is meant to thicken. Arguably, you, the reader, will have to develop your own postscript in accordance with the interpretative community of which you are knowingly or unadmittedly a part. For it is such an interpretative community that finally provides the only appropriate context for determining the truth or falsehood of the prophetic plowshare passages and the persuasive arguments of this study.

I offer here one testable response to the otherness of reading the same data in similar or very different contexts. Like Plato, I too hope to win the rhetorical battle against the alternatives. Whether that indeed finally happens remains an open question. In the meantime, Isaiah's words of invitation remind all of us of the one who alone will finally determine the truth or falsehood in the rhetorical battle about to be waged (2:3–4a):

> "Come, let us go up to the mountain of the LORD . . .
> that he may teach us his ways and that we may
>   walk in his paths."
> For out of Zion shall go forth Torah,
>   and the Word of the LORD from Jerusalem.
> He shall judge between the nations,
>   and shall arbitrate for many peoples.

I

CONTRADICTION, COMMUNITY, AND CANON

ONE

Contradiction and Intertextuality

Prophet against Prophet

They shall beat their swords into plowshares and their spears into pruning hooks.
                                                                    —Isaiah 2:4/Micah 4:3

Beat your plowshares into swords and your pruning hooks into spears.
                                                                    —Joel 4:10 (Eng. 3:10)

The Bible contradicts itself. This has become a truism in academic circles, aptly described by Daniel Boyarin as "now practically a commonplace that the narrative of the Torah is characterized by an extraordinarily high degree of gapping, indeterminacy, repetition and self-contradiction."[1] This is more elaborately expressed in the words of James Sanders:

> The fact is that the Bible contains multiple voices, and not only in passages recording differences between disagreeing colleagues (so-called true and false prophets), but between the priestly and the prophetic, between Wisdom and tradition, between the orthodox and the questioning voices of prophets such as Jeremiah in his confessions, between Job and his friends who represented aspects of orthodoxy, between Qohelet and the Torah, between Jonah and Nahum . . . , among varied voices within a book like Isaiah, between Paul and James, and even among the Gospels with their varying views of what God was doing in Christ. And these are only a few of the intrabiblical dialogues one might mention. One needs also to recognize the measure of pluralism in the doublets and triplets in the Bible, the same thing told in quite different ways, making different even *contradicting* points.[2] (emphasis added)

Acknowledging the Bible's "self-contradictions" still sends discomfort through the ranks of many who read the Bible as Scripture. Since the days of

13

Tatian's *Diatessaron,* attempts have been made to impose a unity upon texts that appear at face value to contradict each other.[3] This fondness for smoothing out contradictory texts lies at the doorstep of fundamentalists of both religious and secular mettle. A religious fundamentalist when reading tries hard to harmonize the tensions within Scripture by obliterating from consciousness the very hermeneutics at work that demand such harmony. Those who assume but do not acknowledge their personal role in claiming Scripture's seamless unity can claim unmediated revelation to what seems obviously contradictory to many other readers. The advantage to such readers is that it relieves them from personal responsibility to negotiate the real and bitter conflicts present all the time in every context, whatever one's commitment to the Bible's inspirational status. In a different way, but one only slightly less reductive, fundamentalist readers of secular and religious persuasion steeped in the last two hundred years of historical critical inquiry have sought to make sense of contradictions and textual fissures by positing multiple hands in any and every disjuncture.[4] They also find real and psychic relief by declaring one hand (usually the earliest) "authentic," the other "inauthentic." The supposed advantage is that such readers will not appear obscurantist because they recognize the obvious diversity in Scripture. At the same time, they discount the canonical authority of the side of the contradiction deemed "inauthentic" by imposing upon the debate their own canons of historical critical inquiry. The difficulty as I see it is not so much that they claim one hand less authentic than another on historical grounds, but that they too often fail to acknowledge their own communal standards of orthodoxy in their claim to be "objective." In fact, they are no less communally bound than other readers. All such fundamentalist readings, whether secular or religious, constitute a loss for hermeneutics. One sees authority only in revelatory seamless unity; the other sees authority as best determined by historical origins.

The Bible's contradictions create a real problem because they strike at the core of definitions of truth and falsehood. Since for many the Bible is sacred Scripture, the "guide for faith and practice," the contradictory "words of God" pose very real and practical dilemmas for people striving to conform to scriptural guidelines.

Prophetic literature gives testimony to a wide range of claims and counterclaims among the various biblical prophets that leaves the reader bewildered about just what is true or false. The "plowshares" passages of Joel and Isaiah (Micah), the focus of a grueling debate about God's intentions for the end of history, are only one case in point. Deciding between the two is no trivial pursuit. In his study of true and false prophecy, Gerald Sheppard concludes that the Bible itself presents the discrimination between true and false prophecy as a matter of life and death. Any claim of divine revelation within Judaism and Christianity hinges on this discernment.[5] There is little difficulty

passing judgment on clear-cut cases of prophetic conflict in which the antago-
nist is sufficiently labeled as "false";[6] the sociopolitical contexts may have
differed but must be reconstructed; and the literary context makes clear who
the true and false prophets are.[7] However, when two canonical prophets face
off in their juxtaposition within the sacred canon, critical judgment is far more
grave. We are left with the uncomfortable dilemma of deciding which
prophet to heed.

Two hundred years of historical critical research have not alleviated the
onerous task of adjudicating conflicting prophetic voices. In fact, it was
historical criticism's methodological roots in the Reformation claim of *sola
scriptura* that gave rise to the Christian version of the problem posed by inner-
biblical conflict. Prior to this, the Church's dogma judged between contradictory interpretations. Various other arbiters would continue to emerge over
time. For example, Erasmus insisted on the discernment of reason. Luther
claimed Christ-centeredness to be the referee. Early Anabaptists extended
Luther's criterion by emphasizing the role of the Holy Spirit vis-à-vis community discernment. Calvin resorted to a Protestant version of the earlier dog-
matic approaches, claiming God spoke directly in Scripture.[8] And so it went.
While the newly articulated doctrine of *sola scriptura* may have liberated Bible
readers from the dogma of the Roman Church, it unleashed a fury of interpretative conflict that in time exposed the very nature of the Bible as a reservoir of interpretative battles.

Historical critical scholars have focused almost exclusively on the genetic
relationships between and behind the traditions in Joel and Isaiah (Micah) in
their study of the conflicting "plowshares" passages. Determining the origins
and subsequent history of the traditions of these texts was apparently, in their
minds, sufficient. However, the various assured results of the historical critics
are at least as conflicting and contradictory as the texts studied. The hermeneutical dilemma of true and false prophecy has only been heightened by
the conflicting conclusions drawn by these historical critical endeavors. In
1970, Brevard Childs finally declared the whole enterprise in crisis since the
impasse had by then become one of text *and* interpretation.[9] The conclusion
sticks.

The emergent call to canonical criticism by James Sanders[10] is one attempt
to remedy the atomizing approaches of the past and suggests a way out of the
present dilemma. As a discipline, it is hermeneutical in thrust and seeks to
account for both the historical critical life of a text/tradition *and* the interpretative journey of a text/tradition all along its route from sacred story to
sacred text.[11] The canonical critical method (as method) does not stop at the
covers of the biblical canon but extends into the life of the believing communities throughout history. In this sense, it is as much a hermeneutic stance as it
is a biblical discipline among other disciplines.[12] The value of canonical criti-

cism, as both method and hermeneutic stance, extends beyond questions of the Bible as canon into other disciplines struggling with questions of authority. For example, a history of traditions not only is important for its own sake but also serves the canonical critical quest by disclosing the hermeneutical shifts that occur as the traditions achieve authoritative, that is, canonical, status. Indeed, *the* focal points for determining *how* the biblical writers understood their own ambiguous contexts and therefore *how* we might better interpret our realities in light of Scripture are the varying perspectives that emerge from comparing conflicting biblical texts or their versions.[13] At the core of the canonical critical approach is a hermeneutic dependent on the acceptance of contradiction as an aid to understanding.

Contradiction: The Nature of Reality and Canonical Process

If the Bible contradicts itself, it does so because the real world out of which it comes is itself contradictory. Sentiment regarding the nature of reality seems to be converging on the contradictory nature of life as we live it. The radical plurality in language, the essential ambiguity of history, antifoundationalist trends in epistemology, the new physics of relativity and chaos, psychologies of decentered egos, and rampant cultural pluralism guarantee contradiction as a fact of life for all but the most naive. Even then, ordinary folks have always experienced life's contradictions every time they come face to face with rage, jealousy, lying, or evil in a loved one.[14]

To intensify matters, the new development from book culture to screen culture portends a revolution in communication unprecedented in history.[15] The screen culture of the common man and woman stands to influence, if not redefine, beliefs in inspiration and authority. Such influence is unparalleled since the printing-press-driven Reformation helped reduce the impact of the long-held dual authority of *magesterium* and *scriptura* to *sola scriptura*. Today the debate is not about one or two authority centers but about many. This evident crisis of authorities simply mirrors today's reality.

The world as it has been understood throughout history is finding itself being deconstructed, literally and literarily.[16] Traditional historical critical studies of the Bible merely reflect the chaotic pluralism of reality.[17] Little wonder that a new critical discipline would emerge that makes virtue out of necessity. At the same time, this new discipline *constructs* a unifying paradigm to counter the psychological and sociopolitical hazards endemic to such a contradictory reality. This discipline is canonical criticism; its method, the canonical process; its paradigm, the canon.

Although the discipline of canonical criticism was first articulated by James Sanders in *Torah and Canon* (1972), a different version was developed by

Brevard Childs in his *Introduction to the Old Testament as Scripture* (1979). The works of Sanders and Childs dawned upon what is increasingly recognized as the horizon of postmodernity. A second horizon upon which canonical criticism appeared was the revolution in text criticism brought about by the discovery of the Dead Sea scrolls at Qumran.[18]

As the scrolls of the Judean desert were studied, the long-held view of canon as a stable corpus gave way to pluriform views of canon(s). Before these discoveries, canon studies focused on the limits of content, the number and order of books making up canonical Scripture, and when the canon gained formal closure. The scrolls of Qumran provided for the first time in one place the whole variety of textual traditions that paralleled the known textual arbiters (e.g., LXX and MT). All this frustrated the assured results of those seeking to reconstruct autograph texts and also undermined the confidence of claims for a definitive shape of *the* canon. After Qumran, the study of canon as shape (*norma normata*) gave way to the study of canon as function (*norma normans*).[19] The study of lists of books gave way to the study of the measure of authority that an ancient community exercised in the context of its use of a tradition. The "what" of canon formation gave way to the "how." Externally, the adaptability of canons of tradition to the needs of differing or competing communities became exposed. Sanders suggested that the very "adaptability of canonical literature may be found in its internal contradictions."[20]

Far from lamenting such intrabiblical pluralism, Sanders celebrates it as primary to the Bible's continuing value among believing communities. With or without Qumran, the phenomenon and value of textual heterogeneity were in full flower among other disciplines as well, not least of which was literary criticism. Description by certain literary critics of the textual interplay of differences as being key to one's understanding of a text now provides a gateway for interdisciplinary dialogue with canonical studies. The description of such textual interplay within this larger interdisciplinary dialogue follows.

Intertextuality and Canonical Hermeneutics

The term *intertextuality*[21] refers to textual language used to characterize important relationships between elements that contribute to acts of knowing (epistemology) and understanding (hermeneutics) as they relate to the use of language (linguistics). An uneasy relationship exists between language, knowledge, and reality. This interplay has been designated the "linguistic turn."[22] There are five basic relationships described by the term *intertextuality*: reality itself, syntax, (con)text, process, and reader.[23]

Intertextuality and Reality

At the broadest level, intertextuality describes in textual language the radical ambiguity of reality in all its contradictions. Perhaps no other literary critic has so graphically connected his literary discoveries to life as we experience it than René Girard. Girard has risen to the rank of first thinker in literary and anthropological disciplines alike. His initial field of inquiry, literature, led him to propose a whole explanatory system of reality. Girard concluded from his reading of literature that social order depends upon a system of differences. These differences are constrained via myth (literature) and ritual (the sacrificial system) and other forms of social cohesion. Graphically, the cohesion originated in a primal lynch mob, what has been termed the mimetic scapegoat mechanism. Reality as we know it from society and religion was constructed in the aftermath of the inevitable (and for Girard, violent) struggle between rival others in what he terms the "mimetic crisis." The crisis was resolved through a communally sanctioned and ever more sacralized scapegoat mechanism bridging the divide between protohuman and human cultures. Blatant conflict at the dawn of human culture gave way to a "poetics of violence" seeking resolution. Thus, intertextuality as reality is potentially, if not always and if not overcome, violent.[24] Conflicts between Joel and Isaiah (Micah) not only replicate conflictual reality textually and socially, but also articulate two ways of resolving the conflict that is as old as time itself. We will return to this dilemma.

More positively, intertextuality also describes through language and texts what we all know to be true about reality. Reality is fundamentally relational. From subatomic quarks to human interaction, reality is interactive and dynamic, not isolated and static. Any attempts to discover an "onion per se" by pulling off peel by peel by peel is futile. Reality is a system of parts capable of coherence only by relating its many and conflicting peelings. So any "prologomenal search for 'scratch'" will prove fruitless.[25] Julia Kristeva, mother of the current use of the term *intertextuality,* has argued that reality is known and understood only in the interrelationships of its parts (i.e., in its intertextuality) and in the interplay of all our constructed and conflictual metatexts.[26]

Intertextuality and Syntax

A second level of intertextuality refers more particularly to the interplay of words in a sentence, even letters and sounds within words.[27] Although this is not the place, nor do I claim the expertise, to untangle the influence of Ludwig Wittgenstein, Martin Heidegger, and Ferdinand de Saussure on questions of language, knowledge, and reality, with the help of David Tracey,

I hope to unravel a bit of Saussure's influence as it relates to the topic of intertextuality.[28]

One additional cue to my interest in Saussure must first be articulated. Heidegger ("language as the house of Being") and Wittgenstein (forms of life and language games) served as two great masters in the study of language, knowledge, and reality. Their contributions focused largely on diachronic analyses of language as language used historically. Saussure introduced a synchronic analysis of language that articulated a theory of language as system. Further, he formed the metatextual horizon (canon as paradigm) against which the poststructuralists, especially Derrida (under Heidegger's influence), challenge him by radicalizing his contributions. My primary aim here is to note Derrida's contribution to the discussion of intertextuality and syntax. But one must go through Saussure to get to Derrida.

Ferdinand de Saussure was interested in language as a system. To be sure, his system was not to be reduced to positivistic clarity: "In language [i.e., the linguistic system] there are only differences."[29] For him, language was not a thing, an object to be studied. Rather, language was an articulated system of differences.[30] Pivotal to my use of his ideas in this discussion is Saussure's insistence that linguistic meanings are unavoidably a matter of social convention. The relation between a word and a concept or a thing (between signifier and signified in the jargon of structuralism) is *in principle* arbitrary.[31]

An indicator of Saussure's influence is that a variety of schools developed that featured the systems approach, which countered the notion of inherent difference in Saussure's famous *logoumenon:* "In a linguistic *system,* there are only differences" (emphasis added). Structuralism, semiotics, and formalism all develop Saussure's systemic approach.

Another quite influential tradition emerged that placed extreme importance on the second part of Saussure's observation: "In a linguistic system, there are *only differences*" (emphasis added). Jacques Derrida, the French philosopher, radicalized Saussure's claims by describing the interplay of language, knowledge, and reality in such a way as to earn the now-formalized description *deconstruction*.

Saussure himself had irrefutably shown that a word like *tree* means "tree" only by being *different* from *she* or *be* or *thee* (in sound) or *free* or *three* (in letter combinations). *Tree* means "tree" by *not* being other like-sounding or similarly spelled words such as *free, three, be, thee,* or *she.* A word only has meaning in its difference from other words; *in contra dictus.* Derrida exploited this observation against Saussure's hoped-for *system* of differences.

Derrida's response to Saussure suggests two important observations pertinent to our current discussion. First, like Saussure, Derrida insists that at the most basic level of language meaning is derived in the *nexus between* two words, in their contradistinction, not in the words themselves. For many in the linguistic guild, this intertextual "onion per se" shows that language is, by nature, *nonreferential*. For Bible readers, this means that at a most fundamental level we must insist on the character of *contra dictus* in and between every biblical word and sentence. In the parlance of canonical criticism, all texts are "multivalent." Further, canonical criticism recognizes that the concept of intertextuality is constitutive of (not merely descriptive of) meaning. The search for inherent meanings in words, ideas, concepts, and sentences is futile. Meaning is derived only *in contra dictus,* in interrelating letters, sounds, words, sentences, paragraphs, or books to each other. Textual meaning, like life itself, is wholly and irreducibly relational (and potentially conflictual). Stated canonically, meaning is derived from the whole of the parts in their intertextuality.

If Derrida radicalizes Saussure's notions of the intertextual differences at the level of syntax, he extends this challenge to Saussure's systemic view of language. In doing so, he offers critical nuance to the discussion of intertextuality and context to which we now turn.

Intertextuality and (Con)text

A third level of intertextuality focuses on synchronic readings of texts in their literary contexts. A synchronic reading concentrates on the interplay between two or more texts or traditions now in juxtaposition by nature of their being in the same work. For example, different sources in the same book or disparate writings in the same canon will take on new and expanded meaning by nature of their new alignment with each other. The stories of Jesus of Nazareth in the New Testament remain less meaningful—perhaps meaningless—without their juxtaposition in a larger context that includes the Old Testament stories. This is particularly true when Jesus stories are read in terms of promise and fulfillment. The formal shape of the New Testament itself, including its very designation as "new," is derived *in contra dictus* to the shape of the older literary form now designated by the generic term "Old" Testament. The focus for such contextual readings tarries on the final form of the text, with minimal attention to the historical contexts that gave rise to the various parts of the whole.

Both Sanders and Childs agree with the new literary critics on this one point: There is a "thisness" to the whole text that ably provides a meaning-producing field quite apart from original intention or historical critical discovery. Such an emphasis does offer helpful correctives to the atomization of texts rampant in the historical critical enterprise. The more holistic views in the new critics' appreciation of texts in context promised relief from the endless ravages of historical-critical searches for original, "authentic" sources and meanings. But this hoped-for relief is only temporary. New questions of equally difficult resolution emerge in the face of the intertextual nature of conflicting contexts, wholes, systems, canons.[32] The ante has been upped. A brief look at Saussure as challenged by Derrida gives shape to the new difficulties.

Even though Saussure had rightfully argued for the arbitrariness of the relationships between words and concepts or things, he remained a believer that self-conscious meaning would emerge in the synchronic unity of these parts. He stayed a "Structuralist" even while providing the sword for the Deconstructionist. In short, Saussure hoped that by focusing on the synchrony of the language *system,* with minimal attention given to historical contexts, the system itself would provide a ground of self-present meaning found in the system, in its structure, or in the unitary sign.[33]

In his challenge to Saussure, Derrida elevated the concept of differential relations to the level of systems as well. He insisted that there is no self-referential system of meaning that is not arbitrary. That is, even the best synchronic systems describing the interplay of reality, knowledge, and language must yield to "self-destructing antisystems, antihierarchies, and anti-identities."[34] Such a deconstructive aim was especially focused on Saussure's unitary sign but could similarly apply to any number of unitary systems, including Claude Lévi-Strauss's unitary structure,[35] Northrop Frye's "self-contained literary universe,"[36] the canonical critic's "canon-as-paradigm," or, tellingly, Derrida's own largely unacknowledged center, his "abyss."[37] The promise of reality's integrity held out by synchronic readings must confront the issue of its own systemic intertextuality.

If the multivalent character of reality, language, and knowledge is not yet obvious to the reader, there is another level pressing for description, namely, intertextuality as process.

Intertextuality and Process

The fourth level of intertextuality highlights the function or interplay of an older text or tradition cited, alluded to, or echoed within its new textual setting. Insofar as our focus is on the *history* of interactions between texts, that is, the history of *how* language is *used* (functions) in time-bound contexts, then Wittgenstein, Schleiermacher, Heidegger, and Gadamer form a "linguistic horizon" (which includes ontology and epistemology) upon which intertextuality as process looms. Daniel Boyarin in reading midrash summarizes intertextuality as process as "the way history, understood as cultural and ideological change and conflict, records itself within textuality."[38]

For example, sometimes the Bible explicitly alludes to earlier texts, such as in the book of Numbers (21:14): "Therefore it says in the book of the Wars of the Lord 'and Waheb in Sufa and the rivers of Arnon.'" More often, biblical citations of earlier works are less explicit. In such instances, noticeable gaps, repetitions, and obvious contradictions provide the data for historical critics to use to posit multiple hands or differing sources. The canonical critical reader, by contrast, might just as easily see one hand capturing the markers of earlier traditions or signifying systems in a "compressed history." What becomes of interest, then, is not the formal identification of a particular genre or structure or source but rather how the earlier and often unacknowledged tradition or echo of a tradition is being appropriated. In many cases, it is these very fissures or contradictions within the text that reveal the conflictual dynamics that led to the text as it is currently read. The movement from a previous system of signification to a new one is what is called here intertextuality as process.

Intertextuality as process in biblical studies—with its underlying developments in the fields of philosophy, epistemology, and linguistics—traces its roots to a much less self-conscious era. Michael Fishbane has shown how, in the scribal activity apparent within the Bible itself, the process of earlier traditions taken up by later traditions began very early in ancient Israel. Later communities were inclined to incorporate legal materials into their histories and oracles and to use them for other exegetical purposes.[39] Fishbane describes this intertextual phenomenon as "inner-biblical exegesis":

> One may say that the entire corpus of Scripture remains open to these invasive procedures and strategic reworkings up to the close of the canon in the early rabbinic period, and so the received text is complexly compacted of teachings and their subversion, of rules and their extension, of topoi and their revision. Within ancient Israel, as long as the textual corpus remained open, Revelation and Tradition were thickly interwoven and interdependent, and the received Hebrew Bible itself, therefore, the product of an interpretive tradition.[40]

Biblical critics long emphasized the importance of and differences between the *traditum* (content, form) and its *traditio* (the process of its use over time) as necessary to the hermeneutical task.[41] Fishbane massively documented these relationships within the Bible even as he depended on the groundbreaking work of Renée Bloch on midrash.[42]

Because the tradition transmission *process* at work in inner-biblical exegesis in fact extended beyond the biblical parameters into early Rabbinic exegesis, a new discipline called *comparative midrash* arose to account for this development.[43] From the beginning, early comparative midrash study borrowed the vocabulary and tools of its precursor, the tradition historical method. Thus, comparative midrash extended the reach of tradition historians into the post-canonical literature. Indeed, Geza Vermes claimed the only difference distinguishing biblical and postbiblical midrash was canonization.[44]

Modern literary theory has also made its contribution to the discussion of midrash and intertextuality as process. Daniel Boyarin, expressing sympathies with Derrida, defines midrash as "a radical intertextual reading of the canon."[45] Sounding reminiscent of Bloch and others, he describes in literary terms what they observed exegetically: "The intertextuality of midrash is an outgrowth of intertextuality within the Bible itself."[46] Such a reading of the Bible, in which potentially every part refers to and is interpretable by every other part, provides for Boyarin a classic example of intertextuality, defined as "the transformation of a signifying system."[47] The Bible is a severely gapped and dialogical text waiting to be filled in by its readers. The role of midrash is the role of every reader—to fill in those gaps. As we have seen, filling in the gaps is a never-ending process. Canonical *process* thus began before the formal closure of the canon and continues right up to the present hour.

Canonical process rests firmly, though less explicitly than modern literary theory, on the insights gained from discussion on intertextuality. Tradition history focused on how and why earlier traditions were being appropriated. Sanders correlated this trend in tradition history with its counterpart in comparative midrash as the centerpiece of his canonical critical enterprise.[48] A guiding force of this study is to integrate Sanders's canonical criticism (here, his canonical process) with similar trends in modern literary theory—trends that emphasize the use and function of texts in the process of meaning production. For Sanders, intertextuality as a "never-ending process" is the diachronic "repetition/recitation/reapplication" of an older biblical text or tradition into a new text.[49] Intertextuality as process is the core of tradition historical and comparative midrash studies.

Sanders suggests meaning is found "in between the lines of a text"—in its function over time. He seems to imply that meaning is discovered less in the text itself than in the difference between how two texts or traditions function in relation to each other. If this is the case, he sounds every bit the literary progeny of Saussure or Derrida with regard to differential relationships in meaning production, though he assuredly claims no such interdisciplinary dependence. In his insistence upon the context-dependent, diachronically read texts as crucial for understanding textual meaning, Sanders also reflects similar concerns among reader-response critics, including the one who deserves the name "founding member," Hans Robert Jauss.[50]

Intertextuality as process describes an aggregate number of symbols, conceptual frameworks, and hermeneutic options for resignification in new contexts. As such, intertextuality as process expands still more the plurality of meanings in any biblical text or tradition with each resignification or repetition. If the radical ambiguity of *representation* of the past by the present has not yet sufficiently heightened the instability quotient of biblical texts, the description of a fifth and final level of intertextuality might do so: the interplay between a text and its reader(s).

Intertextuality and the Reader

The examination of intertextuality as the interplay between a text and its reader(s) warrants two observations. On the one hand, the potential for increased textual anarchy is assured. On the other hand, a sign of the only real constraining dynamic on the text's field of possible meanings becomes manifest. The latter observation will be developed fully in the next chapter.

The potential for increased textual anarchy becomes understandable when the (psycho)dynamic relationship between reader and text is highlighted. Every reader is himself or herself a composite "text" of sorts, full of already interpreted earlier texts. In literary circles and here, Roland Barthes's influence is noteworthy. Extending his observation that a text is "a tissue of quotations drawn from innumerable centers of culture" that can be written or nonwritten, we can readily speak of the "experiential text of self." Our own life experience can be described as a whole complex of signifiers and meanings: "The reader is the space on which all quotations that make up a writing are inscribed."[51] When the reader-hermeneut as "text" engages another text, what emerges is an act of intertextuality that is no less complex than every other level of intertextuality so far described and that gives full meaning to the term hermeneutics.[52]

This is not the place for a history of general hermeneutics, or even of biblical hermeneutics in particular. What may be helpful is a brief encounter with the makers of the modern mind on the problem of hermeneutics in understanding the intertexuality of reader and text. Schleiermacher, Dilthey, and later Heidegger, Gadamer, and Ricoeur represent the philosophical context for the problem of hermeneutics. In the area of theology, the thought of Fuchs, Ebeling, Bultmann, and Barth, to name the most celebrated, represent ongoing hermeneutic conflicts.[53]

Schleiermacher and Dilthey were preoccupied with what was *behind* the text, especially with its history, authorship, and *who is expressed* in the text, over against *what* a text said. Heidegger moved the discussion from epistemology to ontology while still focusing on the *who* questions posed by Schleiermacher and Dilthey. For Heidegger, the *Dasein,* the "being-in" the world, was the situated being. "Being-in" the world necessarily conditioned any interpretation (everyone is a "text" full of pretexts). Heidegger raised to new heights questions of objectivity and subjectivity. Inasmuch as every subject (person) purporting to be the measure of objectivity is an "in-habitant" of this world, his or her claim to objectivity is radically circumscribed.

Bemused by foundations, Heidegger never returned to epistemology, leaving such questions to his most famous student, Gadamer. Gadamer's contribution emphasized that a human being finds himself or herself always within a tradition and that the act of understanding is historically bound by that tradition. Any reading of a text would always involve a collapse of distance, a "fusion of horizons" between text and interpreter that must be addressed.

If not already apparent, such ruminations emphasize that all understanding is an act of intertextuality between text and reader, between past and present, between two quite distinct horizons of reality encountering and interpreting each other.[54] The more people reading the biblical text, the more potential there is for varied readings of every sort. Indeed, later psychological studies on perception reinforced just such an understanding of the text-reader (observer) dynamic. The meaning of texts, then, is dependent upon the differential relationships between various readings and their readers, even contradictory readings, but no less so than upon those between Saussure's letters and sounds within words themselves. The truth of meaning-gaps between reader and text is now well established and unavoidable, undergirded as it is by history, philosophy, experience, and the nature of language. "*Inter*textuality" reigns between reader and text, even as it does at all other levels of our description.

Conclusions: Canon and Chaos

Four conclusions are drawn from this study on intertextuality. In the first place, contradiction, as situated in a discussion of intertextuality, can now be seen as necessary for understanding instead of a barrier to it. The loftiest and most noble meanings are known to us only *in contra dictus,* that is, in contradistinction to other signifiers, which in turn are known in their differential relationships, and so on. Even ultimate meaning is always already deferred meaning, since every object signified (even the concept of ultimate reality) is itself a signifier (a word whose own meaning is determined in a differential relationship).

When it comes to judging the truth or falsehood of conflicting prophets, language, history, interpersonal relationships, and even reality itself, given their endless intertextualities, unmitigated ambiguity is guaranteed. But there is no alternative language, history, way to relate, or reality. Positively speaking, the very pluralism in the heart of language, history, relationships, and reality manifestly ensures the odds of survival of such meaning-full literatures as the Bible. That "the Bible is adaptable for life"[55] remains the key to its ongoing canonical authority.

A second conclusion from this study of intertextuality insists that any appeal to determinate meanings in a word, sentence, or the combination thereof in what has traditionally been called a "text" has to be abandoned.[56] Exegesis must admit to tracking usage of words in contradistinction to other uses, not in extracting "self-present" meanings from texts. *Full* meaning is always deferred and is derived only in context (diachronically and synchronically). Since meaning is discerned in the play of difference, texts can never be considered simply on their own terms but must be considered with reference to just about everything. A starting point for finding meaning—not a given by any text per se—is the recognition that meaning, like beauty, truth, and justice, is a transitory cultural construct. A shift in focus from what a text *means* to what a text *does,* from content to function, is a necessary corollary for understanding.

In the third place, the intertextuality of all texts and readers-as-"texts" argues against having one's "text" and "misreading" it too. One cannot make a consistent argument for the "integrity of the text" (i.e., textual constraints on readers) as a means of claiming universality and objectivity for one's method while also claiming freedom from the tyranny of the text by emphasizing the reader's role (i.e., *how* a text is appropriated) in the production of meaning. Canonical criticism as it is now articulated stands vulnerable to this judgment. This criticism will be addressed later in this study.

A fourth and final conclusion arising out of this study on intertextuality focuses on how we use language. The use of language is neither system alone (canon as paradigm) nor use alone (canonical process), nor is it a "differential nonsystem" (Derrida's deconstruction); rather, it is discourse. By way of example,[57] if a narrative contains story (*what* is said), it also contains discourse (*how* it is said). As such, discourse entails many factors: the sequence in which events are related; the use of irony, repetition, and symbolism; and so on. A reader must reconstruct the meaning of the narrative not only in view of its content but also keeping in mind the particular way in which it is told—its hermeneutical thrust. One can conclude from such observations that stories that contain the same basic events, characters, and settings may be told in ways that produce radically different narrative meanings. This is a foundational insight shared by canonical criticism.

One can see why David Tracey, attributing his formulation to Paul Ricoeur, discovers "discourse" as "a reality beyond individual words in the dictionary, beyond both synchronic codes (*langue*) and individual use of words (*parole*); it is to rediscover society and history."[58] Important for this conclusion is that language as discourse is an acknowledgment that every discourse expresses conscious and unconscious ideologies, which in turn suggests that neither text nor reader is the source of meaning production. Rather, both are situated in "interpretative communities" past and present that negotiate their intertextuality. Such a conclusion offers both a liberation from the near past's extraordinary commitment to the historical critical paradigm and to scientific "objectivism," as well as a recommitment to the more distant past's literary and typological readings, though now on an altogether different footing.

The radical intertextuality of language, history, relationships, and reality might rightly be called the new chaos theory of Bible reading. Such disorderly reading conduct argues for the making of canons as a necessary and ordered response. Before detailing the rise of canon as a limiting hermeneutic paradigm, some thoughts on the reader situated in the "hermeneutic community" (the arena of meaning and canon production) are warranted.

TWO

Reader Response and Community of Interpretation

THE previous chapter signaled the vaporous quality of determinate meanings in texts, arguing instead for the radical intertextuality of all texts, indeed, of all reality. If the case was made at all, it raised the possibility for intertextual anarchy, seemingly placing us far from hope of ever confidently understanding the meaning of prophetic truth claims of Scripture, much less of ever evaluating the truth or falsehood of conflicting biblical prophets. Hope for finding the way out of this potential interpretative morass was suggested but not explained. The proposed hope hinged more on restraints placed upon the *reader* by his or her *interpretative community* than on the text's ability to constrain the interpretative options. We were left asking literary theory and canonical criticism to again provide assistance in finding our way from that suggestion toward its explanation.

The Bible as Story

If story is an "absolutely essential aspect of the Old Testament,"[1] then the insights of literary critics are paramount.[2] The study of the Bible as literature (story) in the past was often narrowly enveloped by historical interests in sources, authorship, and dating. It is clear to story-readers everywhere, if not to modern biblical exegetes, that the fact that a story may have some basis in history does not in itself explain the story's full spiritual, symbolic, truth-filled meaning. A story maintains great value for us many times precisely because it transcends its historical basis. The cruel, questionable story of Abraham's near sacrifice of Isaac is a case in point. Elie Wiesel claims this story contains Jewish destiny in its totality: "Every major theme, every passion and obsession that make Judaism the adventure it is, can be traced back to [this story]."[3] Wiesel's claim indicates that a story about the near sacrifice of a child has significance well beyond its merely historical meaning. Although such a practice has been outlawed for millennia, clearly the Akedah maintains its hold on literary giants and gnome readers even today. It would take James Muilenburg, in his presidential address at the Society of Biblical Literature meeting in 1968, to finally swing the doors of rhetorical and other literary approaches to the Bible wide open.[4] Serious Bible readers can only be thankful he did so.

If one understands the century-long hegemony of historical critical scholarship over biblical studies, one cannot underestimate the shift that occurred in granting the Bible its formal place as story. Without fully claiming with James Barr that the Bible "cannot be identified at all with history," one can still insist with him that as story the Bible "belongs to a literary form and cannot be removed from it without danger."[5] The Bible as story (literature) presents itself to the literary critic for scrutiny and recommends two fundamental particulars not always associated with the historical critical enterprise. First, increased weight is given to the final form of the text over its compositional layers or referential status.[6] Second, a methodology less prone to circumvent the act of reading or hearing the text is required.

Canonical criticism as a discipline germinated in the late 1960s along with the meteoric rise of the literary interest in the Bible. It should not be unexpected, then, that canonical criticism would converge with modern literary criticism on the very two points described above: respect for the final—in this case, canonical—form of the text and interest in the reception of the text by its readers. To this latter common interest we now turn.

Reader-Response Criticism

Meeting the Reader

Reader-oriented criticism is a logical consequence of the increasing distance placed between the text and its author(s) by literary authorities in the middle of the twentieth century. New Criticism and, later, structuralism were part of this shift in focus.[7] Meaning had earlier been sought in authorial intention and/or historical context, whereas for the New Critics meaning was thought to inhere within the text itself without reference to external context. In the late 1960s, another shift occurred that placed the reader, over against the author or text, at the center of meaning production. Underpinning this new emphasis on the reader were new assumptions within the philosophy of language and epistemology. As described in the previous chapter, language was no longer seen as referential and knowledge was said to lack foundations.

Since the basis of all the historical critical methods heretofore was the genetic principle that "insight into the origins and development of a phenomenon *contains the key* to its understanding" (emphasis added),[8] accent on the final form and its reception remained under suspicion. Canonical criticism was not exempt from suspicion because it redefined the historical moment on which biblical criticism had focused. It declared itself to be "a confession on the part of biblical criticism that it now recognizes that the true *Sitz-im-Leben* today of the Bible is in the believing communities—heirs to the first shapers of this literature—whatever the provenance . . . of the original forms and early literary units."[9] Sanders appears to have transferred the locus of meaning to those who received the text (its readers) in whatever moment, insisting that the same thing going on now in believing communities was going on back then. He thus collapsed the horizons of understanding in true Gadamer-like fashion.

Since Sanders did not completely disavow the historical in his method, Edgar McKnight poses an appropriate question: "Is it possible that the historical mooring of the hermeneutical enterprise in canonical criticism is a limitation that must be transcended?"[10] For me, if not for Sanders, the answer entails both a "yes" and a "no." In the literary field, Hans Robert Jauss, having struggled with similar questions, would, no doubt, appreciate such an ambiguous reply. To him we look for help in gaining perspective on this question.

Literary History and Canonical Process: Hans R. Jauss

In response to the move among literary critics of the 1960s to shun the historical nature of literature (New Criticism, structuralism),[11] Hans Robert Jauss, in his monumental work, *Toward an Aesthetic of Reception,* sought to restore history to the center of literary studies.[12] However, his return to historical interest was not an aping of historical quests for first and subsequent causes of production, nor was it simply *describing* a text or tradition "historically."[13]

New Testament scholar Krister Stendahl had sought diligently to distinguish between "what the text meant" and "what it means," between its description and its application.[14] Of course, for Stendahl and others, "what the text meant" has always been viewed more authoritatively than "what the text means." Suggesting "what a text means" was usually seen as a pastoral function for less intellectually rigorous settings, such as the weekly sermon. It was not an issue for the academy, whose task it was to do the more fundamental "objective" research. The interpretive bias in such an approach was seldom noticed, given the historical-critical commitment to "origins" (authorial intent, date, and so on) as the "objective" category of meaning production contrary to all later "subjective" categories. In similar fashion, E. D. Hirsch, to whom biblical scholars fearful of rampant subjectivism often appeal, became the literary counterpart to Stendahl, drawing a line in the sand of interpretation between a text's "meaning" and its "significance."[15]

Jauss became suspicious of such "essentialist" tendencies oriented around "objectivist" ideals for recapturing historical "facts." To the degree that study of the production or the structure of literary texts was pursued at the expense of their *reception* over time, including the reception of the reader-historian attempting the reconstruction, his suspicions stand justified. For Jauss, "literature and art only obtain a history that has the character of a process when the succession of works is mediated not only through the producing subject, but also through the *consuming subject*" (15; emphasis added). He coined the phrase "aesthetics of reception" (*Rezeptionsästhetik*) to describe this new emphasis, explaining:

> The aesthetic implication lies in the fact that the first reception of a work by the reader includes a test of its aesthetic value in comparison with works already read. The obvious historical implication of this is that the understanding of the first reader will be sustained and enriched in a chain of receptions from generation to generation; in this way the historical significance of a work will be decided and its aesthetic value made evident. (20)

Not surprisingly, Jauss underplays any notion of canon in the classical sense of a formal aesthetic incarnation of a universal essence (xi). His interest in the dynamic and dialectical *process* of canon formation, along with his own largely unacknowledged reaction against German literary orthodoxy, precludes commitment to any canon per se. Jauss criticizes his teacher and major influence, Gadamer, for his perceived commitment to a canonical idea of tradition (*norma normata*).

Jauss's literary historiography demands a conscious mediating role between past and present. Instead of simply accepting the tradition as given, the historian of literary reception must rethink *how* "canonical works" affect or are affected by current conditions and events. Such a stance would argue that past meaning is to be understood only as part of present practices. As a student of Gadamer, Jauss calls on "experience," not neutrality, in writing a literary history. He accepts the "fusion of horizons" rather than opting for objectivist attempts at "pure" description over time.[16] It seems the experienced and self-conscious pastor-reader could offer depth of reading to otherwise sterile historiography.

What is new with Jauss is not his disclaimer of objectivity, though such nuance is too rarely demanded of historians. Rather, it is his emphasis on the impossibility of any openly stated or recorded proposition to capture the historical consciousness of a given period—even those purporting to do so in the period in question. Without necessarily meaning to, Jauss here comes close to a psychoanalytic description of the historical unconscious. Every vantage point contains a restricted range of vision due to its situatedness. Jauss calls this the "horizon of expectation." The "horizon of expectation" of all parties participating in a text's meaning production (authors, texts, and readers) simultaneously reveals and represses what can be known in an encounter. Literary historiography is akin to archaeology of the text.[17] Through a process of "dialogue" between and among the varied "horizons of expectations," the possibility of description becomes clarified (or perhaps muddied), even though none of the experiences may ever become fully explicit.

Knowing the complexity of his proposal, Jauss grounds his theory of literary history methodologically in seven theses. First, the prejudice of historical objectivism must be removed. The historicity of literature rests on the preceding experience of the literary work by its readers, not on an organization of supposed "literary facts" (20). Second, from a preunderstanding of genres, forms, and themes of already familiar works in the same historical moment, one can lessen overzealous psychologisms (22). Third, the horizon of expectations of a work allows one to determine its character by the kind and degree of its influence on a presupposed audience. A change in horizons is then monitored over against an earlier, albeit reconstructed, horizon (25). Fourth, by reconstructing a past horizon of expectation, one can now pose questions that the text gave an answer to and thereby discover how the contemporary reader could have viewed and understood the work (28). Such a stance avoids considering meaning to be eternally present in the text and immediately accessible to the interpreter. Fifth, demand is made to insert the individual work into its "literary series" in order to recognize its historical position and significance in the context of the experience of literature. One work's following another can solve formal and moral problems left behind by the last reception and present new dilemmas as well (32). Sixth, the intersection of synchronic and diachronic planes of reading provide a check-and-balance system for locating constant and variable formulations within the overall historical reconstruction (36). Finally, the social function of literature becomes manifest where the literary experience of readers impinges upon their own life situation, which impacts their understanding of the world and affects their social behavior (39).

Parallels between Jauss's description of literary history and the canonical process as articulated by Sanders are noteworthy. Whereas Sanders would not join Jauss's wholly negative assessment of formal canons in literature, including Scripture, he would agree with Jauss concerning the canonical process itself. Jauss is "freer" than is Sanders to dispense with canons on literary grounds because literary criticism has no canon equivalent to that of the church that requires a similar faith commitment. However, Sanders echoes Jauss's literary history in describing canonical process functionally: "A written canon has antecedents in the very process by which the concept arose, that is in the function of authoritative traditions when there was as yet no written literature deemed canonical in the sense of *norma normata* or shape."[18] Indeed, for Sanders, the various canons available to the Jewish and Christian believing communities are shaped more by their function than by any set number or order of books.[19]

The never-ending process "canonized" in the Bible is that of the recitation and reuse of earlier traditions by later tradents. There are very few passages of Scripture that do not in some sense build on other Scripture. One task of canonical criticism, then, is to discern the unrecorded hermeneutics that lie among all the pages of Scripture. This discernment, for Sanders, depends upon describing these shifts in use over time using traditional historical-critical methods (history of traditions) and comparative midrash analysis. On this last point, Sanders parts company with Jauss by not accounting fully for the "collapse of horizons" that, as was noted, Sanders purported to accept.

It is clear, for example, that Sanders agrees with Jauss that the meaning of a text does not lie in its original moment of production or in its reception at any one historical hour or in its content alone. Rather, its meaning lies in its use over time. Like Jauss, Sanders sees this historical *relecture* as describing the intersection between the synchronic and diachronic planes of reading all along the way. The hermeneutic continuum advanced by the literary history of Jauss and by the canonical process of Sanders achieves, for Jauss, a "trans-subjective horizon of understanding,"[20] and for Sanders, a "theocentric monotheizing pluralism."[21] This might best be described as fully contextual exegesis.

Both Jauss and Sanders see in this variegated process the means for the development and the correction of a system of understanding whereby the scope of the genre-structure is determined.[22] Said differently, the Bible contains its own self-correcting apparatus (*norma normans*) that helps determine its shape as canon (*norma normata*).

The similarities between Jauss and Sanders do not stop in their positive correspondence. The problem for one is also a problem for the other.[23] The problem for both does not lie in their procedures for relating literary texts or traditions to their social matrix, which follow fairly accepted methods in their respective fields. What is difficult for them, given their stated commitment to the collapse of horizons, is the attempt at maintaining the transcendental horizon (Jauss) or the monotheizing principle (Sanders) by implying its empirical objectifiability. The methods necessary for objectifying these over-arching categories require a neutral, if not transcendent, position from which these observations can be made. Both Sanders and Jauss seem to ask us to bracket our own historical situatedness and accept their metacategories, despite their claim to escape just such a historicist paradigm. To the degree that both rely on an objective principle *referred to* by the texts themselves (manifestly apparent to all who would read the texts), each appears to fall back into errors his hermeneutic approach sought to overcome.

Part of the dilemma for both Jauss and Sanders lies in their approaches to reconstructing the various "horizons of expectation" and reception of a text or tradition along its hermeneutical route. Both set out to accomplish this reconstruction with evidence or signals from the works themselves. Both feel secure in their reconstructions because of the self-correcting apparatus of their respective (canonical) processes. Corrections are clarified through alternating hermeneutical stances. However, these self-correcting systems are vulnerable to the common belief of Sanders and Jauss that the textual and generic clues provided by the texts themselves, at least in theory, establish the "transsubjective" or "monotheizing" horizons of understanding.

This is not to say that proceeding in this way is uncommon or that I do not largely agree with the metacategories of either. It is not, and I do. I'm suggesting, rather, that both Jauss and Sanders are at cross-purposes with their expressed intentions. By reintroducing an objectivist understanding of the text as a means of providing necessary restraints on various reconstructed receptions along the hermeneutical route, both Jauss and Sanders seem to be at odds with their fundamental hermeneutical positions. Sanders had argued, after all, "that the *true Sitz-im-Leben* today of the Bible is *in the believing communities*—heirs to the first shapers of this literature—whatever the provenance . . . of the original forms and early literary units" (emphasis added).[24]

The dilemma confronting Jauss and Sanders is not trivial. Indeed, it shows just how difficult it is to extricate one's method from a horizon of expectation that has for centuries operated under a particular paradigm.[25] That the paradigm is shifting is certain, as the rise of canonical criticism and reader-response criticism itself makes apparent. However, remnants of the old paradigm are heard in the ongoing appeals to inherent textual restraint proffered by biblical and literary theorists who otherwise accept the new reality. In the domain of literary criticism, no theorist better exemplifies this dilemma than Wolfgang Iser. In appreciating his contributions, decisions of hermeneutic importance will surface and require definitive response as to where the locus of restraint for determining canonical authority truly lies—with the text or with the community or between the two.

Between Text and Community: Wolfgang Iser

Wolfgang Iser's works have received a very popular reading.[26] This may be, in part, because of his amazing skill in weaving into his theory of

meaning production matters of ontology, history, psychology, and epistemology, while still offering a "good read." To the central question facing
contemporary literary and canonical critical interpreters alike—What is the
source of interpretative authority, the text or the reader?—in typical fashion
for him, Iser answers, "Both."

In his most popular work, *The Act of Reading,* Iser argues that classical
models for understanding texts—those seeking inherent meanings in texts—
ignore the crucial role the reader plays in actualizing a text's meaning (18,
21).[27] The goal for Iser is not simply to exegete a text for its treasures but to
"reveal the conditions that bring about its various possible effects," effects
that demand the participation of the reader in whose experience "the text
comes to life" (19).

On the one hand, Iser seeks to avoid identifying meaning with a formal,
objective self-sufficient text (à la the New Critics), while on the other hand, he
endeavors to restrain idiosyncratic reading-experiences of individual readers.
The role of the text is to "designate instructions for the production of the
signified" (65). The role of the reader is to follow these instructions. In the
process of this "dyadic interaction," understanding is produced (66–68).
Actually, what is produced by this interaction is an event, a happening. The
relationship between the reader and text is not a partnership in which each
bring their respective portions of meaning to the "table." Rather, neither text
nor reader contain meaning (as an embodied object), but meaning is produced in the *process* of interaction between text and reader. The text can be
grasped not as a whole but a series of changing viewpoints, each one restricted
in itself so as to need subsequent viewpoints. The reader then "realizes" an
overall situation through this give-and-take. The text-reader relation functions as a "self-regulating system" to guard against arbitrariness.

For Iser, the "act of reading" entails accommodating the "gaps" and "indeterminacies" or "blanks" in all literary texts. For example, from one scene to
the next in a plot line or in inconsistencies between two texts by the same
author, "blanks" are left that must be filled in by the reader according to his or
her "individual disposition" (165–172, 182–187). In the previous chapter, a
case was made on linguistic grounds for just such "blanks," a point not lost on
Iser. Iser variously calls this filling in the blanks left by the structure as "grasping the text" in a *Gestalt*-forming, *Gestalt*-coherent, or consistency-building
process (121, 123, 127–130). But, and this is not unimportant for Iser, *the
reader is restricted by the very structure of the text*—even a text that, in the nature
of all texts, allows for different ways of fulfilling *its* potential (37). Iser concludes that "while the meaning of the literary work remains related to what
the printed text says, . . . it requires the creative imagination of the reader to
put it all together" (142).

In some ways, Iser represents on the literary scene an amalgam of the two
leading canonical-critical approaches within biblical studies, namely, those of

Sanders and Childs. Childs is primarily concerned with the final, fixed form of the text, which transcends the communities that produced it.[28] Unlike Iser, Childs *does* seek norms *embedded in the text* itself. However, with Iser, he suggests that the overall structure of a book provides the (theological) construct that becomes (potentially) normative for all communities, those who had a hand in producing the text and its subsequent readers. In giving the text an authoritative role in circumscribing possible readings, Childs and Iser are comparable.

Sanders, on the other hand, emphasizes the believing communities' roles in the process of canon production and to that degree is closer to the aesthetic-response side of Iser's reading act. When Sanders suggests that the biblical text (canon) was shaped in Israel's quest for survival in exile and by Israel's need to define its communal identity in light of the exile,[29] he reveals his "existentialist" commitments.[30] In much the same way, Iser suggests that it is in the reader's "experience" that the meaning of a literary text is constructed or "concretized" (18–21).

On matters of canon and authority, the attractiveness of Sanders's approach parallels that of Iser's.[31] Like Iser, Sanders endorses the reading community's influence over the text while guarding against idiosyncratic readings by insisting on the text's stability. Indeed, a hallmark of Sanders's canonical approach is to contrast and complement the stability and fluidity in text and canon. This interplay between the stability and adaptability of the biblical text is a maxim almost everywhere present in the works of Sanders.[32]

Sanders has recently emphasized the limitations of any statement regarding a text's so-called stability quotient in spite of the many communal efforts to achieve a stable text. The ninth-century Masoretes went a long way in "constraining" the text with vowel and accent markings and scribal notes, creating a "hedge" around the text-as-artifact. Even then, their marginal notations (*masorot*) preserved textual anomalies that show the tenuousness of statements about a text's stability.

Notably, Sanders's suggestions belie where the center of restraint indeed rests, namely, in the interpretative communities preserving *their* texts for themselves.[33] Whether among Samaritans, Hellenized Jews (Septuagint), Masoretes, Catholic or Orthodox ecclesial bodies, or Lutheran reformism, it is increasingly clear that no two manuscripts are exactly the same. In fact, there are sometimes thousands of discrepancies among them, often reflecting the community transmitting the text. To the degree that "scholars engaged in textual and canonical criticism can now usually reach agreement on the earliest canonical stage of a biblical text in antiquity"[34] (so Sanders), such agreement implies, if not dictates, that the restraining factor in determining the stability of the text-as-artifact is the community (scholarly or otherwise) transmitting the text. As has been suggested previously, the meaning-potential of the text-as-artifact is even less stable. Here Sanders comes closest to abandoning earlier statements about how Scripture "contain[s] within it the grounding needed for the community" and/or references to the text offering the needed restraint for keeping one's methodology "responsible." As is more fully argued below, and as Sanders seems wont to do, the proper place to locate restraint lies in the community of interpretation, not in the text-as-artifact.

By now, it should be clear that Sanders and Iser seem to accommodate both sides of a controversial dichotomy defended within their respective fields: the so-called objective status of the text versus the subjective status of the reader. In literary circles, a line has been drawn between those "subjectivists" who are thought to be subverting the rule of common sense (Derrida, de Man, Bloom, Miller, Fish) and those "objectivists" fighting the good fight against nihilism (Abrams, Hirsch, Booth, Graff, Crews, Shattuck). In biblical studies, the whole historical-critical enterprise has set itself up to defend exegesis over eisegesis and objective constraint over subjective autonomy.[35] Sanders and Iser in their respective fields straddle both camps. They defend the spatial dimension of the text as an object with a particular *shape*—for Iser, the shape of the "designated instructions," and for Sanders, *norma normata*. They also defend the text's temporal dimension by arguing for the production of meaning as a *process* that the text only sets in motion—for Iser, the "act of concretization," and for Sanders, *norma normans*.

The appeal of these approaches lies in their pluralism. Both theorists seemingly manage to hold the middle ground between those who would embrace notions that texts have but one correct reading and those who would argue that texts have as many correct or legitimate readings as there are readers. In other words, Sanders and Iser legitimate the plurality of significances for a text while constraining infinite and arbitrary interpretations. In sum, Fish's words, intended for Iser, might now also apply to Sanders:

> His theory is mounted on behalf of the reader, but it honors the intentions of the authors; the aesthetic object is constructed in time, but the blueprint for its construction is spatially embodied; each realization of the blueprint is historical and unique, but it itself is given once and for all; literature is freed from the tyranny of referential meaning, but nevertheless contains a meaning in the directions that trigger the reader's activities; those activities are determined by a reader's "stock of experience," but in the course of their unfolding, that stock is transformed. The theory, in short, has something for everyone, and denies legitimacy to no one.[36]

In the end, both theories stand vulnerable to the very distinctions upon which they depend for their most appealing features: the distinctions between the determinate and indeterminate nature of texts, the distinguishing characteristics between subjective and objective methodological categories, and the nature of the dialogue between text, reader, and community. For his part, Sanders's affirmation of the role of the "interpretative community" contains within it the promise of addressing some of these vulnerabilities. It is a role he surely recognizes: "The text of the Bible is based upon the numerous manuscripts of both testaments which have been inherited from ancient and medieval believing communities. We are directly dependent on *those communities* for the text *we attempt to establish* for reading and transmission today" (emphasis added).[37] Due, perhaps, to his own horizon of expectation, Sanders has not yet fully embraced his own stated commitments.

Deficiencies have been suggested but not yet fully explained. Literary criticism and canonical criticism hold promise of explanation in their appeal to the authority of interpretative communities.

The Community of Interpretation

In a remarkable and largely unprecedented exercise in self-criticism, Stanley Fish opens his collection of essays, *Is There a Text in This Class?: The Authority of Interpretative Communities,*[38] by tracing his own development as a literary theorist. He opens with a programmatic manifesto for an "affective stylistics" and closes (ten years later) with a recantation of some of his earlier assumptions. The book is structured a bit like an autobiography, which displays many of the same questions raised by the canonical-critical enterprise. Indeed, to understand Fish and his transformation is to appreciate the central arguments of my attempt to link decisions about authority and meaning to decisions about true and false prophecy, textually and so also in life.

Fish's opening essay (1970), in keeping with the horizon of discussion set by the New Critics, asked the question, "Is the reader or the text the source of meaning?" (1).[39] He answered the question by showing, first, that the text was *not* a self-sufficient depository of meaning and, second, that something else was—namely, the reader. Rather than make his case for the indeterminacy of the text on linguistic grounds, as I sought to do in the previous chapter, Fish, like Jauss and Sanders, noted that the spatial plane of the text camouflaged its temporal dimension. A text is a compressed history in which meanings are actualized in the reading experience over time. Fish then argued explicitly what Sanders and Jauss in their own contexts had suggested to be the case—that the text, though more visible, actually acquired its true significance *only in* the context of reading and rereading. So he replaced the structure of the text with the structure of the reader's experience as the determinant for understanding a text's meaning. He admitted here to hedging his bets, as Iser and Sanders would continue to do, by arguing the text's stability quotient on the one hand while dislodging its preeminence as the container of meaning on the other (3). Meaning now emerged in the interplay between the text and the response of the reader.

He soon realized that granting the reader such authority also meant that potentially there could be as many reading experiences as there were readers. So Fish sought constraint by pressing Chomsky's notion of "linguistic competency" upon the readers themselves. Just as speakers of a language share an internalized system of rules, so must it be with readers (5). "Informed" (i.e., "competent") readers, those sharing similar internalized rules for reading, would also share in objectifiable meaning experiences that would guard against subjective and idiosyncratic readings. In order to argue for a common reading experience, however, Fish was obliged to posit an object in relation to which the readers' experiences could be declared uniform. That object was the text, not in terms of its content (as in "container" of meaning) but in terms of its structured potential.

Like Iser and Sanders, Fish was able to argue both for the integrity of the text as a means of claiming universality and objectivity for his method and against New Critical formalisms. Or so he thought. Fish did not see that the explanatory strength of his construction was also its weakness. Arguing out of both sides of his mouth proved exhausting at least and flawed at best. It seemed both sides were arguing against separate criticisms. When someone would argue that his emphasis on the reader would lead to interpretative anarchy, he argued for constraints upon readers by the text. When someone saw in his method simply an extension of the New Critical emphasis on a text's stable objective character, he would argue for the readers' role in meaning production and the readers' freedom from the text's tyranny (7). In the end, Fish would finally admit that neither the text nor the reader could claim independent status in such a way as to serve as an objective constraint upon the other. The authority of the text and that of the reader fell together under the weight of the interpretative community's authority in which both were situated.

The authority of the text was dislodged by Fish's analysis that the formal features in a text were in fact the product of the interpretative principles for which they were supposedly evidence:

> I did what critics always do: I "saw" what my interpretative principles permitted or directed me to see and then I turned around and attributed what I had "seen" to a text and an intention. What my principles direct me to "see" are readers performing acts; the points at which I find (or to be more precise, declare) those acts to have been performed become (by sleight of hand) demarcations in the text; those demarcations are then available for the designation "formal features," and as formal features they can be (illegitimately) assigned the responsibility for producing the interpretation which in fact produced them. (163)

Fish produced a series of analyses by prominent literary critics committed to the text's objective integrity. In each case, he showed how the interpretation arrived at was not so much *derived* from formal structures of the text as it was merely *asserted* in terms of the grammatical and lexical categories employed in analyzing the text. Across the literary aisle in biblical studies, James Kugel undertook a review of various scholarly analyses of symmetry, rhyme, meter, and genre in the Psalms and in some biblical narratives. Although the scholarly readers Kugel studied all insisted upon the text's inherently stable character, he showed by their dissimilar conclusions how much convention had actually helped determine their perception of what structures were said to be found in the text. Kugel would conclude with a strong warning against universalizing any of our "conventions," including such assured categories as formal genres, because "texts are written and read in an environment of convention."[40]

As a student and great admirer of one of the form-critical and exegetical giants of today, Rolf Knierim, I can attest to having attended many a seminar in which students and teacher wrestled endlessly over a text's inherent structure. The irony of such verbal jousts was our expressed intent to discover the conceptual world of the author(s) behind the text for the larger task of doing biblical theology. But we had to go through the assured results of our exegetical structure, which rested on the foundation of inherent textual meaning, which in turn provided support for making claims about the conceptual world behind the text. Indeed, if Kugel is correct, and if the varied structures that were brought forward in those exegetical classes are at all indicative, it might have been an equally viable discipline to compare the conceptual world of the readers of the texts with our various reconstructed exegeses. Instead, after some great rhetorical battles, we generally submitted our exegetical readings, *as it eventually should be* within a learning context, to the referent authority among us. This generally was not the text.

To pretend that communal "conventions" influence only the naive readers and not the "objective" readers of "enlightened" academies is to conceal the truth-bearing mechanisms at work in honest inquiry. To expose the convention is not to ridicule it but to appreciate its power. On this point, from a completely opposing angle, Harold Bloom is correct to speak of the "anxiety of influence" that animates truly canonical works—and, I would add, truly masterful exegetical constructions. With Fish, I would not argue against formal categories, but neither can it be argued that such categories simply inhere to texts or "lie innocently in the world." Rather, categories themselves are constructed by interpretative acts (13).

Although the textual side of the reader-text dialogue faced tough questioning by Fish, he went on to dislodge any notion of independent status of the reader as well. Readers, like texts, were every bit products of their varied communities. Harold Bloom seems to disagree on both counts. He not only argues for the aesthetic autonomy of the canonical text but also goes out of his way to argue for the autonomy of the reader. Notwithstanding the seedbed of antifoundationalist sentiment centered on his own campus at Yale, to which he and others defending inherent aesthetic value are a critical counterpoint, Bloom still sees no inner connection between any social group and the specific ways in which he has spent his life "reading, remembering, judging, and interpreting" what was once called "imaginative literature." He bluntly concludes: "I myself insist that the individual self is the *only* method and the *whole* standard for *apprehending* aesthetic value" (emphasis added).[41] Immediately he seems to about-face by lamenting, "But, 'the individual self,' I unhappily grant, is defined only against society," and then goes on to explain in the same breath how the literary critic (a self-reference?) is no solitary worker of white magic on an enchanted island. Indeed, "criticism . . . is a kind of theft from the *common stock*" (emphasis added).[42] When all the rhetorical dust settles, his implausible deniability notwithstanding, Bloom's very defense of the *Western* canon places him squarely within a canonical *community* of reference, the West. If you are from the East (and all that implies), this is no small admission.[43] Without a hint of irony, Bloom defends his very choice of Shakespeare as "the secular canon [of the West], or even the secular scripture," by appealing to a clear consensus among the Western traditionalists *and* their opponents, the canon-openers, on just this point.

That Bloom feels a need to defend and preserve the Western canon is the strongest argument against an inherent canonical aesthetic between its covers and a strong argument in favor of the canon-making authority of interpretative communities. Again, somewhat ironically, the fraying of a generalized communitarian sensibility, especially in the academy, arises in part from the very individualized canonical autonomy of the reader that Bloom so favors. Although I agree that such fragmentation must be addressed, appealing to an *irreducible* aesthetic value offers no solution. To argue aesthetic value is not necessarily to claim its inherent status, as Bloom seems to think. Aesthetic value is a communal activity even when defending literary canons. Defense of the inherent nature of that aesthetic is not required. Indeed, it is a side road, an epistemological error, a fruitless search for "scratch." Canons must be negotiated by communities arguing over relative value, not asserting irreducible status to one's value-laden commitment, be it an autonomous text or reader.

When Fish finally concluded that the interpretative community, rather than the text or the reader, was the source of meaning production (14), it was no small shift in his thinking. For him, interpretation became the master category in theoretical discourse.[44] The text no longer had to compete for authority against its reader and vice versa since both were subject to the authority of the community in which they found themselves situated.

A corollary to Fish's elevation of the interpretative community to "canonical" status was to eliminate the subject-object dichotomy as being the only framework within which critical debate could occur. David Bleich had earlier argued from the world of science and psychology that even such notions as "objectivity" were learned in community.[45] Internalized *objects* in the infant's mind are constructed via interaction with and *in contra dictus* to (my term) its mother to finally *produce* representational intelligence. Bleich states, citing Piaget:

> The individual can only achieve his inventions and intellectual constructions insofar as he is the seat of collective interactions that are naturally dependent, in level and value, on society as a whole. The great man who at any time seems to be launching some new line of thought is simply the point of intersection or synthesis of ideas which have been elaborated by a continuous process of cooperation, and, even if he is opposed to current opinions, he represents a response to underlying needs which arise outside himself.[46]

Interpretative communities relativized the object/subject dichotomy, being both and neither. Fish concludes: "An interpretative community is not objective because as a bundle of interests, of particular purposes and goals, its perspective is interested rather than neutral; but by the very same reasoning, the meanings and texts produced by an interpretative community are not subjective because they do not proceed from an isolated individual but from a public and conventional point of view" (14).

The grounds for what was real and normative were now said to occur within interpretative communities, and what was thus normative for one community might be seen (if seen at all) as altogether wrong by members of another. In other words, for Fish, "There is no single way of reading that is correct or natural, only 'ways of reading' *that are extensions of community perspectives*" (16; emphasis added).

Truth claims are relative, as Fish confesses. For ethical reasons, arguments to determine the better alternatives must be employed. Indeed, such negotiation is central to any study of true and false prophecy, a subject developed in more detail below.

By this point, Fish's communitarian reading stance said a great deal methodologically. It required one to determine from which of a number of possible perspectives a reading might proceed. Such a determination would not be made once and for all by neutral arbiters. Rather, decisions would have to be made and remade whenever the interests and goals of one community replaced or dislodged those of another. For Fish, the task of criticism was no longer to decide between interpretations by subjecting them to some test of disinterested objective criteria but instead to establish by political and persuasive means the set of interpretive assumptions from the vantage point of which the evidence (and the facts and the intentions and everything else) would hereafter be specifiable (16). In effect, the reader would specify the vantage point using what Foucault called "rules of discourse." Such rules of discourse in canonical criticism were constructed with the help of comparative midrash, displaying the many reading options on a continuum of unrecorded hermeneutics.

Fish moved from having felt the need to constrain interpretation lest it obscure texts, facts, and intentions to viewing interpretation as the source of those very factors. Previous battles waged over authority to control interpretation, whether by claiming a text's inherent stability, the autonomy of the reader, or authorial intention, were now seen as *products of* interpretation (16). In short, Fish had redefined the activity of criticism from a discipline of demonstration (i.e., description) to that of endlessly negotiated persuasion (17). Not unlike the conclusions in chapter 1, there drawn on linguistic grounds, here Fish shifted the conversation from one of "facts" to one of *discourse* about "facts"—a discourse narrated by the community of interpretation.

Under Fish's model, questions still remain about texts, authors, genres, standards, values, disputes, and canons, but those questions must now be addressed within explicitly acknowledged and defined discursive communities. My agreement with Fish that meanings of texts are finally the products of interpretative communities, past and present, does not lessen the essential task of validation. How does a community choose between rival reading strategies? What are the sociopolitical dimensions in making such choices? How does the exercise of power and control shape decisions? Who judges between competing interpretative communities? In short, how does one go about deciding whether a prophet is true or false? Before taking up these concerns in subsequent chapters, it remains for us to conclude this one.

Conclusions: The Readers' Canon

(Hi)story, Truth, and Canon

The Bible read as "story" recommends new ways of constructing meaning. Truthful meaning need not derive from authorial intentions or historical background—that is, from reference points that are external to the text. On the other hand, in the act of reading itself, meaning can derive from any point along the road to and including a text's final form. If the primary component at work in interpreting texts is the reader situated within his or her interpretative community, then the nearly canonical status of the historical-critical method must be seen for what it is: a community-based orthodoxy.[47] In summary, there are rival reading communities, equally valid, challenging the interpretative strategies of historical criticism, not the least of which are those of reader-response and canonical criticism.

Stephen Moore, in his recent book, *Literary Criticism and the Gospels,* masterfully defends the legitimate place of a reader-responsive reading at the table of biblical studies. He is well aware of arguments here defended regarding a reader's place within a larger community of interpretation. However, he only obliquely refers to his own reading community as that group "suspended between the loss of old certainties and the discovery of new beliefs."[48] Well and good. Such an anemic stance, however, shortchanges the very real sociopolitical claims at stake between the many and varied and sometimes mutually exclusive readings conjured up by those very groups "suspended between." It is not good enough to just defend opening up the biblical guild to other new methods. All readers at the table are politically and ethically required to go beyond method defense to argue for the "better" saying (Proverbs) so constructed by whatever reading method. How to do just that remains the primary task of this study and will be addressed later.

At the beginning of this chapter, canonical criticism as a method faced a formidable question: "Is it possible that the historical mooring of the hermeneutical enterprise in canonical criticism is a limitation that must be transcended?" A response can now be made: Yes, but with some clarification.

Yes, the historical mooring of canonical criticism must be transcended if such a history continues to be reconstructed without sufficient regard for its own "horizon of expectation" as determined within its interpretative community.[49] The observations of Michel Foucault prove helpful to this new way of reading history (a new historical-critical reading?). Foucault distinguishes traditional historical analysis with its emphasis on genesis, continuity, and totalization from his own historiography, which he calls the "archaeology of knowledge."[50] He views his historical "dig" as "nothing more than a *rewriting*"—a regulated transformation of what has already been said—"the systematic description of a discourse-object in contradiction to other discourses" (emphasis added).[51] His interest is not so much to define ideas, thoughts, themes, and representations that are revealed or concealed in discourse, as it is *to describe the discourses themselves as practices obeying certain rules for a specific context irreducible to any other*. To the degree the canonical-critical method of Sanders attempts to describe the "unrecorded hermeneutics" of biblical tradents diachronically, and declares the *function* of such authoritative moves (over content) to be what is truly canonical, he resembles Foucault. To the degree that both Sanders and Foucault depend on contradiction as a sign of hermeneutic potential, they converge. However, Foucault departs sharply with traditional historians who "seek in the great accumulation of the already-said, the text that resembles 'in advance' a later text"; who "ransack history in order to rediscover the play of anticipations or echoes"; who "go back to first seeds or forward to the last traces" in order to "reveal in a work its fidelity to tradition." He sees all this effort as "harmless enough amusements for historians who refuse to grow up."[52] We need not agree with Foucault in his outburst to see the danger he is combating, that of placing a hierarchy of value on a statement's fidelity to *majority* tradition and not simply trying to establish the regularity of its occurrence within a discursive sweep. He does offer a cautionary, if blunt, reminder of the power of tradition to undermine truth and the historians' complicity insofar as they do not recognize their own contingent readings.

Foucault believes textuality is contextualized from within a set of rules that is always subject to historical transformation. History, for Foucault, then, is a web—a series of disjunctive, discursive formations that neither authors (that is, original intention) nor writing nor readers can master. Each discourse has rules of formation, not based on universal, a priori Kantian-like categories but based on historically contingent moments (both in terms of the author and reader). However, in contrast to Derrida, all is not lost in an abyss of meaning. Rather, along with the traditionalists, Foucault advocates deploying, if for heuristic reasons only, some form of the principle of determinacy. Otherwise, criticism cannot offer itself as a cognitive activity because the refusal of determinacy is the refusal of knowledge. Equally important to Foucault (and because of Derrida!) is that such a determinacy is not located in a text or tradition or any other "ground" but is simply located in the historically contingent rules of discourse. As such, the discursive formation partakes simultaneously of the synchronic and the diachronic: "It rules time, but only in time and for a time." This map of discourse exists as a "problematic unity" that contains the means to its own transformation and appropriation.[53] I have argued in keeping with, if not altogether following, Foucault on this latter point: These "rules of discourse" are defined by the "interpretative community" of which one is a part. This is no small assumption and lies at the heart of the central goal of this study: to distinguish truth and falsehood in prophecy and to determine the irrelevancy of speaking truth while not being *dans le vrai* (so Foucault).

A second "yes" to the question of whether the historical mooring of canonical criticism must now be transcended is supplied. Yes, that is, if sufficient discrimination is *not* made between what may be said historically about Scripture and what should be said canonically about it. Sanders himself clarifies: "History and canon are not coextensive terms. Something may be canonically true without having been historically true."[54] Or vice versa.

For example, to introduce historical-critical questions into the order of books of either Testament certainly raises interesting chronological questions related to that order. Those same historical questions, however, could just as surely disrupt the interrelationship of the literature as set by the canonical communities arranging those interrelationships. A different truth-chemistry would emerge in reading the same texts historically than occurs when reading them according to their canonical shape. It makes all the difference in the world whether one reads the Book of Joshua as the endpoint of an early historical credo (hexateuch) or as the first book in the second section of a three-part canon. Since Joshua is one of the most violent books in the Bible, the first purely *historical* reading might argue for, and too often has, a sociopolitical climax of bloody proportion to (any of) Yahweh's promises. The second *canonical* reading would understand the Book of Joshua as having been deliberately excised from the historical credo and the first canon of Scripture, the Torah.[55] As such, the Book of Joshua, as it now stands within the canon, introduces a failed history, not a victorious climax to Yahweh's promises of land. The canonical reading is thus a significant sociopolitical statement on the part of the early canon-makers in exile. Any historical reading, then, must fully appreciate its own historical situatedness, naming its history as one reading among many, if it wishes to provide canonical criticism with a modest but important historical mooring.

Perhaps, as Sanders suggests, the Bible *is* the "product of a very peculiar history, the essential characteristic of which must not be overlooked, and a history which continues today in Jewish and Christian believing communities."[56] If so, as argued here, what is truly peculiar to the Bible's history is not so much the product accounting for that history as it is the peculiarity of its believing communities. Said differently, *all* histories are sustained by their own (even peculiar) communities of interpretation.

Canonical Autonomy of the Reading Community

In order to fully appreciate the reader's role in meaning production, it has been necessary to restate arguments for a "demythologized" text. Such a move is not new, though the reasons here may be. The purpose of demythologizing the text in this context is to discover the reader's role in the text's authority. I am not impugning the value of "myth" in any way. The Bible as sacred story is, after all, the believing community's myth, a book believed to contain particular truth value. It is precisely by communal agreement that this book has gained canonical status. The community displays its role of canon-maker in remythologizing the text on a new plane.[57] In the postmodern context, such remythologizing is a grace given to all metatextual discursive communities, especially those defending the Bible as sacred Scripture. While such grace is welcome, it is not without consequence. By arguing on behalf of the community's role in all meaning production and by defending its authoritative role in naming the Bible as canon, we have also undermined the notion that the text, as text, has any *inherently* divine status. Textually, it is better to describe Scripture's divine status, if one wishes to, vicariously so, not so in substance. Theologically, condemnation by the first commandment would thus also be averted.

Is it now too much to ask, with Schuyler Brown, the obvious: Apart from a reader and a reading, is not a text simply ink on paper?[58] I do not wish to diminish what Daniel Patte calls the "multidimensional power-authority of the text."[59] However, I do wish to suggest a *sequence* of power-authority that passes from those who initiate the reading process (we, the readers) to the inert text. It is in our initiating the reading process that we give life back to the inanimate text on the page. Insofar as it is a written text, fixed on pages, the text then may claim a position of power in relation to us as a conversation partner with multiple meaning-producing coherences from which we then *produce* a coherent meaning (or coherent meanings) that matters to us and, we hope, to others. Still, the sequence of power-authority remains reader to text, and for the believer, God (through God's Spirit) to reader to text. As the Apostle Paul comments in his letter to the Corinthians, "You show that *you* are a letter of Christ, prepared by us, written not with ink but with the Spirit of the living God," and again, "The letter kills, but the Spirit gives life" (2 Cor. 3:3a, 6b; cf. Jer. 31:33). Could it be that no "text," in the end, can be substituted for the people of God?[60] If it truly is the reader—and for believers, the Spirit-filled reader—that finally gives life to so many "words-on-the-page," it is time to accept the Copernican revolution in interpretative theory. The determinacy of the text without a reader must be declared an illusion.[61]

Such a commitment is not unimportant because to the degree both Iser (literary critic) and Sanders (canonical critic) appeal to the text's determinacy for claims of interpretative constraint (and methodological objectivity), their systems falter. For example, without their dependence on the text's determinacy, they could not say that the reader's activities are constrained by it; they could not, in the same breath, honor and bypass history by stabilizing the structure the text contains; and they could not free the text from the constraints of referential meaning yet say that the meanings produced by countless readers are part of the text's potential.

In point of fact, the restraint placed upon a reader does not come from a determinate text; rather, it comes from the interpretative community whose norms and interpretative strategies create the conditions in which it becomes possible to pick formal patterns out—patterns that are then said to restrain the reader.[62] In other words, determinacies and indeterminacies are the *products* of an interpretative strategy that requires them, therefore neither component can constitute the independent given that serves to ground the interpretative process.[63] Of course, the believing community may still wish to claim spiritual inspiration for its norms, thus assuring divine guidance in the process.

Even then, testing the "spirits" remains a necessary injunction of even the most pious commitments as the hermeneutic "rule of Paul" demands (1 Cor. 14:29; Tim. 6:3; Titus 1:10–16).

A further corollary must be stated here. Biblical exegetes have long claimed to simply extract meaning *out of* texts, in contrast to their opponent eisegetes, who are said to *impose* "subjective" meanings *onto* texts. Distinctions between exegesis and eisegesis aside, whatever meanings these terms end up having relate directly to how a particular community uses them. For instance, the historical-critical reading community defines "eisegesis" as any reading that does not coincide with its own norms regarding irreducible meanings treasured in texts waiting to be mined.[64] Another interpretative community might see those very readings that insist on finding original intent or historical causation in discerning a text's meaning as simply "eisegesis" of another kind. The premise stands that the interpretative community provides both the freedom and the restraint upon readers reading texts, including the Bible. The call here is for a new self-understanding in biblical studies that demands new rules of eisegesis as well as exegesis.

Questions abound that are worth asking in regard to critical exegesis under the scrutiny of a postmodern lens.[65] Is critical exegesis the interpretation of the text as text alone? Or is it not as plausible to accept that exegesis is always the interpretation of existing interpretations of the text? Should the goal of exegesis be imagined as the production of *the* singular legitimate meaning of the text? Or is it plausible to accept the polyvalent nature of all texts and that the goal of exegesis is the critical display of the many and varied critical (and naive) understandings of the text? Could it be that there is a methodological relationship between so-called critical exegetical readings and precritical (ordinary) readings at the level of "intuitive hunches" about the text that are then confirmed or not through additional reading? Given the fluidity of reading options and the constructive nature of all readings, it would appear that the most important task becomes one of critical judgment of any and all readings from whatever vantage point. Readings can no longer be defended as true or false by appeals to the method one might use to read meaning into or out of authoritative texts. Rather, critical judgment of conflicting truth claims must be negotiated between the readers, whatever their reading method. This act of judgment might best be understood as the truly canonical act. As will be defended more fully, such canonical adjudication begs for a communitarian negotiating stance.

A canonical status must now be granted to the interpretative community insofar as it is the community that gives meaning to words on paper and it is the community that determines their relative value. Certainly there is precedent for such a claim not only in the Oral Torah tradition of Judaism but also in the *magisterium* of the Roman Church. Even the Protestant reformers initially defended the idea of "canonical autonomy" for their own local communities of faith. Of course, technically, there is no radical autonomy for individuals or for communities. I use the term "autonomous" narrowly to emphasize the community's own authority quite apart from necessary textual legitimation and to note the historical "fact" of the believing community's priority over the text in meaning production and validation. Even though all of us enter the story of "the people of God" sometime after the beginning and before the end, it is, after all, *we* who enter, reading the story for ourselves. In this sense, even those who defend an inerrantly inspired Scripture still *submit themselves* to such a claim and then live accordingly. The communitarian authority for making claims matter has been described by John H. Yoder as "the hermeneutics of peoplehood."[66]

As Yoder has shown, historically, both Martin Luther and Huldrych Zwingli in 1523 made the case for the canonical autonomy of the local congregation. Both defended their claim by arguing from 1 Corinthians 14:26, 29 that the Apostle Paul authorized such autonomy of discernment in the face of conflicting prophetic claims. For Luther and Zwingli, the argument proved useful as long as it justified the independence of what they were doing locally against the bishops of the Holy Roman Empire. Ironically, their appeal to the church's "canonical autonomy" had its roots in the Roman Church's own tradition of appealing to the very same Pauline statements to establish the earlier conciliar apparatus. Luther and Zwingli had no concern about being branded "heretical" until, of course, their localized "canonical autonomy" obliged them to counter the "canonical autonomy" of the mother church. The cycle would repeat itself when followers of Luther and Zwingli began to express their own "canonical autonomy." The "rule of Paul" did not become a part of the life of the Swiss national church but was retained programmatically by the early Anabaptists and the British Puritans.[67]

Nathan Hatch has argued for a similar development regarding the concept *sola scriptura*.[68] The concept itself was a helpful tool when used by the Reformers as an important form of protest against the Roman Catholic Church's coercive control over possible reading options. The very same concept soon became dangerous, even to the Reformers, when the common folk began to use it in earnest for their own counter-readings. Protestant leaders from Calvin and Luther to Wesley and Whitfield were finally compelled to "fence in" the concept against the threat of theological anarchy. In effect, they exercised their canonical autonomy as an interpretative community in order to maintain their identity as such.

Stanley Hauerwas radicalizes Hatch's observations for our time, arguing that the Reformers' problem is no longer our problem: "When *sola scriptura* is used to underwrite the distinction between text and interpretation, then it seems clear to me that *sola scriptura* is a heresy rather than a help to the

Church. When this distinction persists, *sola scriptura* becomes the seedbed of fundamentalism, as well as biblical criticism."[69] Scripture cut away from its source of authority, the canonical community of faith, simply loses its meaning. This is especially so since to claim inherent divine status as the basis for one's authoritative claim is simply to join every other counter-Scripture in doing the same. Claiming such simply begs the important judicial question in a postmodern, religiously ecumenical world in which different Scriptures must also struggle to gain the upper hand in any rhetorical battle of persuasion. To argue, then, for such a community-based meaning producing authority is to defend a truly catholic (little "c") authority that recognizes in principle and in practice the "priesthood of *all* believers" (1 Pet. 2:9; Exod. 19:6). The same claim calls for a communitarian negotiating stance among differing "priesthoods" and their own "divinely inspired" Scriptures. Indeed, a close reading of the prophets and the apostolic writings (especially Paul) details the struggle each had with questions of legitimacy in the face of alternative claims of validity. Why should it be any different for us?

Wilfred Cantwell Smith, in his comprehensive new book, *What Is Scripture?*, expands the argument even more broadly, suggesting a new understanding of scripture based on comparative insights. Such comparisons suggest that "no text is a scripture in itself and as such . . . people—a given community—*make* a text into scripture, or keep it scripture: by treating it in a certain way" (emphasis added).[70] For Smith, as for me, "scripture is a human activity." That is not to say, for me, that it is not also a divine activity or to defend Smith's contention that "scriptures are not texts."[71] His conviction, based as it is on a thorough comparative study, certainly underscores the priority given to the canon-making community as a generalized human activity. Elsewhere, Jacob Neusner suggests, with respect to the different Judaisms, that all have selected for themselves an appropriate and useful past, that is, a canon of useful and authoritative texts.[72] That is the order of priority for Neusner: "The system creates its canon."[73] In his provocative manner, Hauerwas summarizes emphatically for his own context, "You do not have or need 'a meaning' of the text when you understand that Church is more determinative than text."[74] I would simply argue that the same is true for the whole "people of God." The people of God as living texts are inspired by God to create and sustain their own canon of Scripture as their guide for faith and practice. Such convictions comport with a truly evangelical view of God's Spirit in the lives of men and women of faith all along the way of canon formation. Again, what is important to understand is the sequence of authority: God to (Spirit-led) human communities to text. Arguably, such a sequence maintains a priority commitment to the First Commandment: "You shall have no other gods before me" (Exod. 20:3).

Since I have earlier described reality as a labyrinth of intertextualities and have posited here a certain canonical autonomy to various interpretative communities, virtually assuring multiple reading options, a sure foundation for judging between contradictory Scriptures and their contradictory readings seems ever more remote and needed. The making of canons by canonical communities yields clues, if not sure footing, to the way out of this textual labyrinth. To those clues we now turn.

THREE

The Fall and Rise of Canons

CONTRADICTORY prophetic passages in Scripture, a focal point for this study, declare meaning to be intertextual and community determined, as noted in the foregoing chapters. Factors of evaluation necessary for judging among conflicting theologies, differing prophetic sensibilities, and contrasting truth claims in the Bible are the same factors that lead to creating canons (references of authority). Such conflicting alternatives, given their scriptural context, invite the question; What is meant by canonical authority?

Other difficult questions whose immediate source can be located in literary theory must also be asked: Why has this text been authorized at all? What institutional purpose was served by that authorization? What power is amassed by asserting that authority? Who recommends these and not other texts? Who controls their circulation? Who speaks for them? How are they evaluated?[1] All these questions find their context in notions of authority and canon and, by extension, in conflicting communities of interpretation, leading to still more questions: Are we now so caught up in the infinite play of meanings that it becomes meaningless to speak of canon at all? How useful, historically and theologically, is the concept of canon?[2] In this chapter, we are urged by these and other questions to explore the rise and fall, the making and remaking, of canons by interpretative communities as signposts to discriminating "true" from "false" prophecy.

The Fall of the Canon: The Problem of Canon

Our contemporary interest in "canon" has much in common with earlier debates.[3] Classically, the plurality of canonical models was matched by a similar diversity of canonical function. From the essentialist canons of Polycletus and Euripides to Plutarch's suspicion of all canons to Aristotle's accommodating "leaden rule," interest in canonical authority has not waned. Harold Bloom, a truly modern canon-maker, suggests that the literary giant Dante *invented* the modern secular idea of the canonical. Ironically, given Bloom's own spirited defense of the aesthetic essence of a truly canonical work, he still makes the claim that the emergent idea of canon is that of "a literary work that *the world* would not willingly *let* die" (emphasis added).4 Understanding the community's role in canon-making is an important step in recognizing the contingent aesthetic quality in every canon. Understanding the ambiguous history of canons must also nuance any categorical distinctions made by modern readers who worry over the erosion of consensus regarding *the* canon, biblical or otherwise.

From sociology to cultural history, from comparative religion to education, more and more disciplines have gained interest in the study of canon.5 The reemergence of interest in canon comes out of a growing concern over the loss of certain, often unacknowledged, loyalties to referent authorities within the various disciplines. The warning coming out of the biblical academy by James Sanders for would-be canon-makers seems eerily prophetic: "When one uses the word 'canon' one must specify to which denomination or community of faith it refers."6 Such counsel need only be extended to include all disciplines, communities, and periods of history.

The "crises on the horizon of *postmodernity*" that have provoked "the demise of 'traditional' canons" will be explained further. In doing so, it is important to remember that categories dividing historical periods (for example, "premodern/modern/postmodern") serve primarily as heuristic constructs to help distinguish the rise and fall and rise of interest in canon.7 Likewise, since we can now speak of many possible canons across the interdisciplinary fields, the focus here will necessarily be limited to those canons converging in the classification "biblical literature." What follows is a particular reading of the history of biblical and literary canons that must be judged, as must any counter-readings, for its persuasive coherence and aid to learning. It is hermeneutically essential, then, that *this* reading of the demise and rebirth of canon be situated in its context, lying as it does at the "end of modernity."8

Crises on the Horizon of Postmodernity

Canonical criticism as a discipline can trace its birth order to much larger shifts in consciousness that can be collectively described as the shift from modernity to postmodernity. This shift has profoundly influenced almost everything, including how to decide between conflicting biblical passages, which is central to the goals of this study. The evolution from modernity to postmodernity began some thirty years ago and has been summed up by Nancey Murphy as having three revisionary moves.[9] First, a shift from foundationalism to holism in epistemology emerged. Second, a shift occurred from a representational view of language—in which primary meaning was dependent on language representing the objects or facts to which it refers—to an emphasis on language as discourse (use/action). Third, a shift in interest occurred from atomism or reductionism, with its emphasis on the individual, to a new communitarian stance. The *irreducibility* of community was this third trend's hallmark.

The horizon of postmodernity, like all paradigm markers, has been accompanied by the language of crisis, indicating a transition to different historical projects and presuppositions.[10] The now-familiar observation that the two Chinese ideograms making up the word for "crisis" are "opportunity" and "danger" describes the functional usefulness of this word for rehearsing the context of our argument: crisis as catalyst, not as resignation. The overbearing crisis for the present study falls under the rubric of "the demise of 'traditional' canons." However, at least five other general crises can be noted that help to explain the fall and rise of attention to canon.[11]

Walter Brueggemann posits a crisis of socioeconomic cast that gave birth to questions about modernity's long-held faith in itself. The continued suffering due to political oppression, social discrimination, ethnic hatred, and economic greed gave the lie to a governing belief in scientific method and technological advances as infallible means for the advancement of the human species.[12] A growing number of scientists were questioning the ideal of a unified science ever more frequently. Not a few came to see the unified order *observed* in nature as very closely tied to kinds of order we *impose* on the world we observe. Unity in science was acknowledged in fits and starts for what it always was: a play of value-laden choices open to political and economic judgments.[13]

Within Western democracies, the effect that the revolutionary mood of the 1960s had on notions of authority linked to categories such as "canon," which was broadly defined up to that time, cannot be gainsaid. The anarchy, real and perceived, in the United States during this period is a case in point. Events at the end of the decade, most notably in 1968, point to the crisis spirit of the time: the assassinations of both Martin Luther King Jr. and Robert Kennedy; the withdrawal of President Lyndon Johnson from the presidential race; the ongoing Vietnam War and, capping off the year, the riotous Democratic convention in Chicago. That little was said in America when the Soviet tanks rolled into Prague, crushing the seeds of democracy there, suggests just how much our internal chaos ruled our concerns at the time. The election of Richard Nixon on a platform of "security" and "order" cannot be underestimated in defining the longing of the country for reasserting its social and political canons.

Globally, during this period, Western political and economic hegemony was losing its authority. Alternative claims to truth were ushered in as "silenced" voices began to share in the power necessary for being heard.[14] Inasmuch as any "canon" had to do with fields of authorized options or certitude, and insofar as they represented control by the centers of Western educational, political, and religious institutions, a turning point for canon studies was sure to emerge with the questioning of Western dominance. We shall return to this point later.

A second crisis defining the "end of modernity" has been described by others, including Brueggemann, as an epistemological turning point. Questions about the means of knowing and perceiving reality are not new but are reiterated in new ways by such a crisis. The term "sociology of knowledge" has become standard shorthand for the modern acceptance of the subject's role in meaning discovery. However, the language of crisis in the arena of epistemology has become apropos, as moderns contemplate just how community-dependent and partisan so-called objective facts really are.

A shining example can be offered in the works of the postmodern epistemologist Willard V. O. Quine. In his "Two Dogmas of Empiricism," Quine explicitly rejects (for the first time?) the foundationalist models of knowledge, whether Hume and Locke's acceptance of the reducibility of experience to words or Russell and Wittgenstein's enhanced category of sentences as containers of experience. Quine's argument (now accepted by many) was that it is the *whole* fabric of what we know that "faces the tribunal of experience": "The totality of our so-called knowledge of beliefs, from the most casual matters of geography and history to the profoundest laws of atomic physics or even of pure mathematics and logic, is a *manmade* fabric which impinges on experience only along the edges."[15] In philosophy Quine reiterates Thomas Kuhn's now-famous basis for scientific revolutions, that community-dependent categories are accepted or rejected *as a whole* in order to make sense of the chaos of empirical data. "Facts" become so inasmuch as experience "fits" the newly accepted paradigm.[16] It is the (scientific) *community* that decides which "facts" are to be thought of as "solid" and which must continue to be questioned. Acceptance of the new paradigm (a canon for thinking about data) relies on its persuasive power and, often, generational shifts in thinking about things. In any event, the association of knowledge and power only exacerbates the crisis since appeals to metacategories of "objective" knowledge usually give way to a contest of wills.[17] Evidence of the crisis manifests itself in longings for "objective" restraints on rampant partisan interpretation and truth-claims, as noted in previous chapters, with appeals to history, text, author, "plain or common sense," empirical research, and so on.

The modern quest for knowledge relied on the hope that any claims to knowing could be justified on the basis of some objective method for assessing such claims. At the horizon of modernity, increasingly accepted was the awareness that no such justification will be available: "There is no way of testing our beliefs against something whose source is not also a belief."[18] For believing communities (of all kinds), this is liberation language even as it is sobering. Whereas the rhetorical playing field has been somewhat leveled, the rhetorical volume has increased. Discussions of canon(s) have sprung up in direct proportion to the felt disarray in previously trusted modes of knowledge, including trust in inherent textual meanings of sacred scriptures. This battle for new canons of understanding of just about everything is at once a cry for a truly new and perhaps more inclusive comm-*unity,* even as the threat of anarchy is ever present in the contested middle-time between old canons of modernity and the yet-to-be-agreed-upon canons of a postmodern world.

A third turning point at the end of modernity that follows closely from the second has been described by Francis Fiorenza as "the crisis of hermeneutics." Although his concern is narrowly circumscribed, as indicated by the title of his chapter, "The Crisis of Hermeneutics and Christian Theology," Fiorenza's observations are true in a more general sense as well.[19] This crisis hinges, for Fiorenza, on two alternative insights. The first, not unlike what has been described by Fish and elaborated earlier, has to do with the "universality of interpretation." Just about everything is interpretation (122). The crisis in hermeneutics also hinges on Fiorenza's contrasting second point, which he labels "the limitation of interpretation." Such limits are now readily admitted, as it becomes increasingly apparent that human subjectivity not only advances truth, meaning, and freedom but also can foster absence of truth, lack of meaning, and the forces of domination. It is precisely the question of determining the limits of hermeneutics that marks the divide between modern and postmodern thought for Fiorenza (125–126).

Fiorenza then concludes that the "traditional" (in modernist terms) understanding of the "hermeneutical circle," even in its broadest application whereby a text is understood against its total historical-cultural context, is inadequate (128–129). Elsewhere, Fiorenza recognizes the significance of James Sanders's hermeneutic triangle (text/traditions, context/situations, and hermeneutics), which moves the authority of Scriptures away from the fixed literal text to the *process* of interpretation and reinterpretation.[20] Taking his cue from Sanders, Fiorenza notes the parallels between the Scriptures' own appropriation of previous traditions and the proclamation and interpretation of the Scriptures within churches.[21] Whereas Sanders's triangle assumes the "hermeneutical circle," Sanders does not articulate the *controlling role* of the *present* horizon. Fiorenza augments Sanders's canonical approach by connecting it to the reception theory of Hans Robert Jauss, which underscores the importance of the later reader. Citing Jauss, Fiorenza says, "The readerly experience of the earlier reader can be recovered only by means of the actual reading done by the later reader, *so the difference between the past and the present must be worked out within the interpretation itself*" (emphasis added).[22]

Fiorenza clarifies in his article on the crisis of hermeneutics that the hermeneutic triangle must also be applied to the later reader attempting to recover the earlier reading (130–131).[23] Combining Fiorenza's insights with those of Sanders suggests that the hermeneutic triangle must function for both ends of the "hermeneutic circle" simultaneously and at points in between, creating in effect a hermeneutic triangle in three dimensions.

Broadening the hermeneutic circle into a three-dimensional hermeneutic triangle *attempts* to offer some "control" to the subjective element of interpretation. Such a broadening, in fact, points to the relativity of the whole enterprise. Theories about texts/traditions, context/situations, and hermeneutics, even while modifying the hermeneutical circle, remain themselves subject to change, revision, and interpretation (131). A simple example makes the dynamic described clear enough. Fiorenza traces the interpretations of the meaning of creation in Genesis over time, correlating the changes in the structural organization of society at any given reading moment with changes in how creation in Genesis is read. He concludes, "Creation does not refer to a pre-given reality or entail an interpretive discovery of an essence or an underlying identity. Instead, the very meaning of creation in Genesis has always been *constructive,* forged in a hermeneutical reconstruction of past traditions, new background theories and new experiences [his triangle]" (132–133). When the constraints upon interpretation and experience are themselves determined by interpretation and experience, the crisis in hermeneutics is complete.

Fiorenza, of course, responds to this crisis by calling for an evaluation, an "interpretative decision . . . as to what is decisive and essential . . . and what is not, what is paradigmatic and what is not" (133). And this evaluative task is both *constructive* and *reconstructive* in nature; it is not simply an act of uncovering an identity already present. Such a suggestion lies at the heart of questions about true and false prophecy taken up fully in the next chapter.

A fourth crisis ushering in postmodernity also found its genesis in the 1960s in what has been described as no less than a "methodological crisis" in literary studies. Not surprisingly, Jauss describes this crisis as a literary revolution of paradigmatic scale.[24] The large-scale changes that have shaped the literary-critical profession in the last twenty-five years especially underscore the disintegration of an earlier consensus in the field.[25] Trends in contemporary critical theory—structuralism, deconstruction, semiotics, hermeneutics, feminism, reader-oriented theories, psychoanalytic interpretation, and political thought, to name a few[26]—underscore the lack of any truly self-evident approach. Even the definition of literature itself has undergone intense scrutiny, foregrounding questions of interpretation and raising others about "authorized texts."[27] Taken together, these and other signs of shifting ground beneath the discipline of literary criticism insinuate that there is a crisis not yet resolved, foreshadowing the plight of canon in a postmodern context.

The "common-sense" consensus among the literati has given way to three decades of seemingly endless challenges to the canons of literature, climaxing in Harold Bloom's reassertion of the Western canon, with its cataloging of "the books and school of the ages." Such spirited defense notwithstanding, these challenges to the Western canon are not simply, as Bloom suggests, "the rabblement of lemmings" hurling themselves off of cliffs. The momentary chaos created by the crisis in literature may appear to be a screaming death-plunge of sorts, and no one would argue that the means to destroy canons is at hand. However, so too is the opportunity to open the old canons to new canonical works or to read old works in new ways. This task, as it has always been, even in the making of the Western canon, is a communal one, of which Bloom's voice may be a principal prophet in his call for a return to an authoritative reference (canon). However, the *means* by which he demands loyalty to the canon have dropped through the hourglass of modernity. The foundation on which Bloom asserts his claims, namely, the individual belief in the irreducibility of the aesthetic in all would-be canonical texts, stands on sinking sand. It does him no good to argue that such an aesthetic can be "recognized or experienced, but it cannot be conveyed to those who are incapable of grasping its sensations and perceptions," or to conclude that "to quarrel on its behalf is always a blunder."[28] Either Bloom is disingenuous in making such statements in a book arguing for his selection of truly canonical works against lesser others, or he naively refuses to acknowledge the necessary truth that all canons are the result of just such community quarrels. Surely Bloom knows that all canons are "battlefields of power." All canons are decided in just such contentious times. It is in the crucible of history in crisis that such canonical battles are won and lost. I, too, hope for and believe in the necessity of canons, be they literary, scriptural, or other referent-unifying authorities, but not on the grounds Bloom requires. His fear may be real and prophetic with regard to the Western (and other) canons, but if his prophecy proves true, it will not be for lack of trying to defend it but because of his refusal to defend it in the language and terms supplied in the new postmodern reality. That would be his failure, not that of the times in which we live. A prophet such as Bloom may not be accepted in his own country for all the wrong reasons, but a prophet whose message fails to take into full account the signs (language, social realities, epistemological categories) of his times may rightly be declared false.

Finally, not only did "the end of modernity" unravel socioeconomic, epistemological, hermeneutic, and literary consensus, but it unleashed what has been described as "biblical theology in crisis."[29] Although this crisis could trace its roots to brawls over history and dogmatics articulated much earlier by Gabler (1787) and Baumgarten-Crusius (1828),[30] the crisis today owes much to the atomizing deconstruction of the "winning" side of those earlier debates (the historical-critical method) to the virtual exclusion of the other side. Whole academies, departments, and curricula were divided along these battle lines. When we speak of biblical theology in crisis, we cannot isolate it from what has been said thus far, nor can we see it as unparalleled by crises extending throughout the theological disciplines generally.[31] It is not my aim here to defend the particulars of this or that formulation of the crisis but to note that biblical theology, as a reborn discipline flourishing throughout the 1940s and 1950s, came under severe attack beginning in the 1960s.[32] By 1970, this "movement" was given focus in Brevard Child's landmark book, *Biblical Theology in Crisis,* which declared the crisis obvious.

Noteworthy to the debate regarding the chaotic status of biblical theology was the coincidence of crises among other disciplines during this time. Likewise, proposals offering ways out of this methodological bog were forthcoming on many fronts.[33] Most particularly, emphases on the canon as a new discipline were prominent among the options outlined.[34] Defending canonical criticism as the most adequate response would have been premature at this stage, since the idea of "canon" itself, in the course of the crises outlined above, had reached its own potential demise.[35]

The Demise of "Traditional" Canons

Any argument suggesting the demise of canons presupposes a time when one could invoke a homogenized entity called "*the* canon." The history of "canon" shows that no such undiluted frame of reference ever really existed, even in the early Christian communities responsible for the *ur*-canon of modern literary studies.[36] On the other hand, the outrage among many in society today over the fact that new approaches are politicizing the age-old canons of life (including the Bible) suggests how successful the hegemony of age-old canons, which represent themselves as "natural" and "neutral," has been— having survived, as it were, by their own intrinsic power.[37] What is being described here as a "demise of 'traditional' canons," then, might more accurately be characterized as the demise of *a perception* that a *particular* canon has transcended the institutionalized interests—that is, the community-based authority responsible for its survival. The unraveling of consensus regarding monolithic perceptions of the canon was effected by four interlocking forces:

the ambiguity of the term itself, new questions regarding old theories about the biblical canon, influence of literary theory on the canonical process, and comparative studies of canon in other religions.

In the first instance, the ambiguity of the meaning and use of the word *canon,* whether in Greek, Latin, or English, whether in biblical or literary arenas, ensured that some confusion would arise with respect to points of consensus and conflict in the debate about canon.[38] Whether the meaning "rule" (norm) or "list" was uppermost in the minds of those who first applied the word "canon" to Scriptures (fourth century C.E.) is in heavy dispute. The varied uses in classical times, as well as good arguments for both understandings in the early Church, suggest both meanings grasp dimensions of the term's ambiguous use. Whether in its more literal sense, meaning "straight rod" or "ruler," its more metaphorical sense of "rule" or "norm," its use by Polycletus, Plato, and Aristotle, or its use within the Septuagint and New Testament, the word *canon* (Greek, *kanon;* Hebrew, *knh*) evokes controversy, as even the most cursory look at the history of interpretation of the concept displays.[39] The emergence of sacred canons augmented the earlier classical understandings of canon.[40] The recurring feature of sacred and secular canons was their use by particular communities to define themselves in contradistinction to others.[41] This last point is central to the raison d'être of canon and anticipates conclusions about the nature of canonical authority as being rooted in the life (survival) of the community.

If ambiguous terminology provided one force in the eventual demise of the traditional view of the biblical canon, a second force is found in new questions about old theories regarding the biblical canon itself. The shattering of long-held assumptions about the unbroken continuity between the writing and collection of scriptural books and about the finality of the Bible's canonical closure is a case in point. Literary criticism and tradition history as applied to the Bible, especially from the late nineteenth century on, which emphasize multiple sources and long prehistories of particular books, threatened the notion of an unbroken link between the original writing of a book and its acceptance as canonical. It became apparent that component parts must have reached canonical status long before the books in which they were embedded were themselves deemed canonical.[42] There was clearly a "canonical habit of mind" long before there was finally a canon.[43]

Traditionally, one discussed canon under the rubrics of *norma normata* and *norma normans,* the former referring to the body of scriptures in formal terms, the latter, in functional terms.[44] It was generally the pattern of traditional approaches to define the *norma normata* (lists of books included in the canon) as a means of setting the limits for understanding the *norma normans* (the measure of the authority that the ancient tradition exercised in the context of its use). By the end of the nineteenth century, H. E. Ryle, relying on the "assured" results of historical-critical work to date, provided what became the classic three-stage theory on the formation of the Old Testament canon. Ryle suggested the Old Testament was recognized as authoritative in three stages, coinciding with the three divisions of the Hebrew Bible: the Pentateuch was deemed canonical in the fifth century B.C.E.under Ezra (Neh. 8); the Prophets, in the third century B.C.E., before the inclusion of Daniel and Chronicles; and the Writings (along with the whole canon) were formally recognized as canonical at the Council of Jamnia in 90 C. E. Ryle's proposal underscored the dependence of canonical discussions on defining "closure" to *the* canon *before* its authoritative function could be entertained.[45]

The discoveries of the Dead Sea scrolls at Qumran (1947) soon broke the confidence in the traditional consensus regarding the historical formation of the canon as Ryle had proposed. For example, the Qumran Psalter varied in content and order from the known Masoretic text of the time, raising immediate questions about the well-defined "limits" of the canon.[46] Double editions of Jeremiah turned up. One edition appeared to be the *vorlage* of a shortened Jeremiah, much like that of the Septuagint version. The other edition was textually akin to the longer Masoretic-like version.[47] The variety of text types and "book" forms operating authoritatively at Qumran in effect consolidated all the diachronic and synchronic canonical and textual problems and their proposed solutions up to that time into a very narrow historical time frame and a very limited geographical area. It became apparent that to speak of *the* canon with the confidence of Ryle was no longer possible.[48] What was clear was that different religious groups within Judaism took different lines with regard to canon. The Masoretic tradition, though ancient, was not the only early canonical tradition with which to contend.

Equally compelling are other biblical canons whose attachments to ancient believing communities are just as persuasive.[49] The question of "Which canon?," then, is not easily answered. For example, there are two major canons of the Old Testament, Hebrew and Greek, which differ widely. The Jewish Hebrew canon and the Protestant canon, which includes the Hebrew, must be distinguished from each other by the inclusion of the New Testament by the Protestants. Of course, from a canonical-critical perspective, it is also right to distinguish the Samaritan canon from the Tanak of later Judaism. One could go on to discuss the Ethiopic and Roman Catholic canons, and so on. In point of interest, if not in fact, the first official church pronouncements formally defining the limits of the canon came after the Reformation—at Augsburg and then at Trent in the sixteenth century for the Protestant and Roman Catholic churches, respectively, and at the Council of Jerusalem in the seventeenth century C.E. for the Orthodox church.[50] How do such late pronouncements affect discussions of what canon, when, and whose?

Ironically, there were always multiple canons with which to contend, though the dominance of the relatively peaceful coexistence of the Roman Catholic and Protestant canons, coupled with the historical-critical consensus on the prehistory of canon, went a long way in staving off the impending "crisis." The pretense of a monolithic *ur*-canon by the church and academia was played out by appealing to common "original autographs" directly linked to individually inspired authors, whose identities were recoverable via historical-critical means. This in spite of the obviously different canons of the Roman Catholic and Reformation traditions, with their roots in the differing traditions of earlier canons (LXX and MT). Also, the use of convenient labels such as "deutero-canonical" eased the apparent discomfort invoked by the logic multiple canons offered. The Dead Sea scrolls laid bare the masquerade that heretofore linked authority issues (i.e., matters of canon) in a one-to-one relationship with "original" authors, that claimed inherent textual meanings to be intrinsic to sacred texts, or that believed in a monolithic *ur*-canon. By contrast, the Dead Sea finds declared unequivocally that single communities can appeal to multiple traditions of authority and that multiple communities create multiple canons.

It has since been argued on text-critical grounds that each textual tradition should be allowed the integrity of its own hearing before it is "pillaged" by text critics to reconstruct a hypothetical "autograph."[51] The argument now stands for the question of canon as well. Modern translators must now decide how best to provide new versions of the Bible that account for the pluriformity of apographs and multiple traditions available today and determine whether readers are ready for such an honest presentation of the current state of affairs.

What the obviously pluriform shape of multiple canons did do was raise new questions about the usefulness of the very idea of canon and highlight the "serious faults of method" surrounding the study of canon.[52] As a result, the earlier emphasis on canon as shape (*norma normata*) shifted to perceiving canon in functional terms (*norma normans*).[53] This shift asserted use over form, discourse over content, community over author, and hermeneutics over all, situating discussions of canon between the modern and postmodern horizons.

Besides the ambiguity of the term *canon* and the new questions raised about the biblical canon after Qumran, a third force effecting the demise of the "traditional" view of canon can be located in the influence of literary theory on the canonical process. The Bible has entered with new determination into contemporary English departments, and literary-theoretical discourse has enlisted the "Bible as literature" in new conversations.[54] If we are to answer the question posed earlier concerning what is meant by canonical authority, we cannot ignore the challenge literary concerns pose to biblical authority by way of their own questions regarding the making and maintaining of literary canons.

Arguably, literary concerns about canon pose a challenge to biblical authority greater than philological and archaeological "facts" ever did. This is perhaps because, as Regina Schwartz observes, "theological questions are more difficult to separate from literary theory than they were from the discoveries of archaeologists and philologists; in part because questions of faith are matters of theory."[55] Schwartz argues correctly that it is difficult to cordon off questions of interpretation when approaching the Bible on literary terms, even though historians and philologists seemed to find it laudable to do just that. However, questions about the multiplicity of interpretations, about the politics of interpreting, about gender and race construction, about repression in the Bible, about decentered subjects, and so on have to be faced by the devout and secular alike when reading the Bible as canonical literature.[56]

More than anything else, literary theory has underscored the nature of canon as process over against that of "shape" in part because "secular" canons are more permeable than ecclesiastical canons. The collective cultural process by which authors or their works come to be recognized as canonical in literary circles, called "canon formation," involves many of the same sensibilities and sorting that biblical texts and traditions underwent on the road to canon. Indeed, *in functional terms,* loose-bounded literary canons are quite comparable to their more restricted biblical counterparts. These close parallels have not always been appreciated because of prior theological claims regarding the uniqueness of the Bible's canonical *shape* (content/*norma normata*).

On the question of canon, the literary community's struggle with defining its various canons, their demise and rebirth, provides a telling example of the canonical process in general and, in particular, of the often concealed connections to the institutional interests defining the canon's shape and function. Arguments scrutinizing the literary canon and the "canonicity" of individual authors are in full bore among literary critics today and are spilling over into other fields. The arguments about canon in literary circles are quickly aligned with arguments about culture, values, authority, education, economics, and ideology. Any discussions of canon cannot avoid the politics of canon.[57] The general charge is that the "standard" literary canon is deeply biased in favor of writers who are white, male, middle class, and Anglo-Saxon and whose works are aimed at largely the same.[58] Not incidentally, the floodgates of critical concern regarding the demise of a monolithic canon of literature have released a deluge of new interest in the biblical canon as well.

A fourth and final force in the near-death experience of traditional views of canon is provided by comparative religionists. In *Rethinking Scripture: Essays from a Comparative Perspective,* Wilfred Cantwell Smith argues for the "common propensity to scripturalize" by human communities throughout the world.[59] He shows that the canonizing *process* (*norma normans*) is not all that different from religion to religion when it comes to the "integrating of former disparate or at least independent components into one reified entity."[60] Although I do not fully accept his claim that it was the Greek classical tradition that provided Greek-thinking Jews the "larger transcending context of the process of the development of classicized or canonized ancient texts,"[61] I fully appreciate the significance of his observations regarding canonical process in the broader religious context (temporally and geographically).[62]

Comparativists have shown, compartively and phenomenologically, in ever more convincing studies of "canons" of "scripture" that the shift in focus from canon as shape to canon as function is warranted.[63] Even the forms and concepts of scripture over the many centuries of Western hegemony, though tending in a certain direction, have continually changed. This fluidity of form is manifest wherever scriptures appear and is as varied in content/lists as disparate religious communities. The *process* of canonization finds close parallels across religious traditions, indicating that the uniqueness of the biblical canon cannot be maintained functionally. Whatever the final form of a given canon, the road there is well traveled by many traditions.

In summary, this section outlines the demise of "traditional" views of canon, both biblical and literary. We have seen that traditional views of canon were themselves situated in contexts of cultural, philosophical, epistemological, and literary influence and were directly affected by the dominance of this or that theory or faith commitment. The traditional view of canon as a list of normative texts (biblical and literary) has shifted to emphasize the function of canon. Such a change in focus was supported by shifting assumptions on the horizon of postmodernity and observations among comparative religionists. Whereas the Bible as canon may be unique, it now appears that its uniqueness lies in the community defining and validating its role as Scripture, not in some unparalleled process of formation or in its ontology per se. A defense of the biblical canon must now be argued on new grounds, the foundations of the old having been cleared away.

The Rise of Canons and Their Canonical Communities

Walter Brueggemann has asked, "Why do we have canon criticism now?"[64] His question is especially telling since the old, normative, evangelical reading of the text—that is, the very notion of the Bible as "inspired canon"—was largely abandoned with the rise of the historical-critical method more than a century ago. Following Brueggemann's lead, I have tried to show that discussions of canon have emerged now, and not then, because of the historical convergence of a series of deconstructive forces creating a watershed in contemporary experience and thought. In light of the demise of traditional views of canon, fallback positions from the (pre-)Enlightenment period are no longer adequate to address the question of canon as we know it at the "end of modernity." However, the anxiety created by the radical ambiguity of the new situation has become the horizon for renewed interest in canon. Certain historical moments of disorientation such as war, riots, or economic or natural disasters cry out for consolidation and for a renewed sense of shared traditions: a search for a renewed communal identity. The need to recapitulate old traditions as a means of transcending the miserable moment provokes a paradigm shift conducive to canonical formation or, in this case, the revival and redevelopment of canonical criticism.[65]

Discussions of canon(s) in a postmodern context must conform to the assumptions of a plural society, unlike the ecclesiastical canons of old that conformed to assumptions of a hierarchical universe. Also, one can no longer speak of canon or canon formation without acknowledging and explaining how much a particular canon's political functions account for its origins and limit its usefulness. On one hand, any such canon would have to be manifestly diverse, refusing to absolutize any single stance. On the other hand, it would have to argue for the necessity of constructing idealizations, however provisional, to counter the practical impossibility of living out the postmodern fondness for deconstruction, itself an often unacknowledged idealization.[66] In summary, such a canon would have to encompass the tensions between historical demand for contextualization arguing from the criterion of power and the aesthetic demand for constructive "idealizations" arguing from literary criteria. This question must be posed: Can the Bible as canon accommodate this tension in the present context?

A case must now be made that such a canonical stance can only happen when both approaches see themselves within historically situated communities of interpretation. In other words, either side must admit to the *context* of its own observations about the text—context directly linked to the hermeneutic "community" to which it is committed. To make the case, let me present a brief clarification of how James Barr and Brevard Childs, two representative claimants in the historicist/aesthetic debate, seem to undervalue their own situatedness, thereby failing to appreciate the larger dimension that might incorporate both. The canon(s) of James Sanders and Frank Kermode go a long way toward unifying the dissimilar stances of Barr and Childs. I will argue that even the *via media* of Sanders and Kermode succeeds not so much because of the "inherent" intertextual nature of their canon(s) as texts as because of the variety of "intertextual" reading strategies native to differing interpretative communities. This last argument will then be applied to the development of the biblical canon with the help of literary theories that emphasize power, politics, and canon formation. As a result, the groundwork for decisions of judgment between two prophets in conflict will have been laid.

The Reading Strategies of Modern "Canon-Makers"[67]

The "canonical criticism" of Brevard Childs has sparked ardent response and some vehement opponents, not least of whom is James Barr.[68] A complete description of Childs's approach is not necessary for our purposes. What is important is to recognize the significance Childs places on the literary, formal reading of the Bible as canon. Childs understands the Old Testament as a literary and theological unit with fixed parameters, arguing, as it were, for a renewed "aesthetic" interest in Scripture as an object of desire in its own right. Of course, Childs's interest in the aesthetic qualities of the Bible as Scripture is more a theological commitment on his part than a literary stance per se.[69] Along with the New Critics in literature, Childs bemoaned the loss of appreciation of the text's canonical shape made manifest by the deconstructing quests of the historical critics. For Childs, the meaning that is canonical for today's reader is the meaning the text has when it is read as part of the canon in its final form. There is, for Childs, a radical break with traditional readings, such as those of the historical critics, that depend upon discovering what a text's author must have meant in the political, social, and economic setting of a text's origin.[70] He does not discount the history of the formation of the canon but relativizes it to the canon in its full, final, and, for him, ultimately valid form.[71]

Naturally, historians like James Barr who see the canon as an arbitrary, late imposition on texts with no relevance to the original readers find Childs's conclusions intolerable. For Barr, it is not the canon that gives the books their authority but the events and persons about which and whom the books report. If anything, canons impede historical investigation. Whereas Childs finds the true meaning in the final canonical form, Barr finds it in the original person or event. The discrepancy between Barr and Childs is the variance between "objective" history and a hermeneutic approach to truth.[72]

What neither Childs nor Barr seems to appreciate fully is that, in true Gadamer-like fashion, both of them, consciously or not, assume a need to relate the individual text to a total context. Barr's preunderstanding requires him to apply the individual text to the total historical situation, which for him is the "true," "objective" historical context. Childs's preunderstanding requires him to discern the text in the unity of its meaning, in its total textual context (the formal canon). Both are guided by preunderstandings growing out of their own "situatedness." Both presuppose some sort of totality to which they appeal as final norm.[73] This confidence—whether in the integrity of the canon or in sentiments for all that is pretextual, that is, for persons and events behind the text—compels a stance appropriately described by the language of faith.[74] In a postmodern context, such an outlook need not be pejorative. Rather, it describes the "ground" of *every* construct in the age of probable reasoning, scientific or theological.[75]

If Childs and Barr represent opposing communities of interpretation within biblical scholarship, James Sanders and Frank Kermode access communities of coincidence at the intersection of literary and canonical criticism. Sanders, the canonical critic, and Kermode, the literary critic, both offer a *via media* between Childs and Barr, a middle passage whose parameters are invoked by the phrase "canon of interpretation."[76] Both Sanders and Kermode juggle competing claims of history (the past) and aesthetic sensitivities (the present) into a convincing canonical synthesis—what Jan Gorak calls "a fluctuating canon hospitable to all possible interpretative demands, except the demand to dissolve the canon itself."[77]

Rather than treating the text as simply a difficult means of getting at history embedded in the whole historical context (Barr) or treating history simply as a precursor to the final form of a text that constitutes its own context (Childs), Kermode and Sanders recommend treating the canon as a stage in tradition whose parameters are ultimately determined by the imposition of a text's intertextuality.[78] The way in which Kermode and Sanders defend their cause is to take the very weapons used by those inclined to destroy canons—historicity, multivalency, pluralism, contradiction—and wield them to guarantee the survival of the traditional canon. For them, the survival of the canon now depends upon the relinquishment of its identity (in terms of a strictly bounded *norma normata*) into the hands of its interpreters (*norma normans*). The canon, thus formulated, is saved for a pluralistic society as "a crowning gift to all [people] to resist every tyranny which would claim them."[79]

The canon's diversity, evidenced by its laudable potential for endless resignifications and new interpretations in ever new settings, subjects it to hermeneutic challenge. That challenge is met by a hermeneutically defined unity. For Kermode, this larger transcendent pattern is finally defined as "mystery"[80] or a sort of "magic."[81] For Sanders, it is described in functional terms as the "monotheizing process," which is equivalent in existential terms to "Reality" and in theological terms to "God."[82] What is different for both Sanders and Kermode from the similar claims of the precritical era is their tentative recognition that these "canons," these "imaginative ideals," these "mythic patterns," these unifying "fictions," are ultimately hermeneutic constructs rooted in the experience of (believing) communities of interpretation.[83]

Kermode and Sanders are a bit equivocal in their stated commitments, as can be seen in their appeal to the canonical text's inherent authoritative claims over the hermeneutic community—a sort of canonical privilege of the text.

What they do not fully appreciate is that the Bible or any other work, *as canon*, does not have authoritative value apart from some communal validation. Even the confession that the Bible is somehow and in some mysterious way divine, as some would claim it to be, is a community-authorized commitment. Or to confess that God has somehow made and declared this text inspired, as I myself am wont to believe, is likewise a community-determined affirmation. Other communities with their own canons say as much and more. Without such validation, literarily or spiritually, it would be just another book on the shelf or a buried tablet in the lost library of an ancient world. I have argued, using the insights of Kermode and Sanders regarding interpretative communities, for the priority of the community in defining its canon. Any control a canon has over its reading community presumes that community's submission to it. Kermode alludes to this when he describes inspired exegetes who ensure the survival of the canon by their willingness to say a thousand times over, "This is valuable, this endures as long as we do."[84] Presumably, such a confession includes the process of its transmission across the generations. The canon of sacred scripture lives by the ongoing faith in its authority by believing communities across time and space.

In their attention to interpretation, both Sanders and Kermode shift away, if subtly, from the canonical object to the institutions and assumptions that render a work canonical.[85] It is ultimately in these institutions, these believing communities, that the question of canon is settled. In this sense, the makers of canons, both secular and sacred, ancient and modern, share in similar myths, fictions, and transcendent constructs necessary to reduce diverse experiences, texts, interpretations, and resignifications to a single hermeneutic order called, in this case, canon. I reiterate: There is no one anywhere at any time who is not engaging in precisely this hermeneutical move. Pragmatic psychological and social factors demand it. As Henry Gates has so eloquently argued, the choice is never between institutions, the mediators of all canons, and no institutions, but what kind of institutions are determining what kind of institutions.[86] Even the deconstructionists have their canon and deem valuable (i.e., canonical) those works that in the process of their writing deconstruct themselves.

Canonical and literary critics alike at the "end of modernity" can fully appreciate the fact that literary (including biblical) texts do not make themselves into canons—people do. The survival of the canon, as such, is community-dependent. Harold Bloom's insistence that it is the intrinsic value of a canonical work that guarantees its survival must now be countered.[87] To argue, as he seems to do, that the survival of a literary piece proves its canonical "worthiness" begs the question. This is especially so if it is in fact the power of a dominant social order that holds the key to the literary work's survival.[88] Of course, as will be shown later, it is not always the power of dominance that enables a piece to survive; a power of a whole different sort can provide the survival mechanism for a literary piece. In either case, it is communal power, not the irreducibility of the text and its inherent content, that keeps it alive. A text's canonical worthiness is, after all, a constantly changing, socially chosen value dependent less on the text's inherent quality than on the readers reading it. What should be clear to almost anyone is that textual excellence, like beauty, lies in the eye of the beholder. Acts of communal power, even as simple as the power to decide what will be read today, lie at the core of canonical formation and the canon's ongoing survival. An inquiry into the canon-making power of the canonical community is in order.

The Canon-Making Power of the Canonical Community

Reference to power has become an essential element in any exploration of canon formation and in the circulation of canonical texts of scripture.[89] Indeed, the biblical canon was forged in the crucible of fluctuating "power-flows" among Israel's prominent neighbors and patrons. For our purposes, "power" will be understood as defined by Max Weber as the chance to impose one's will against the resistance of others; power is the tension between interests, ideologies, classes, or individuals.[90] These contests of wills take place within larger structures that are themselves also constituted by power relations.

One does not have to fully concur with the general conclusions of J. Blenkinsopp in his work *Prophecy and Canon* to appreciate the truth in his categorical claim that "what we call 'canon' is intelligible only in the context of conflicting claims to control the redemptive media and, in particular, to mediate and interpret authoritatively the common tradition."[91] Explaining canon in terms of power differentials works well for historians and those of radical historicist persuasion.[92] However, an unequivocal stance on the matter, as defined historically, may prove to be too reductionistic to explain power of a different sort—namely, "the ethical *force* of imaginative *ideals*" (emphasis added).[93]

In our setting, the historicism of Barr and the theological aestheticism of Childs provide the alternating contexts possible for articulating the canon-making power of interpretative communities. The language of power thus provides the discursive conditions for understanding the following discussion of power. To begin with, the role of power in the biblical canon's formation will be traced *historically* as "the will to power." A counter-reading of canon formation will then be traced *aesthetically* as the "power contrary to power." The contributions of both biblical and literary disciplines will center our query.

In their recent book, *Power, Politics, and the Making of the Bible,* Robert and

Mary Coote detail the history of Scripture as a "history of power and power-ful organizations."[94] Beginning in David's court, literature and ritual were used to buttress David's legitimacy and rule. This literary kernel, containing traces of all three sections of what came to be the Tanak, became the first in a long line from David to Constantine whereby scriptures were used to legiti-mate a change in rule (25–27).[95] The turning points in canonical history were linked to the building of the Temple, the restoration of the Temple under the Persians, the destruction of the Temple by Rome, the re-creation of the Temples by Constantine, and the legal canonizations under Roman Law, the Church's canon law, and the Babylonian Talmud (162). At every point along the way, layer upon layer, revision upon revision, the Bible was formed out of power struggles between "rich men, who were its primary consumers and dominate its history" (11). During this 1,800 years, society was hier-archical and pyramidal, the relatively few elite landowners and rulers at the top and the many poor and powerless at the bottom. Each pyramid of power was bound together up and down by claims and responsibilities and common response to external threats (12).

The development of Scriptures grew out of the same process of interpreta-tion that would later be applied to the final form, thus ensuring that the "canonical state of mind" from the start was operating under a "will to power." Gerald Bruns explains:

> The distinction between canonical and noncanonical is thus not just a distinction between authentic and inauthentic texts—that is, it is not reducible to the usual oppositions between the inspired and the mundane, the true and the apocryphal, the sacred and the profane, and so on. On the contrary, it is a distinction between texts that are forceful in a given situation and those which are not. From a hermeneutical standpoint, in which the relation of a text to a situation is always of primary interest, the theme of canonization is power.[96]

Not sufficiently addressed by either Coote and Coote or Bruns is how the exile and the destruction of both Temples (587 B.C.E. and 70 C.E.) influenced the biblical canon's formation in ways antithetical to the power motives that may have brought it together. Coote and Coote do acknowledge the incor-poration of concepts in Scripture that were antithetical to the power elite but suggest these were mostly theoretical political platforms that came back to haunt future elites (via the prophets, for example) when Scripture bounced from ruler to the ruled in subsequent generations (18). That is, the self-interest central to a model of power-centered canon formation occasionally backfired.

What seem to Coote and Coote to be exceptional vulnerabilities in a history of power plays I would argue are not exceptional at all but crucial to under-standing the very type of power used in the Bible's formation. The points at which the very survival of Israel/Judah mattered most were those of intense canonical formation, when even the elite found themselves powerless to change their social and political reality. At those times, the elite canon-makers were finally persuaded that even their identity no longer rested in land or power-based entitlements but in "mere" words that told them who they were. In a remarkable twist of historical irony, the "winner" of the power struggle over canon formation had become a *literary* document.

One would not expect such a concession from Coote and Coote or Bruns insofar as literary texts pressed into canons remain, for them, primarily impressions of power propelled by power criteria. There is, however, a certain kind of political power available primarily to the powerless, the vulnerable, those in exile whose identity is a matter of survival, that may not be accounted for by a total embrace of power criteria as defined by the radical historicists. In describing the canon-making power of the interpretative community, this second type of power has been accurately characterized as the "ethical force of imaginative ideals"—a "power contrary to power."[97] Such imaginative ideals need not be apolitical or unpragmatic. In a book edited by Vaclav Havel, *The Power of the Powerless: Citizens against the State in Central-Eastern Europe,* an essay by Havel serves as an imaginative ideal in the face of neototalitarian states.[98] The essay is widely seen as the theoretical basis for the Solidarity movement that emerged out of the joint Czechoslovak-Polish literary dissident efforts. Clearly, not all literature worthy of the name canonical is so labeled because powerful rich men are its primary consumers and dominate its history, as Coote and Coote seem to suggest. Such a force derives from aesthetic idealizations that are no less basic to the concept of canon than are the differential power categories outlined above.

Providing a contrast to power-based criteria for canon formation, Hazard Adams in "Canons: Literary Criteria/Power Criteria" builds a case for literary power that is "contrary to power" in what he terms a "visionary antitheticality" (756).[99] He concludes that a total embrace of power criteria, even in the name of a heroic resistance to tyranny, results in the annihilation of the self as a "free" agent for choosing which canon-defining community one wishes to call one's own. He lays at the feet of Foucault and Lacan this negation of the individual in favor of the ubiquitous play of external power plays (752). Adams asserts that, in contrast, the individual's relative personal power to choose his or her canon-defining community conserves the will of the individual to dissent.

Here is not the place to debate the age-old wars of "determinism" versus "free will." I have argued earlier, standing alongside Fish, that the individual who chooses not to participate in one community of discourse, is nevertheless always and forever a part of some alternative community of discourse, acknowledged or not. However, I agree with Adams against Foucault and

Lacan here that the individual does have a relative power of his or her own not totally determined by the play of external power conflicts. With this relative power comes personal choice to dissent or to transfer from one community of interpretation to another. In other words, on the continuum that runs from Fish to Adams to Foucault/Lacan on the question of freedom of the individual, I fall somewhere between Fish and Adams, albeit closer to Fish. What can be said is that the individual conscience and will are "free enough" to choose between alternative ways to use power. Of course, having said that, I am simply admitting that my hermeneutic community informs such a belief in the relative "freedom of the will."

Adams is not trying to evade the historically situated reality that canons of all types are "battlefields of power" (so Bloom). In fact, he readily admits that literary canons are "probably mainly, the product of invocation of power criteria" (751). Having said that, he argues that they are not entirely so, do not need to be, and ought not be. At the same time, literary criteria should not be fully embraced as an alternative. The elevation of literary criteria to universal law in a formalist sense can only be attempted by surrendering to their own version of power (752). If he wishes to maintain the importance of the aesthetic dimension in canon formation, Adams appears to have painted himself into a corner, and he admits as much by asking, "Can there be an antithetical canon with all the implications of power criteria in the term 'canon'?" (754).

He answers the question with a yes and no of sorts by showing that some works are included in the modern literary canon(s) that stand opposed to power trends, harboring antithetical characteristics in spite of the motives that may have brought them into the canon (754). In effect, Adams is arguing for antithetical criteria to counter situations in which power criteria negate literary criteria or the much rarer instances in which literary criteria negate power criteria (751). He posits the possibility of a "pure [antithetical] aestheticism" (751) that might be considered, in the words of James Sanders cited earlier, "a crowning gift to all [people] to resist every tyranny which would claim them." In this way, Adams can admit a canon that would forever remain "dissatisfied with stasis." At the same time, such a canon would reject "the concept of pure flux that disregards the necessary moments when one must stop and formulate a reading only eventually to go on" (758). His new antithetical aestheticism suggests that the spoils do not necessarily go to the strongest but may, in fact, go to the weakest, whose "visionary antitheticality is a power contrary to power" (756)—the power of "antithetical persuasion" (758). The familiar hermeneutic of suspicion and Sanders's hermeneutic of "prophetic critique" are examples of what Adams here calls "antithetical persuasion."

Akin to Adams, but more expansive in argument, is Charles Altieri's *Canons and Consequences: Reflections on the Ethical Force of Imaginative Ideals*.[100]

Altieri calls for a correction to power categories that fail to account for the fact that literature can contribute to the social good in noncoercive ways (3–4). He proposes a model of provisional reverence or communally negotiated authority necessary to avoid simply applying values of pure self-interest or social manipulation to our situation (7). Altieri would agree with Adams on the need for a renewed "aesthetic" dimension to stand alongside the new historicism characterized by certain "imaginative ideals." Standing with Adams at the horizon of postmodernity, Altieri sees these idealizations from their *ethical* genesis, not as mere universal abstractions. These are not the old, ahistorical ideals in any sense but rather abstractions from history that allow us to track certain features of another's cares (ethics) and even explore idealizations we might share (17).

Whereas Adams declared his "ideal" to be an "antithetical visionary stance," Altieri's canon (of the past) is a provocateur that reveals imaginative configurations (both negative *and* positive) that show us what is at stake in the most radical contemporary experiments (15). Rather than celebrate Nietzsche-inspired versions of the will to power (with all its negations), Altieri argues for a more compassionate, although no less antifoundationalist, humanism that defines interests that empower us to envision a "public life built on principles of reciprocity, appreciation of differences, and the capacity to negotiate those differences by cultivating concerns for justice" (12). It is a call to a communal civil life.

Altieri's canon, like all canons before and since, is communally negotiated. New canons must be fought over and must meet the challenge of all previously formulated canons. New canon-makers must defend the communal criteria by which their proposed canon hopes to come to exist. This does not presuppose that the former canonical communities were aware of the challenges they undertook or were posing for all would-be canon-makers in their lineage. It does argue for some sense of community spirit that counters Nietzsche's bald "will to power." Indeed, part of a community's survival depends on the will to limit one's power, not in order to "honor some abstract command but to achieve freedom to enjoy a sense of intimate belonging or to characterize oneself as accepting reciprocities that demonstrate one's commitment to community" (315). In contradistinction to Adams's hermeneutic of suspicion directed toward all canon-making communities, even those provisionally accepted as one's own, Altieri offers a more positive, cooperative hermeneutic of commitment also necessary to the canon-forming enterprise. Sanders's language of "constitutive support," emphasizing as it does providential care and endorsement of the basic institutions of life, reflects an important hermeneutic perspective in the canonical process.

Doubtless the play of difference between history and aesthetics is the difference between alternative plays of power (both kinds) situated in differing canon-making communities. The rise and fall of interest in canons, like the making and remaking of canons themselves by alternative interpretative communities, foreshadow the canonical function at play in adjudicating so-called true from so-called false prophecy. Although discourse on true and false prophecy awaits scrutiny in the next chapter, the implications of what we have discussed in this chapter remain to be synthesized.

Conclusions: God and Canon Power

Canon, Crisis, and Hope

This chapter ends where it began, asking the question, What is meant by canonical authority? It was shown that any response to the question must now take on a different cast from earlier responses to the same question in light of the deconstructive moves taking place in many fields, not least of which were the biblical and literary disciplines, over the last thirty years. Old authorities and ways of knowing that depend on revelation, the inherent sacredness of a text, human reason, and experience (psychological, social, phenomenological, comparative, gender-based, or metaphysical) that were considered foundations of past claims to authority were found to be the straightforward play of value-laden choices open to social, political, and economic judgments.

The concept of canon itself, long a symbol of a "natural" and "neutral" basis of authority—surviving, as it were, by its own intrinsic power—was shown to be the less than innocent product of interpretative communities. The play of differences that had radicalized the plurality of language and the ambiguity of history now widened the playing field to include multiple contending canons, unraveling any consensus of a monolithic perception of *the* canon, biblical or otherwise.

The several crises emerging in almost historical coincidence (ca. 1960) undermined confidence in authority generally and canonical authority in particular. These crises marked a shift in horizon from modernity to postmodernity, whose frame of orientation was characterized by communally negotiated and constructed frames of orientation as varied as the communities creating them. To describe the situation as unbridled pluralism is appropriate. Such a pluralism provides certain strengths not always appreciated under more monolithic constructs: opening human experience to the widest possible diversity of powers; giving voice to the canonically silenced; and ensuring a rich variety of options for living. In such a scheme, the various communities, values, canons, and gods all have a certain integrity of their own that is worthy of reflection and interaction.

Life under the deconstructive forces at the "end of modernity" parallels in fascinating ways the polytheistic framework of a much earlier period, for both benefit and peril.[101] Since there is no perception of a single high god or supreme principle beyond all others to provide a sense of unified "world-picture," there are no clear criteria for arbitrating between competing values. In addition, there is no focus for an overarching commitment that might provide an integrity to the participants and communities so situated. Such a rich and varied panoply can threaten disintegration and chaos when conflict arises between factions in the absence of any clear-cut adjudicator.[102] Life under this framework can become pretty much a matter of reaction against competing powers (and gods). The self, as noted earlier, is then determined by power struggles external to it (so Lacan, Foucault).

This study has noted that the anxiety created by such a situation has served to advance renewed discussions of canon. New conceptions of canon must account for the advantages of a pluralistic (polytheistic?) frame of reference while advancing the argument for a still more comprehensive framework that might overcome the tendencies toward anarchy and fatalism (annihilation of the self, loss of personal responsibility) characteristic of such radical pluralistic "world-pictures."

Reference to canonical authority can no longer be merely asserted but must be defended with the full acknowledgment on the part of its defenders that the criteria they adduce for such acceptance begins with a confession. In the past, confessional commitments have been ridiculed and subsumed under claims that were equally confessional, though thought not to be so—claims thought to be self-evident, commonsensical, objectively scientific, or universally defensible. The future of any canon lies in a developing maturity and acceptance among its makers of their responsibility in creating communities of cooperation, coherence, and civility *out of which* canons might emerge that are worthy of invitation to "outsiders" willing to join such a community guided by such a canon, secular or religious. Herein lies the hope of the canonical process, in that it requires not just the rhetoric of persuasion but also a persuasive ethic that this canon and not another is worthy of the name. As such, canon becomes a paradigm for living. The idea of canon still offers a political, social, and potentially spiritual model for living in fractious times. For those claiming the Bible in its many canonical forms as their guide to faith and practice, the postmodern context comes as blessing. For those who long for a return to the unquestioned foundations of the past, that blessing may come in disguise. Whereas the old evangelical commitments to persuading others to join one's canonical community must give way to new models of persuasion on different "grounds," the playing field of discourse has now been opened wide for doing just that, and it is a playing field more level and egalitarian than ever before.

The challenge to the people of God is the challenge of becoming a truly ethically based (covenant) community: to prove in practice what it has always said it believed about the Bible as its canon. *How* a community lives under the influence of its canon may be the key to any acceptance of *what* its canon proclaims as true. One such claim central to the biblical canon holds the key to its survival. The ongoing survival of the Bible as canon lies in its mythic and moral claim of the one God over its many and conflicting parts. Therein lies its greatest hope.

Canon and the One God

I return then to the canonical construct of James Sanders, who argues for what he calls the "monotheizing process" intrinsic to canon formation. Important to understanding Sanders's proposal, situated as it is at the brink of postmodernism, is the acknowledgment (a methodological self-consciousness) of several particulars. First, Sanders's proposal is *a* reading, one among a number of other possible readings of the Bible as canon, each of whose claim must be argued for by the community committed to its advancement. For example, another reading of the Bible as canon could argue from its ability to deconstruct itself, *including its own canonicity,* as the ultimate criterion of its canonical power. Still others could argue for a polytheistic reading of sorts, insofar as the text is read historically without regard to its role as canon in defining its monotheistic stance. Indeed, the monotheizing process, as a conceptual apparatus for framing life under its authority, has certain disadvantages (as well as benefits) that might argue against it. These disadvantages, which will be spelled out later, suggest the possibility of its rejection by certain reading communities.

A second factor in understanding what Sanders means by the canon's "monotheizing process" lies in a reading that emerges out of a context of radical deconstruction and crisis at the "end of modernity," as was argued earlier in this chapter. This was no small factor in proposing a reinvestigation of canon that focused in a new way on canon as function (supporting its pluralism), while maintaining the importance of its shape (supporting its unity). Indeed, Gorak is correct to suggest that Sanders's canonical proposal "validates the biblical canon for a plural society," unlike the canons of the early church fathers that conformed their assumptions of canon to a hierarchical universe. At the same time, Sanders affirms the power of the canon to suggest the ultimate shape and destiny of the believing community.[103] In this sense, Sanders's proposal is as much a *constructive* enterprise as "pure" "exegetical" description based on modernist (i.e., historical-critical) assumptions.

The postmodern context influenced still a third methodological factor for understanding Sanders's monotheizing proposal, though here I am extending

Sanders beyond what might rightly be called his own.[104] Insofar as Sanders's construct can be said to be an "imaginative ideal" emerging out of abstractions from history (ethos!) over against a purely ahistorical symbol (mythos), it is properly situated at the onset of postmodernity. Sanders's "monotheizing process" derives from the symbol "God" as inherited from ancient Israel's developmental relationship to "other gods."[105] Sanders describes this canonical process as unfolding in four historical shifts, from depolytheizing to monotheizing to Yawehizing to Israelitizing. The temptation was always present to move from rampant pluralism to narrow parochialism. What happened, of course, was that Israel's canon ended up undermining Israel's own denominational tendencies with its stronger monotheizing force in the compressed canon.

By the time of the exile, the cumulative effect of attributes and names associated with God throughout Israel's history constructed the belief in God as the sole power creating and governing the universe (Gen. 1 and 2; Isa. 44:6, 45:6, 12). Thus, in the face of much evidence to the contrary, the universe was believed to be ordered by the purposes and acts of the one and only God. For Sanders, this God-construct emerged canonically in the literary juxtaposition and compression of the many gods into the One. Such a reading, of course, serves as a strong argument in favor of the claim that what came to be (and can be) said as true canonically speaking may not have been (and may not be) true historically.[106]

The canon, in drawing together the many into One, provided a focus that brought order to what was (is) a chaotic interplay of powers and supplied an ultimate frame of reference for orienting life. In other words, the theological construct "God," in its monotheistic conceptualization, could now be said to correlate with an existential construct arguing for an "integrity of reality," which in turn compares to the unifying function of canon and the unified structure declared in its shape.[107] Of course, like all constructs, this one is defined in the context of an interpretative community who must defend it against its challengers. It is very possible, for instance, to argue that humans are simply pawns subject to the whimsy of ever-changing cosmic forces or to argue for some other version of life that emphasizes the pluralism of our choices and decries any attempts to discipline them in morally responsible ways.[108]

Indeed, the most serious disadvantage of the monotheizing hermeneutic lies in the fact that its reach is totalitarian—that is, it claims to have implications for all dimensions of life, including so-called secular ones.[109] God, on high, orders and determines all else. Such a characterization of God can all too readily slip into oppressive hierarchical attitudes and actions, the evidence of which is strewn across the historical landscape. Polytheisms, for their part, at least allow for many gods with different interests, authorizing different claims on differing communities and individuals, thus relativizing one another's interests. By contrast, Kierkegaard's interpretation of the Abraham/Isaac story (Gen. 22) shows the danger in accepting the claims of God operating within the construct of a radical monotheizing hermeneutic.[110]

Sanders, of course, recognizes the potential disadvantages of his construct of an all-powerful "God" and so qualifies God on moral grounds, using the theologem: "the freedom of the God of Grace."[111] Such a conceptualization of God emphasizes, as it were, a self-correcting interplay between God conceived as Creator and God conceived as Redeemer.[112] In addition, any potential for God-human role confusion within a monotheizing hermeneutic is corrected by stressing that God's absoluteness must be conceived of in such a way that it always and forever calls into question every human claim about God. In effect, he implicates God as the supreme relativizer of all human activity, including the biblical canon and all that it contains: "The only really unifying factor in the Bible is . . . the oneness of God, to which all the parts, in one way or another, when joined together, point and testify."[113] No one part expresses in itself the whole.

The advantage of Sanders's monotheizing hermeneutic is that it provides an ultimate unifying *construct* under which the debates between historicists such as Barr and theological aestheticists such as Childs can be negotiated; power criteria and literary criteria can each find their reference; both the hermeneutic of suspicion (Adams's visionary "antitheticality") and the hermeneutic of commitment (Altieri's "imaginative ideals") have their place; and canon-making communities can locate a center from which to negotiate their differences. Indeed, whether some version of a particular canon is endorsed or whether all canons are cursed under the monotheizing hermeneutic, one can see how each combatant in fact hears and is dependent, even if unknowingly, on the other's contrary argument in order to complete his or her own. Michael Fishbane in his book *The Garments of Torah* describes the Bible in much the same way Sanders envisions the canon as paradigm—it is "a model for the pluriform visions of humanity and in so being it functions a prophetic role keeping humanity aware of idealistic ideologies and ideological idealizations."[114] The function of canon as a monotheizing process, accordingly, allows for a realistic norming process within pluralism rather than "assuming (with modernism) that pluralism is the end of all norms, or (with orthodoxy) that norms are the end of all pluralism."[115] However, given the very real and possibly totalitarian claims that the biblical canon's monotheistic thrust could endorse, a final word about the canonical process and power is necessary.

Canon and the Power of the Powerless

It is important to note the primacy given to meaning production as derived from the *Sitz im Leben* (real-life living situation) of those periods of intense canonical formation of the Bible. It was mentioned earlier that the exile (and the post–second Temple period) provided the crucible out of which the canon was given its relative shaping. For Israel to survive under such persecution, it needed for its source of survival an indestructible element in society (unlike the Temple or any other religious icon or "vessel") that would be commonly available, highly adaptable, and (unlike land) portable, if necessary. Only a story could respond to all four criteria. Only the Torah did.[116]

A book of words, reconstituted as canon (Torah and Prophets) by a disarmed, dispossessed community in exile, became the paradigm judging all forms of coercive power used to decide the identity and survival of a people and its canon. Of great canonical significance for the Bible is its canonization of the raucous debate "between its covers"—a debate made physically powerless in exile in the form of "mere" literature. In doing so, it functioned (and continues to do so) as a paradigm of praxis for all other conflicts. It is a canon whose authority derives from its *performance* as a "democracy of words" (arguments) over against virulent forms of willful power imposing itself on another. Its very form and function as canon dominate its own violent content. Excising the most virulent conquest book in the Bible, the Book of Joshua, from its first canon (the Torah) and placing it as an introduction to a failed history (Joshua–2 Kings) argue in miniature what can be said more generally: that the canonical form and function overwhelm the Bible's own violent tendencies.

Gil Bailie, following the anthropological and literary insights of René Girard, argues persuasively that the Bible's anthropological distinction lies in its empathy for victims over and over again. This, he suggests, overpowers the Bible's own attempt to mythologize its violence and venerate it as divinely decreed. All cultures, as evident in their canonical literature (myths undergirding sacred violence), have had to choose between confronting the truth about their violent measures in suppressing the opposition, on the one hand, and enjoying the camaraderie such sacred violence generated, on the other. He summarizes: "What is distinctive about the Bible is that it is the first literature in the history of the world to grapple with the moral dilemma this choice represents."[117] The canonical community in exile chose to face this moral dilemma when it determined the extent of its first canon of Scripture and the form of its second component part, the Prophets. Any reading of the Bible's content must hermeneutically incorporate the authoritative function of the canonical process. As has been argued, what is truly canonical about the Bible may be its lessons in *how* texts are to be read (how texts function) over their content.

A canon whose authority derives from its *performance* as a book of conflicting *words* models for us first principles in communal negotiation. Such a canon insists on nonviolence as a first principle (rule of order) in any canonical dispute. If the exile and rebirth of Israel are any indication, ultimately, inscripturated words—powerless in form yet politically potent—can stand within the community of commitment against all invading armies. I grant the fact that such a canonical claim, born as it is from my own communal context, must also face the challenge of other counter-readings claiming canonical authority.

Clearly, the goal of canon should never be to remove crisis or conflict from reality. It is not perchance that Plato frequently used metaphors of war, hunting, and athletic competition to describe philosophical investigation. For Plato, philosophy belonged to the political domain of persuasion, and he played to win.[118] However, though the biblical canon is by nature conflictual, a "battlefield of differences," it demonstrates in form and function that crises must be negotiated in and between canon-making communities in a non-lethal, noncoercive manner in which the only weapon is word against word; the only battle, persuasion.

II

NEGOTIATING READINGS IN TRUE AND FALSE PROPHECY

True and False Prophecy in Canonical Criticism

I HAVE attempted thus far to describe the paradox of reality as interpreted through the bifocals of literary and canonical criticism. I have maintained that conflicting readings are both inevitable (the linguistic argument) and necessary for understanding (the epistemological argument). I have further argued that the role of belief in *all* forms of understanding makes disagreement inescapable. Belief also provides *all* disciplines with a starting point for constructing liveable models for evaluation and testing, in turn raising questions about canons and their communities.

The ontological consequences of this description suggested further that previous depictions of the mode of existence of texts as autonomous objects did not do justice to their intertextual nature or to their reader-dependent status. Situating texts within their respective reading communities, whether original audiences or present-day readers, raised further questions as to the authority of these interpretative communities and their canons.

All in all, though some ground was cleared by way of describing the rise and fall of canons, it became increasingly apparent that the clash of canons and their canon-making communities was *functionally* equivalent to the clash of prophetic ideologies that instigated this study in the first place. In effect, by necessarily placing the discussion of prophetic conflict in its larger, community-dependent canonical context, it would seem we have traded a narrower set of questions for a broader set whose answers are no less critical to both: Can authority be detached from questions of context and use? Can any interpretation claim universal correctness? What grounds are there for choosing between alternative readings? Is Nietzsche's claim that "there is no truth, only an array of interpretations" itself a truthful statement? How does the play of power affect the value of a reading? What are the social and political effects of a particular reading? Whose interests are being legitimated by what ideology? In short, can one distinguish a true prophet from a false one? If so, how?

As in previous chapters, data will be gathered from the fund of literary and canonical discussions to assist in responding to these and other questions of adjudication.[1] After reviewing the story of research on true and false prophecy, an apology on the ethical force of canonical criticism as the best method for negotiating conflicting readings will be articulated.

The Unfolding Story of Research in True and False Prophecy

The story of Old Testament research in true and false prophecy is influenced by the perspective from which prophecy in general was viewed.[2] The criteria for judging between conflicting prophets as manifest in the unfolding drama of research illustrate just how dependent such criteria are on the readers' own reading contexts, claims of neutrality and objective analysis notwithstanding. In addition, the very search by these scholars for criteria to withstand the test of universality will be shown to be fruitless, though telling.

Age-old questions about how to discern true prophecy from false are not lacking. Criteria based on factors such as the lack of a prophecy's fulfillment, the particular sociopolitical setting of the prophet, whether a prophet was specifically labeled true or false, or emphasis on the spiritual and psychological motivation of the prophet often assume an either/or explanatory stance with regard to distinguishing a "true" prophet from a "false" one. These and other questions may need to begin to address the ambiguous multidimensional possibilities involved: Does a false assessment of the historical situation turn a true prophet into a false prophet *for that particular historical hour*? Is false or true prophecy a permanent state, or can true prophets become false and false true, regardless of their title, motivation, or call? Were prophets ever completely assured of their own status, or did they walk "the razor's edge between certitude and doubt" all their days?[3] Are canonical prophets always true in every context, or must critical judgment be passed on them in every new context, including their present canonical context and our own? If so, how?

The story of prophetic research follows the path of interest from prophet to message to audience, as does the naming of criteria. Like all (hi)stories, the story of research in true and false prophecy is more complex than is suggested here. To be sure, curiosity about these three interests (prophet, message, audience) overlapped in time and content, though a case can be made for the chronology being described here. This pattern is also suggested by the direction literary theory has taken in the last century, with its early emphasis on authorial intention, then on text/tradition, and finally on the response of the audience. By way of anecdote, the prophetic literature itself seems to move from attention to the lives of the prophets in the older prophetic tales to the more message-centered classical prophecy, while exilic and post-exilic prophecy returns to prophetic lives as affected by opposition from their audiences.[4] Canonical criticism provides new accent to the story of prophetic research into true and false prophecy, a story now ready to be told.

The *Standard* Account of the Search for Criteria

Early studies in prophecy focused almost exclusively on the personhood of the prophet, culminating in Wellhausen's elevation of the prophet to the noblest member of Israelite society.[5] As a result, determining the falsehood of a prophet often centered on the prophet's intentions. A false prophet was shown to be false by virtue of the prophet's cultic and nationalistic tendencies, fanatic demagoguery, moral looseness, primitive spirit, and so on. Gottfried Quell in 1952 put an end to those arguments by defending the personal integrity of Hananiah, Jeremiah's prophetic adversary (Jer. 28), who had been labeled "false" (*pseudoprophetes*) by the Septuagint.[6] It became apparent that the prophet's character could exact only ambiguous proof of a prophet's claims to truth.[7]

If the prophetic person was not the key to prophecy, perhaps the prophet's message was. Emphasis on the speech forms of the prophets ensued, with special attention to salvation and judgment oracles.[8] At the same time, accents based on the Word of Yahweh over against the Spirit of Yahweh were defended.[9] Sources of tradition behind a prophet's message were also being highlighted, whether legal sources, wisdom, covenant, or holy war. In searching for message-centered criteria to distinguish the true prophet from the false, research focused on fulfillment or nonfulfillment of the prophecy, its revelatory form, and other concerns of content. None of these proved to be a safe bet in determining the true prophet from the false one. For example, whether a particular prophecy "came to pass" or not was of little help in establishing truthfulness since all failed prophecies could easily be projected into some indefinite future. History is replete with examples of the rearticulation of such failures for a public wanting to believe.[10]

Gerhard von Rad, in his study of false prophecy, ruled out messages centering on social matters, the cult, retribution, or foreign relations with Yahweh as candidates for determining falsehood.[11] Instead, he narrowed the focus to the single issue of weal or woe. He pointed out how a word of weal for Israel used by Isaiah was the same word of hope later used by Jeremiah's *opponents* and earlier by Micah's *antagonists* (1 Kings. 22). What appeared to be a true message in one historical moment was apparently false in another. The historical context *alone* decided the matter for von Rad.[12] Emphasis on the historical context of the message led still others to surmise that false prophecy was simply good theology (Zionist, establishment, royal theologies) voiced at the wrong time.[13] Klaus Koch moved the discussion of true and false prophecy forward beyond particular forms, whether salvation or judgment (or others), showing how closely the forms between both parties in conflict conformed to one another.[14] Once again, the criteria for validating the truth or falsehood of a prophet's message seemed lacking.

The study of the prophets moved again, this time in the direction of audience response, which was actually a return of sorts to Hermann Gunkel's interest in the vox populi. In 1971, James Crenshaw extended the work of Adam S. Van der Woude on the popular traditions presupposed by a prophet's audience.[15] Crenshaw concluded that the failure of the prophetic movement to provide valid criteria to its audience in defense of its distorted view of Israel's history as being under God's control sealed the fate of prophecy. In a separate study, Crenshaw (1981) determined that the "embellished account of Israel's history," as outlined by the prophets, "a story so far from the truth" of what actually happened, "sowed seeds of skepticism at almost every turn."[16] The result was chaos: an increased polarization of prophet against prophet, people against prophet, claim against counter-claim.[17] As a result, the public found prophecy lacking and turned elsewhere for spiritual direction. For Crenshaw, apocalyptic and wisdom literature filled this void.[18] Crenshaw seemed to close the door on the possibility that any biblical criteria might aid the discernment of true and false prophecy, since prophecy itself had failed.

Crenshaw ends on a note of irony, predicting the demise of the biblical theology movement of his day precisely because of the movement's inability to explain "to the people," as it were, its own criteria of validation. His argument rests on the claim that the biblical theology movement, like the prophetic movement of old, awarded claims about God's control of history (salvation history) that history itself could not sustain. Earlier in the present study, a case was made for this "crisis" in biblical theology as one marker of the shift in horizon from the modern to the postmodern period in biblical studies. However, unlike Crenshaw, who is skeptical that any criterion can be of value if it is historically conditioned, I have argued that it cannot be any other way. If biblical theology's claims about God's control of history were rhetorically weak, it was because biblical theology was forced to argue its case from a perspective that failed to appreciate its own narrative account. The radical skepticism of Crenshaw regarding historical claims to truth shows his link to a modern epistemology that has not yet realized that its own quest for universal value markers is what is truly in decline. Still, if the story of scholarly research into true and false prophecy had reached its denouement, it called for a better account of the unfolding drama. The rise of interest in canon coincided with the deep skepticism voiced by Crenshaw and others and suggested new possibilities.[19]

Canonical Hermeneutics in True and False Prophecy

From the perspective of canon studies, James Sanders first added his own chapter to the story of research on true and false prophecy, followed a decade later by Brevard Childs and his student Gerald Sheppard. In his article "Hermeneutics in True and False Prophecy,"[20] Sanders affirms the emphasis by scholars that the historical context was immensely important in terms of validating the prophetic message (95). He suggests, however, that asking the typical historical questions of context and tradition-use alone does not adequately address the problem of criteria as evidenced by the scholarly impasse. He reasons that if it could be shown, using tools of historical research, that "both parties invoked the same theology at the same time addressing the same situation, then hermeneutics would have to enter the picture" (96). By addressing the question of *how* texts were used, Sanders moved the discussion beyond earlier fixation on prophetic intention, message content (theology), historical hour, or audience reception. For Sanders, the truth or falsehood of a prophecy depended on the hermeneutics employed in relating each of these factors to each other.

What Sanders set out to do in this programmatic essay was to develop a method for determining the hermeneutics of prophecy, an avenue that had not as yet been adequately explored. According to Sanders, ancient Israelite prophecy is best understood in the interrelationship between three major factors: ancient traditions (texts), situations (contexts), and hermeneutics.

Texts are said to be "the common authoritative traditions employed and brought forward (re-presented) by the prophet to bear upon the situation to which he or she spoke in antiquity" (89). By contexts, Sanders means "the historical, cultural, social, political, economic, national, and international situations to which the prophets applied the 'texts'" (89). Hermeneutics is defined as the "ancient theological mode, as well as literary technique, by which the application was made by the prophet, true or false, that is, *how* he read his 'texts' and 'contexts' and *how* he related them" (89; emphasis added). Elsewhere, Sanders elaborates on the two basic hermeneutical or theological modes that were used by the biblical writers as being either constitutive or prophetic.[21] In essence, the constitutive mode reads a situation or tradition affirmatively, while a prophetic mode reads the situation or tradition and challenges it. A constitutive mode is one of "supportive guidance," while a prophetic mode is one of "corrective guidance."

Sanders has diagrammed this whole interaction as a "hermeneutic triangle," in which those three factors account for only one side of the reading horizon. The reader-scholar's hermeneutics and context, I suppose, are assumed to be relatively "objective" by definition. Spatially, then, Sanders proposed a triangle in two dimensions (flat). I suggested earlier and reiterate here that the story of varied scholarly readings concerning the question of criteria marking true prophecy from false now argues for a third dimension of Sanders's two-dimensional hermeneutic triangle. The same three factors (text, context, hermeneutics) must now also be defined for each new *reader* in the equation. In essence, one must consider *at least* six interactions in every reading and perhaps many more along the way between "there and then" and "here and now." In spatial terms, the hermeneutic triangle must now be seen as a three-dimensional figure taking both horizons of the reading experience into account at all times. Even without adding the third dimension to his triangle, Sanders still concurred with scholar-readers before him that there never had been clear-cut criteria by which to determine the true from the false prophet (103).

Sanders advanced the discussion of true and false prophecy by arguing in effect for an "indirect criterion" based on evaluating the *hermeneutics* of the prophet. In doing so, he moved the argument from one over form (content) to one over function. What finally mattered for determining the truth claims of a prophet was *how* a text or tradition was used in a specific context. In any historical context, a (biblical) prophet always seemed to operate using either the hermeneutic of prophetic critique or that of constitutive support, proving the historical critics right in their lament about criteria. However, within the compressed (hi)story of the canon, these two contradictory hermeneutic stances were now juxtaposed, fixing the limits of true and false prophecy. A true prophet, now from a canonical perspective, would have to *function* under the auspices of these two contradictory stances, each serving as a check on the other.

In literary terms, what held these otherwise centrifugal forces together was nothing less than the power of the canon. In theological terms, these contrary forces were bound together by God, all other power being inadequate to the task. Affirming God as the creator of all peoples undergirded the mode of prophetic critique, whereas affirming the God of grace of a particular people in a particular historical context suggested constitutive support. A true prophet, for Sanders, was one who held both affirmations together in canonical tension, if not in actual history. Sanders called this function of canon the "monotheizing process" (103). It was the source of the canon's ongoing power and life-giving message in a pluralistic, polytheistic world.

Brevard Childs, in his study "True and False Prophets,"[22] finds fault with Sanders's study in several ways, not least of which he blames on Sanders's "existential interpretation . . . with its somewhat loose connection to early

Barthian theology" (136). Such influence aside, Childs disagrees with Sanders on a more crucial point that, for our purposes, must be addressed: Sanders's reliance on dynamic analogy in addressing the question of true and false prophecy.

Behind Sanders's interpretation of canonical hermeneutics lies the assumption that the hermeneutics of the ancient readers can provide guidance to the modern reader in *how* to apply a biblical text or tradition in the changing context. If, admittedly, one cannot directly make such an application "stick" by simple analogy at the level of content, Sanders claims one can do so at a functional level by dynamic analogy. Childs correctly concludes that Sanders assumes that "by studying the Old Testament and its hermeneutics, we can learn how to apply a correct hermeneutic in our own time" (137).

Childs is highly critical of Sanders's position, arguing that the canon never functioned in the way Sanders suggests prior to the Enlightenment, with its sterile, historicist reading of the Bible (137). Further, Childs argues that seeing a "simple analogy" between the prophet's functional use of texts and traditions and our own use of them helps not a whit since "we are not prophets nor apostles, nor is our task directly analogous" (137). Childs believes that to focus on the *use* of texts by prophets, and, by extension, our own *use* of texts, "subverts the essential role of the canon which established theological continuity between the generations by means of the authority of sacred scripture" (137).

The complaints of Childs hinge almost solely on the importance he places on the *final* canonical shape of the text. In my opinion, his argument does not hold. Better said, it holds only insofar as one accepts his particular assumptions. To say that prior to the Enlightenment the Bible was read in quite different ways from subsequent historical-critical readings is one thing. No one argues this fact.[23] It is quite another thing to say that those precritical readings, and all other readings since, are not every bit as dependent on their own historical context. To be sure, precritical readers in most cases may *not* have read the texts historically in the way Enlightenment-influenced readers self-consciously did. Precritical readings, however, were no less dependent on the historicality of their reading, even as they read texts typologically, allegorically, or otherwise. Childs is surely aware of this but seems wont to insist, nevertheless, that *the* correct way of reading Scripture depends upon the way it was read at the point of its final canonical shape.

Unfortunately for the logic of Childs's argument, he is left in the uncomfortable position of defending the Masoretic shape of the Bible as being the true canon over against the other final shapes, of which there are not a few. In defending the Masoretic canon over against others, Childs finds himself in a situation not dissimilar to that of the prophets and apostles and other biblical peoples. He, like them, must advocate for his canon over against the alternatives. Prophet or not, apostle or not, on the question of adjudicating readings in conflict, modern readers, including Childs, find themselves, *by means of* dynamic analogy, kin to their counterparts in Scripture.

The emphasis Sanders places on the process of canonization over questions of final shape solicit an additional criticism by Childs. He believes that such a reading subverts the essential role the canon as sacred scripture plays in providing theological continuity between past and present (137). The weakness of Childs's argument rests on the assumption that it is the text as scripture, and not its readers, that provides the primary role for theological continuity. This is not the place to reargue that question; I simply wish to suggest that to the degree one gives the text priority over its readers as the guarantor of theological continuity, Childs's argument against Sanders is strengthened. However, placing the burden of continuity in the hands of the reading community on which every text is finally, in some fashion, dependent strengthens the interpretation of canonical hermeneutics by Sanders.

Although Sanders himself would not extend his proposal to such an extent as suggested here, I have done so, relating text to context to hermeneutics to the reading community as a logical premise. To the question of *whose* text, *whose* context, and *whose* hermeneutics, the answer assumed by all, though logically followed through by few, remains: those of the readers in community, then and now. It is true that in contrast to the thought of Childs, and, to a much lesser degree, that of Sanders, the implications of emphasizing reader-in-community over text, context, and hermeneutics undermine a certain classic Protestant view regarding the a priori role and authority of sacred scripture over its readers. I would contend, however, that the truly essential bearer of theological continuity between generations has always been the living, breathing readers of sacred scripture. In that sense, the believing community is the keeper of the flame of continuity, insofar as books not read, even sacred books not read, are books not transmitted to a new readership. At best, and I mean this positively, to argue for the *sacredness* of a text as the basis for its ongoing theological continuity is itself a confessional stance of a confessing community. It has always been so, though now, for the first time since the dawn of the modern era, such honesty of confession need no longer be deemed a hindrance to debating conflicting truth claims. In a postmodern context, evangelical confessions about scriptural authority need not be any more or less confessional than other confessions, be they scientific, historical-critical, or otherwise. Childs, and to a lesser extent Sanders, wants theological continuity to rest upon a more certain foundation than that of a confessional community. Such foundations will always prove illusory and, in the end, no less community-dependent.

His commitments to the final shape of the Masoretic canon notwithstanding, Childs does contribute substantially to the discussion of true and false prophecy by way of his comments regarding Jeremiah 28, the *locus classicus* of the problem. Although Childs is vigilant in differentiating the original prophetic setting from the later traditions about those events, including the final canonical shaping, he concludes that the collating of Scripture in the postexilic period established "a new criterion" based on the recognition that "God had demonstrated by his action that Jeremiah was a true prophet" (140). Now, at long last, the community of faith would have at its disposal a "scriptural norm" to discern the will of God and to distinguish between the true prophet and the false (142). The canonical construal in its final editing declared the criterion of truth to be that which aligned itself with the words and moral character and deeds of Jeremiah.

Childs offers a well-reasoned commentary on how the final redacted form came to speak its own word of discernment regarding true and false prophets. However, he circumvents a number of important problems in finding criteria by focusing narrowly on how the later context of Scripture framed older issues in a very different way. In his acknowledgment (against Crenshaw) of a degree of continuity between the criteria used in the original situation of prophecy and the criteria at work in the collating and formation of Scripture, Childs again comes close to Sanders's notion of dynamic analogy. Paradoxically, he disallows that same possible dynamic to be at work between those readers defining the final form of the text and any subsequent readers. Apparently, for Childs, when canonical form took final shape, canonical function ceased.

Gerald T. Sheppard extends the work of Childs in his "True and False Prophecy within Scripture."[24] Without a hint of irony, Sheppard seizes on Childs's "understanding of the *function* of prophecy and its transformation" and offers some needed clarification by way of anthropological, sociological, and political insights into the nature of "true" and "false" prophecy (264, 266–280).

Sheppard, following the insights of Robert Wilson, I. M. Lewis, and David Petersen, notes how the distinction between "true" and "false" prophets was helpful to ancient societies as a way of defining the loyalty certain persons had to some particular group or groups in conflict (266).[25] Not unlike the checks and balances placed on shamans and prophets in other ancient cultures, accusations of false prophecy were used in ancient Israel to maintain a balance between social innovation and identity, between chaos and community coherence. Adherents of certain prophetic circles believed their own prophets were "true" and *assumed* their criteria were adequate for distinguishing their prophets from others. Concludes Sheppard: "The criteria for evaluating an instance of 'prophecy' make sense only from within the domain of a socially defined support group and its marginal sympathizers, with their own recognized 'true' prophets and idiosyncratic role expectations. . . . The criteria could and did change over time and through social circumstance" (267).

Sheppard returns to Jeremiah 28 to expose the inadequacy of attempting to formulate "ideal" isolated criteria for adjudicating prophetic claims. He shows that the argument between Jeremiah and Hananiah was not settled in the abstract but was a highly political and clear-cut matter: "To what group or groups of prophets has God spoken and at what price is one ready to share allegiance to the 'truth' treasured by that group?" (270). Sheppard argues against Crenshaw's radical skepticism that there was hopeless uncertainty presented in Scripture concerning prophets in conflict. From the perspective of the post-exilic adherents to Scripture, a judgment had been made between Hananiah and Jeremiah (and other canonical prophets) that formed the basis by which the message and character of biblical prophets were now claimed as reliable criteria for all subsequent generations (270).

To the degree Sheppard argues that truth is produced only by virtue of certain forms of constraint defined by a community's "politics of truth" (Foucault), he undermines Childs's insistence on the final form being the final criterion. What can be said is that *from the perspective of* the types of discourse the post-exilic community accepts along with the mechanisms, techniques, and procedures that enable it to distinguish true from false statements, Jeremiah and his kind are considered *by the community* to claim a universality unmet by any other prophets. Insofar as Childs and Sheppard are persuaded by the post-exilic community's perspective, they can speak of a "new scriptural norm" for distinguishing true and false prophecy (271). However, Sheppard's main point must not be overlooked: "As the social performance of prophecy changed, so the criteria for evaluating it changed" (268). The criteria inscripturated by the post-exilic community do not automatically have power over all subsequent (or previous) criteria established by other faithful communities, unless those communities choose by dynamic analogy to claim the same criteria (and canon) for themselves.

To his credit, Sheppard suggests that the various presentations of criteria for discerning true and false prophecy preserved in the Old Testament argue against a monolithic hermeneutic of any kind, including that of James Sanders (267)—and, I would add, that of Brevard Childs. The monotheizing hermeneutic with its constructive and critical dimensions defended by Sanders and the final canonical form of Childs must, like all other claims, defend themselves against their detractors. In this sense, Sanders and Childs, along with all the characters in the unfolding story of scholarly research on true and false prophecy, model the very dynamic that is played out between conflicting prophets within the biblical texts themselves.

In this story of research, as in the biblical accounts themselves, the persuasion models of literary-critical inquiry coincide with the sociocanonical claims regarding power. Both reading groups function without transcendental norms, in keeping with the postmodern reader. Accordingly, "everyone is obliged to practice the art of persuasion" in defending his or her claims to truth.[26] The canonical-critical program now stands ready to oblige that charge.

The Ethos of Mythos and the Politics of Canon

To the degree that canon formation is fundamentally about the preservation and transmission of text and tradition from one generation to the next or across cultural and language groups in translation, *choosing* one tradition or text over another to pass on or preserve constitutes a verdict of ethical gravity. Since choice is an arbitrary act and since alternative choices can always be made, to choose this text or tradition and not that is an ethical act.[27] Mythos (the story of who we are) is here subsumed under ethos (the story of how we are to live), inasmuch as an argument can be made for the priority of ethics over ontology. Emmanuel Levinas argues that since being is always being in relationship with another, ethics and ontology are essentially coterminous. As such, we can never speak of existence before ethics. Indeed, we speak ethically in the instant of existence because existence is always existence-in-relationship. For Levinas, even abstract thoughts are ethical: "Thinking is itself an ethics."[28]

To speak of canon is to speak ethically. Decisions of inclusion and exclusion are themselves ethical acts. Evaluation and validation of certain references as authoritative are canonical functions, as is deciding between a true prophet and a false prophet. Rolf Knierim's search for criteria for making such judgments as the primary task of *doing* Old Testament theology is laudable and influential in the quest for what is here being described as an ethic of canon.[29] However, his criticism of canonical criticism on this score is only partially correct. To the degree that Knierim argues against canonical criticism for its failure to address matters of adjudication, suggesting as he does that the canon has merely "finalized the problem," Knierim misreads canonical criticism. It is precisely in the centrality that canonical criticism places on discussions of true and false prophecy that the issues of adjudication are spotlighted. The "problem" in the canonical-critical program may be its less-than-adequate defense of the ("scandalous") particularity that necessarily accompanies all truth claims (and "falsehoods") in the context of the plurality of readings. Likewise, the "problem" may include its failure to tie its program into the broader discussions in canon and theology on the question of adjudication. However, Knierim's belief that the biblical canon has merely "finalized the problem" is true only if we fail to see how the canon as paradigm and the canonical process are themselves constructive claims about how adjudication is to be carried out as much as definitions of what content is to be believed as true. Indeed, to suggest that the process of canonization may be what is truly canonical is to request clarification of the relationship between conflicting readings within the canon itself.

The argument canonical criticism has with Knierim is *not* with his call for adjudication. Rather, the argument hinges on the question of whether it is possible to define the criteria in such a way as to claim a universality for those criteria beyond one's own peculiar claims to their universality. Furthermore, the argument about what a text means in itself must be negotiated between reading communities and cannot simply be assumed to be "there" for the exegeting. Thus, adjudication will involve the description of a text's content as well as the evaluation of that description for theological purposes; both exercises are tied closely to the norms (canons) of the community of which one is already a part, academic or otherwise. As will be argued more fully later, such a "peculiar claim" can never achieve the kind of universal validation (truth) that Knierim (and others) seems to deem possible.[30]

So, I do not disagree with Knierim's concern that the canon is indeed loaded with hard-fought battles over its content and limits. I do disagree with his contention that the canon, as canon, does not offer clues as to *how* such adjudication must happen, clues that point to the reading communities' ethical responsibility to read rightly, clues that point away from inherent substance-critical exegesis to a communally based ethics of reading. For now, it is right to understand that the formation and content of the canon are very much political activities spawning conflicts over power. It is a sad fact of history that the struggle over interpretation of texts bears with it life-and-death struggles of extreme consequence. In a postmodern era in which a single "objective" truth has given way largely to truth as a rhetorical art within competing discursive communities, there is all the more reason for adjudication to be centered in ethics, albeit a narrative-based ethic.

It is of limited help to construct a totalizing mythos about the oneness of God, or the integrity of reality, or any other form of "transtribal validation,"[31] including the suggestion that the "universality" of one's criterion makes it the "better saying,"[32] without recognizing the moral (i.e., ethical) implications of such a proposal. There are those who would find fault with any form of adjudication because the inherent ideology of adjudication itself is problematic when it carries with it notions of neutrality or insofar as it bears with it a definitive, totalizing discourse.[33] For example, is it moral to propose a uniform logic that *might* iron out contradiction by subsuming it under the categories of a comprehensive theologizing hermeneutic (canon as paradigm), even if its intentions are precisely meant to allow for the pluralism of reality without succumbing to the chaos of nihilism? Asking the question about the morality of the theologizing hermeneutic is not meant to impugn the claim to truth of this construct. Indeed, such a hermeneutic will, with modification, be argued for later. However, in asking the question, one is compelled, precisely by the nature of a pluralistic universe in which opposing interpretations compete for dominance with social and political consequence, to defend one's theocentric mythos on ethical grounds. Every mythos is always and forever embedded in ethos, even as every ethic relies on the mythos of its particular community of discourse. The circularity of such a position is not unlike that of the well-known hermeneutic circle. The challenge of keeping this circle from becoming a vicious one must now be articulated.

Canon as Paradigm: The Force of Story

The idea of "telling stories" is central to the postmodern understanding and is key to the canonical-critical enterprise. The idea of the "force" of story is expressed by the rabbis as central to midrash. For example, the rabbis feel quite pressured by the announcement in Ecclesiastes that "the words of the wise are like goads" (12:11).[34] In a different though parallel vein, Simone Weil argues that the Iliad is a poem of force.[35] Such compelling stories now being told, though originally limited to the category "literature," have spilled over into other disciplines as well. Increasingly, authoritative stories are less distinguishable from what was once considered knowledge: scientific "truth," ethics, law, and history.[36]

As McClendon has shown, such an understanding of understanding has been an embarrassment to the modern mind, as registered by the term "hermeneutic circle." We imagined that if we could disown our particular place in our particular story for claims of neutrality and objectivity, and if we distanced ourselves from the traditions and texts being read, it might be possible to arrive at a purer vision of the truth.[37] We imagined we might discover some abstract, non-narrative-based proposition "out there" or a non-narrative-dependent understanding of reality *as it really is,* which we could then use to determine the truth or falsehood of our claims or those of another.

In Old Testament scholarship, two competing epistemologies play themselves out one against the other, often to a critical impasse. One might be termed a "positivist-inductive model," the other an "idealist-deductive model."[38] Both models in verifying their claims depend on modern assumptions of objectivity, the first in its ability to induce its claims from a precise observation of the "facts" of reality, the second in its a priori stance as to the categorical imperatives of human reason. Insofar as James Sanders (model one) and Rolf Knierim (model two), and others, are compelled by their stance within the modern horizon's demands for a supranarrative based on objectivity, neither will be able to "see" the opponent's point. The blindness each shows toward the other is inevitable since Sanders believes his theory to be a picture of reality as it really is (model one), while Knierim believes his to be an objective statement about reality as deduced from reason (model two). Of course, neither Sanders nor Knierim fits neatly into either category. But to the degree they do, they remain at the border between the modern and post-modern horizons of understanding. There is a third alternative, described here in the language of the literary critics and narrative theologians rather than the more standard epistemological categories of the philosophers.

The Enlightenment narrated its own particular story in such a way that discussions about rationality and truth have been defined by that account ever since.[39] This standard account has been described by Hauerwas as going something like this: First there was religion in the form of stories, then philosophy came along in the form of metaphysics, and finally science evolved, with its exact methods. Each stage was deemed more *reasonable* than the last.[40] Given such a narrative framework, it was natural to view a story-based ethic or a narrative-dependent truth as being prescientific in its ratio-nality and too particular in its claims. In describing this standard, "enlight-ened" account of modernity, Hauerwas shows the fallacy of a rationality that supposed itself narrative-free. In fact, when the standard account is told, it becomes rationally clear why other stories that do not offer universal proposi-tional statements about truth or any other value, stories that do not offer non-narrative-based categorical imperatives (Kant) about what is good or evil, are deemed irrational. The criticism being leveled here from the standpoint of canon as paradigm (an identity *story*) is not in any way against rationality as such but against an "enlightened" rationality that ignores its own narrative dependence. What is being defended here is the narrative *form* as a *form* of rationality. Narrative form functions as rational discourse by[41] a connected description of action that moves to a point at which behavior is purposeful, even if not predictable; by asking "What happened next?," which allows for a structured intelligible response; and by the unfolding of a "character" that yields literary patterns as the plot unfolds.

When James Sanders suggests that "God has a story too," it is not simply a clever title for a book of published sermons.[42] Rather, it is a central construct throughout his work in canonical criticism that bears with it the ethical force of an argument for the coherent meaning of all other constructs about reality. Its truthfulness is defended on hermeneutic and literary grounds in and through the stories of the Bible that tie the contingencies of the whole biblical story and those of our lives together.

On literary grounds, the Bible has long been read as a single, great story united by characters, setting, and plot, at least up until the modern period.[43] The ultimate "implied" narrator of the Bible story, sometimes explicitly so

(Exod. 19:3–6, or in many psalms), is God. "As" Scripture,[44] it is the tale of God speaking throughout its many sources, forms, and historical contingencies. Indeed, the compressed history of the many views of God over time have been shaped canonically to argue for its now being a narrative about the one God, even a biography of God.[45] Said differently, "The claim to be able to tell such a story amounts to the claim to be in the position of God."[46] Such a description may offend some on theological grounds, but Sanders means it in the first place as a literary truth.

But literary truths do have their political fallout! Since the authority of Scripture and canon as paradigm derives its intelligibility from the existence of a community that knows its life depends on this story and its transmission, an ongoing community is required to defend this story against others. Such a narrative must therefore account for how it may improve on other competing stories. One such defense derives from seeing how the many stories of the Bible, all patterned on stories available to them in their times and places, were gradually relativized to one overriding and ordering relationship with God.[47] In a sense, the moral force of this story and its rationality lies in the fact that it is a story about the formation of one story out of the many, whose main character holds in check all would-be contenders to divine omniscience, projected or real. Insofar as its human readers identify with the human characters of the story, and not with God, the story provides for its readers its own self-correcting apparatus.

When a community of readers makes such a story canonical for its own existence, the community declares itself guided by two fundamental characteristics, both of which help to define it ethically as a truthful community (i.e., not given to self-deception), even as it recognizes the limits to its own claims to truth. The first has been called by James McClendon the "principle of fallibility";[48] the second is defined here as the principle of advocacy.

The principle of fallibility is manifested in the canonical story every time a tradition or text can be shown to have been turned on its head or rerouted by a counter-reading. Such a claim to fallibility asserts that "even one's most cherished and tenaciously held convictions might be false and are in principle always subject to rejection, reformulation, improvement, or reformation."[49] Such a story-formed perspective sees less need to find the truth hiding in the various conflicting points of view than to become a person of character who no longer evades the truth that confronts him or her: "truth the relentless hound, I the hare."[50]

If the ethic of fallibility finds its presupposition in the canonical story-form, so also does the ethic of advocacy. The full narrative contains in compressed version the widest possible range of debate between many different stories and counter-stories jostled across three millennia, each needing to argue for its space—or, more accurately, each needing the advocacy of a particular reading community. One might argue that the "deep structure" of the story-formed shape of the canon frames a "grammar of persuasion seeking assent."[51]

If inherent to the ideology of adjudication lies the potential for a coercive totalizing hermeneutic,[52] the principle of advocacy by definition undermines its totalizing effect. Advocacy requires a declared stance, a commitment to a particular perspective, a conviction worth defending, while at the same time recognizing its own vulnerability. To be in the position of advocating for a particular construal of reality over against alternative views necessarily admits potential falsehood. The ethic of advocacy inherent in canon formation provides its own question mark concerning all claims that the canon is a coherent story about the one God. Such a claim must be advocated over against others that might conceivably read the biblical canon as evidence of polytheism, chaos, competing values, or a text deconstructing itself. To suggest that the biblical canon as God's story bears with it the seeds of its own potential falsehood might in fact be the strongest argument in favor of such a reading of the book we call Scripture. As Nicholas Lash has declared, in keeping with the greatest commandment of Torah, "Faith in God, and God *alone,* is inherently iconoclastic."[53]

Even a canonical story about God falls short of the truth made imaginable by such a story, summarized by Sanders as "the freedom of GOD of grace."[54] As will be advocated below, such an expression describes in a nutshell canonical hermeneutics in true and false prophecy. Although he argues elsewhere for a priority of "theologizing" over "moralizing" when reading Scripture as canon, Sanders overlooks the ethical claim that even such a general statement of priorities suggests. Perhaps it would be better to hear Sanders's summary as a statement of theological ethics or ethical theology situated in story rather than a directive to do theology *before* doing ethics. In his summary phrase, Sanders himself seems to admit to the potential danger lying beneath the surface of his own totalizing hermeneutic—what he calls elsewhere the "monotheizing process"—by plying qualification to an all-powerful Creator God on *moral* grounds: God conceived as Redeemer (God of grace) provides a self-correcting interplay to God conceived as Creator (God of freedom), and vice versa.

Canon as Process: The Particularity of Truth

The importance of historical situation and context in the cause of judging true and false prophecy cannot be overstated.[55] Foucault argues that "truth . . . is produced only by virtue of certain forms of constraint" defining a community's "politics of truth," which entail the types of discourse it accepts and the events and mechanisms, techniques, and procedures that enable the community to distinguish true from false statements.[56] In other words, truth is narrative-dependent. In the world of the prophets, *how* a prophet construed his reality coupled with *how* he voiced available traditions and texts to persuade his audience to hear him and ignore his prophetic counterpart are key components of a prophet's repertoire for claiming to be true. For example, the prophets exploited the wilderness-wanderings tradition for positive and negative effect, depending on the rhetorical points they wanted to make.[57] Such use of earlier traditions for opposite effect shows, again, how the function of a tradition was as important to the biblical prophets as its content when constructing what they deemed defensible truth claims. The particularity of a prophet's claims understood by a particular community is clearly central to discerning the truth or falsehood of a particular prophet.

At the threshold of modernity, in the now well-worn phrase of Lessing, "an ugly, broad ditch" opened up between these "accidental truths of history"—here, the canonical process—and the "necessary truths of reason."[58] The logical challenge of Lessing's unhappiness with particular proofs not proving general truths was shared by many a biblical theologian seeking ever more comprehensive criteria for judging between prophetic claims to truth. Indeed, Lessing's unhappiness broadened into a more generalized alienation of the modern reader from the Bible.

The estrangement between the biblical story and its modern readers, with all good intention, was overwrought. Claims for an "objective" reading by means of a professed neutrality and allegiance to the "necessary truths of reason" were misguided. Indeed, it was modernity's embarrassment over the Bible's particularity that drove some people to seek validation beyond themselves in the first place. Such shame is still in need of explanation, as it remains a stumbling block to the central claims of canonical hermeneutics in true and false prophecy, namely, that "truth" is narrative-dependent and linked inextricably to the Torah story and, for the Christian, to the Torah-Christ story.

To questions of particularity, pluralism, and validation, John Howard Yoder, the Notre Dame historian and moral theologian, offers an important general response in an article circumscribed by its title, "On Not Being Ashamed of the Gospel."[59] For our purposes, we might register similar sentiment with the more general phrase, "on not being ashamed of one's particular confessional stance." Yoder argues that the embarrassment of particularity can be located in a "learned personal psychic defense against a constantly repeated experience of being overwhelmed by ever 'wider worlds'" (286). Ironically, experiences in these "wider worlds," which are the cause of this quest for validation, are themselves just more subcultures, some even more narrow than those worlds left behind. There is always a wider world (a universality) claiming its truths to be self-evident (286).

Yoder links the fear engendered by the vulnerability of particularized truth claims to a compelling urge to make such claims irresistible, even coercive.[60] In short, "the hunger for validation is the hunger for power" (287). In his critique of moral theologians since Schleiermacher, Yoder notes how their urges to avoid vulnerable truth claims presuppose the standard account of there being just one "public" and commonly accessible meaning system. The mandate defended by these moral theologians has been to restate their convictions to make sense to this one "wider" "public."[61] In so doing, they have largely implemented the standard epistemological context of "establishment" in four ways: (1) believing in a "public" "out there" that is singularly accessible to regulate or validate "facts" as true or meaningful; (2) believing that this system can validate statements about morality or value; (3) assuming that one can determine what a normative "public" reading truly is by "objective" empirical readings; and (4) defining "public and shared" criteria as true, self-validating platitudes if these are trusted by all and doubted by no one.

Certainly these "establishment" theologians, as so defined, would themselves be horrified by such a label, even more by the notion of a state-sponsored imposed truth. Just the same, Yoder tweaks them just a bit, suggesting that "their definitional moves still project the assumption that they want to restate their claims so that every reasonable person will have no choice but to agree" (203). For Yoder, rejection of truth may in fact be a part of its validation, a move foundationalists cannot follow since they specifically tailor their message for a world "out there," which will presumably listen to them and eventually agree with their version of truth as long as they speak its language. Yoder provocatively concludes: "The search to avoid particularity by some mental move of definition or some kind of empirical data gathering is by the nature of things a wasted effort. It cannot be done" (289). Yoder may overstate the case about the waste of such an effort. He does acknowledge that the intent of "transtribal validation" is noble in its respect for those to whom it wishes to communicate.

The alternative to Yoder's critique of an "epistemology of establishment" that "seeks to adjust its own knowledge to the 'wider world'" is to adopt the stance of the biblical writers in their encounter with their wider worlds. They did not grant their wider world privilege over them. Rather, they faced the challenge posed by engagement with the wider world as at least equal partners and assumed worldly language, saying things with it that *could not have been said* by those wider worlds. For example, the "God of Abraham" was *proclaimed* (a constructive rhetorical move) by the biblical writers as the god of the Near Eastern sages, and by extension, they would, no doubt, have claimed the same for today's "philosophers." The biblical writers refused to filter abrahamic language unchanged through wisdom's (philosophical) funnels. The Bible thus preempted the language of the sages and philosophers, then and now, by saying things they could never say (296). Such images as "election," "Yahwism," and, later, "Incarnation" were also defended rhetorically simply as "good news" to be received. As to securing validation from the "wider world," the biblical tradents did not automatically submit themselves to the canons of intelligibility that were in force before the events to which they gave witness happened.

What Yoder is defending is what other narrative theologians and literary critics have suggested and what canonical criticism assumes: "There is no universal agreement, only competing claims to universality, one of which is our own."[62] To reiterate the thrust of this discussion, we need no longer be "ashamed" of either particularity or pluralism. Both are part of what it means to be historical. There is *no* "public" criterion that can bypass this fact. That does not mean, however, that we need not be ashamed concerning the ethical force of our stories. Those ethical readings still need to be defended and negotiated, perhaps now on new terms.

What, then, is the temper of truth? For starters, canonical hermeneutics would argue that truth is context specific and narrative based: no one can elevate truth to an independent standard. Even the relativist cannot declare his or her own relativist stance as necessarily true. As McClendon rightly concludes, one cannot even hoist the relativist flag to a general principle of relativism, since defining reality as relative is itself story-dependent. Whatever criteria are defended as defining truth will be bound up in the particular story of the narrator of those criteria and of his or her community.[63] Adopting the story-form with its own rationality provides a short way of explaining why canonical hermeneutics in true and false prophecy is irreducible to a logic of validation.[64]

In canonical-critical terms, the search for truth is explored using the hermeneutic triangle in three dimensions whereby text and context are brought together by way of a hermeneutic that is either prophetic or constitutive, depending on whether stress falls on the freedom of God or the grace of God. This interaction must, at every point along the path of a text's reuse, take into account the specific context of the audience while simultaneously accounting for the context of the reader who is reading. So defined, the canonical process might be described as a form of "fully contextual exegesis," with its functional aggregate of metaphors, symbols, concepts, values, and behavioral norms all included in the conversation. The story that unfolds as a result of this process cannot provide a universal criterion to say which other stories are true or false. Criteria cannot be grasped without a paradigm instance, and that is not possible without the story of such an instance. A complete account of how a text or tradition functions would be a narrative recounting of how the various readers came to judge certain stories better than others. Insofar as stories unfold imaginative possibilities for how to create and relate to the world, the reader is then required in his or her own time and space to show how this construal compares to the alternatives and to judge between them.[65] Such judgment cannot be done in advance or for all time.

Defining a community's "politics of truth" involves telling the community's story—or, again, "the search for criteria always ends up being a search for society."[66] The community of interpretation (the believing community) is a political entity by virtue of its need to make decisions, assign roles, and distribute powers. The courage required for a community to undertake such political risks in constantly remembering and reinterpreting its past, judging between alternative "biblical" traditions or texts in the process of defining and refining its canon(s), has always been formidable. Indeed, recognizing the authority of Scripture "as" Scripture, the Bible "as" canon, is to defend a particular kind of polity as defined by a particular polis.[67] Such defense is rarely safe or simple.

That we no longer consider the kind of noncoercive conversation between radically conflicting texts in Scripture as an ethical or political model to which we are still called shows how much the definition of canon as (limited) *content* has dominated the definition of canon as *function*. What canonical process argues is that practice matters,[68] and what matters is conformity to the practice of canon. How it functions is canonical over against how it correlates to some external rule or theory regarding the content of interpretation. That we no longer consider the canon functionally modeling an ethos worth imagining for ourselves shows how wide Lessing's "ugly broad ditch" has grown.

In our rush to leap across Lessing's great divide to argue for a universal ethic that depends on "pure reason" or "nature" for its claims, and not on the narrative memory and ongoing story of the believing community of Scripture, we have unwittingly adopted the "standard account," the "establishment narrative," as our own. In our relief at landing on Lessing's side of the ditch, we have forgotten that Lessing was, in the context of his now-clichéd metaphor, requesting help to make the leap in the other direction.[69] The modern "standard story" that he helped inaugurate kept Lessing from seeing what the postmodern story now makes clear—that the ditch has been filled in, the great divide narrowed. That same "blindness"[70] has kept many from seeing the political relevance of the "Bible as canon" as providing the narrative ethic necessary for negotiating between all would-be prophets (and/or canons) in conflict. Defense of the politics of such an ethic follows.

Readings in Conflict: The Politics of Canon

The coexistence of conflicting readings and conflicting stories spawns conflicts over power. The literary theorist Paul B. Armstrong, in his book *Conflicting Readings: Variety and Validity in Interpretation,* details this dynamic.[71] From a literary-critical perspective and without the language of one working with biblical texts, Paul Armstrong unknowingly describes many of the epistemological, philosophical, and hermeneutical dynamics involved in Sanders's canonical hermeneutics of true and false prophecy. He differs mainly with Sanders over the ultimate unity of reality. Armstrong's ontological "ground" remains that of ultimate difference and conflict, whereas difference is ontologically penultimate for Sanders. For Sanders, as for me, God is the ground of reality's unity and coherence—in Sanders's parlance, the Integrity of Reality. However, for me, if God is understood functionally ("God is covenant love") and ontology blurs into ethics at the level of Godness (Levinas), then I would simply express Sanders's sentiment as God, the Integrity (understood ethically) of (little "r") reality. Armstrong and Sanders do agree, against me, on a text's determinacy in constraining the variety of readings conjured up by a multivalent reality (whether ultimately or penultimately so). As is clear by now, I would situate a text's determinacy, if any, in the community norms dictating how the text is to be read. Such semantic hairsplitting suggests distinctions between Sanders and Armstrong, neither of whom have interacted across their respective disciplines, the importance of which will aid expression in what follows when I speak of a politics of canon.

Although Armstrong agrees with Foucault's assessment of the interrelationship between knowledge and power, he is less convinced than Foucault that power necessarily undermines interpretation.[72] Not all power need be devious, distorting, coercive, or critical. It can be creative and constructive, what is described by Armstrong as "hermeneutic power."

The irony of hermeneutic power, for Armstrong, is that it requires limits on itself to be maximally effective: "It is in the *epistemological* self-interest of authority to limit its claim and to encourage its own contestation" (135). Since interpretation is a constructive task that appropriates material for its purposes, resistance to appropriation aids the interpretative task. Thus, rigorous testing via conflicting points of view is epistemologically advantageous.

Fundamental to Armstrong's quest for truth is an attitude of contradiction. The reader must defend his or her hypothesis (reading) in a sort of power play, while being simultaneously aware of its limits. Any hypothesis about meaning must be held with conviction while maintaining a certain tentativeness about it as well (139), what McClendon deemed "the grammar of persuasion seeking assent."[73] To never commit oneself to any particular vision of "resistance and hope" is to allow one's commitment to unbridled pluralism to become simply a "passive response to more and more possibilities, none of which shall ever be practiced."[74] Not mincing literary judgment, Simone de Beauvoir, cited by Tracey, labels such mushy pluralism "the perfect ideology for the modern bourgeois mind."[75] To avoid the totalizing discourse rightly feared by Foucault, especially when committing oneself to a particular conviction, we must enter the paradoxical ethos of vigorous advocacy with a willingness to change our minds (139).

Important to negotiating readings in conflict is the contradictory, though pragmatic, stance that hermeneutic communities must be both hierarchical and egalitarian. Such a hierarchy could be one of negotiated ideas at the center of a community's system of beliefs or one based on the role of certain figures, teachers, or leaders who enjoy special status. These centers or figures are held in check by the array of interpretations competing for recognition (144). For example, Jeremiah was compelled to legitimate his authority so that the audience would accept his claims and not those of other prophets (such as Hananiah) vying for the same authority.[76]

From the perspective of radical individualism, to the extent possible, Armstrong's comments about hierarchies might evoke suspicions of tyranny. On the other hand, from the perspective of establishment readers, the radical freedom demanded for every voice appears anarchic. Armstrong offers no alternative to this dilemma but merely asserts it as a given. From the perspective of the canon-shaping community, there is another possibility.

The hierarchy suggested by a communitarian claim does not reflect the fairly rigid kind of domination and control in which orders are imposed from above. Rather, it is a more dynamic ("alive") system, wherein signals of information and transaction move back and forth among all levels, ascending and descending. This stratified order of the systems theorists is a dynamic balance (homeostasis) between self-assertive and integrative tendencies throughout nature. The importance of this stratification is not so much a transfer of control as an ordering of complexity. The philosopher of science and physicist Fritjof Capra has inverted the traditional hierarchical model from a pyramid to that of a "systems tree" symbolizing the back-and-forth flow of power in both directions.[77] Social scientist Aaron Wildavsky speaks of a "movable hierarchy," though he recognizes this articulation comes close to an empirical contradiction.[78] However, it was just this diversity of political forms that "saved the Hebrew culture from an early demise" by providing the needed structure and flexibility to become the "shock absorbers of Judaism."[79]

In a slightly different way, Max Kadushin and W. V. Quine attempt to avoid traditional hierarchical models by suggesting a systems approach in dynamic and organismic language. Kadushin, exploring the rabbinic mind, relates four value-concepts (God's justice, God's love, Torah, and Israel) "organismically," not hierarchically. All parts are vital parts and not dispensable, based on the model that every organism needs all its parts to fully live. In fact, Kadushin slides into the realm of ideas, away from the dilemma posed by operational language, by articulating a "mental organism." He tries hard to avoid any hint of hierarchy, though he admits these ideas function in systematic patterns.[80] Philosopher Quine pictures one's belief system as a web. Beliefs most likely to be given up in the face of recalcitrant experience are located at the edges. Beliefs less subject to revision fall nearer the center. The beliefs at the edge are interconnected with more elements in the rest of the system. When experience necessitates some change in the system, there are many ways to revise—though ultimately the decision will be made such that the system as a whole will adjust to a new homeostasis.[81]

The alternative, then, to an individualism tempted to assert hierarchical truth claims arbitrarily is not established authority so much as an authority in which the individual participates and to which he or she consents. Freedom of confession becomes the alternative to anarchy. By definition, such a (canonical) community would have to be voluntary and distinct from the total society. Otherwise, the only means of being an individual would be through rebellion. Testing practical moral reasoning different from the rule of the established majority would be impossible.[82]

It is *within* the canonical community that canonical hermeneutics of true and false prophecy provide the forum for necessary critique and support. Even the great Old Testament polemics against the nations, foreigners, and others external to the community serve primarily as rhetorical devices of legitimation *for the prophet* in making his case *within* ancient Israel against competing views.[83] Such externally directed comments presume a stance within the community of Israel. Within believing communities, then and now, the debate falls out along lines not unlike those Armstrong suggests, between those arguing for maintaining the status quo and those wanting change. The status quo crowd argues for the necessity of stasis to maintain a group's identity. In truth, a relative coherence is necessary for one community to quarrel with another. Those wishing more freedom from the tyranny of the established order fear the silencing of weaker voices (145–149). These two contrasting readerly groups of Armstrong (and others) are translatable in the language of the canonical hermeneutics as the "hermeneutic of prophetic critique" and "constitutive hermeneutics."[84]

The hermeneutic of prophetic critique emphasizes God's freedom as Creator of all the world and of all humankind. As such, all forms of power (political and rhetorical) are subject to criticism. Translated in broader philosophical terms, this is the well-worn "hermeneutics of suspicion," of which the Bible as canon remains a prototype. Constitutive hermeneutics, on the other hand, emphasizes God's grace and commitment to the promises made as the peculiar and particular Redeemer of a particular ongoing community or group. Such a hermeneutic finds its comfort in the regularity of life, presupposed, for example, by the scientific method's demand for repeatable observations. Translated in broader terms, one might call this a hermeneutic of trust.[85]

Since universal transparency is impossible, the juxtaposition of various stories, complete with their various levels of blindness and insight, provides a self-correcting apparatus against the hegemony of either (144). At the same time, as has been acknowledged earlier, it is impossible to escape the domination of some sort of hermeneutic paradigm. Negotiating a hierarchy of consensual ideas, or, better said, a centered web of communal convictions, reinforces a sense of internal coherence necessary for group identity (even survival), whereas internal debate allows for sifting of priorities. Indeed, listening to the voices of outsiders also offers challenges to the interpretative practices of the community.[86]

A classic example of this balancing act is illustrated in the internal negotiations between the political factions in post-exilic Judaism that led to the formation of the Torah—a "constitution" of sorts and the product of external pressures on Israel's Persian overlords. The editors of this "single" Torah sought to give an overall "shape" to the collection while respecting the individual contributions of each tradent group (the so-called "P" traditions, deutero-prophetic, and deuteronomistic group[s]).[87] It can be argued on sociopolitical terms, as well as on Armstrong's terms of epistemological self-interest, that vigorous interpretative conflict increases the ability of readers to choose the constraints to which they are willing to submit (145). On the other side, voluntary restraint to the anarchy of ideas, even if temporary, carries with it the political wisdom for the order and community cohesion necessary for submitting alternative points of view for testing.

In political terms, Armstrong's theories of conflicting readings and those of canonical hermeneutics argue for the inescapable contradiction of a certain kind of democracy: an arena of noncoercive coexistence and productive conflict (149).[88] That the descriptions of Armstrong, along with those of the canonical process, parallel the *beit midrash* of rabbinic lore cannot be gainsaid. As Gerald Bruns so keenly describes it, "The *beit midrash* is not to be imagined as a preserve of serene logic where a liberal pluralism neutralizes the force of disagreement, it is a place where power flows in multiple directions, and the struggle for control . . . is fierce and sometimes laced with insult." Universal consensus is certainly *not* part of goal. In effect, this is a literary-political argument for understanding the biblical canon as a paradigm of democratic debate within a voluntary confessional community.[89]

Conclusions: Truth in Canon Politics

Truth and Canon

The story of true and false prophecy is no less than a story of a politics of truth whereby a transcendent moral norm is claimed in conversation by two or three or more who stake their claim on truth in contradistinction to competing claims by other communities and their prophets in other times and places. The careful reader will see in this compact summary an avowal of the claims of canonical criticism.

A truth of the canonical-critical method was made apparent in its recognition that truth itself is a contingent value and, like all others, has its own history. The review of the unfolding drama of biblical research in true and false prophecy demonstrated that the criterion for distinguishing true from false prophets was not just a contingency of the prophets' own time and space but was determined by the reading context of readers in another time frame, including those of the subsequent generations or of the present-day reader. Thus, in a context that focused on the prophetic person or role, truth criteria were defined in personal terms. So, when focus shifted to the prophetic message or audience, the criteria shifted accordingly. This did not make the criteria any less true (contra Crenshaw) but merely reiterated the narrative-dependent nature of truth.

A second truth of the canonical-critical method was to refocus the discussion of true and false prophecy away from criteria rigidly bound to the text (tradition), or its context, or to the hermeneutics employed. Rather, all criteria must embody the interaction between all three angles of vision, in what was called a monotheizing process. The shift focused on the *use* of the text or tradition: what the text *does* in a particular context (past and present) over against what it says for all time in every context. It is not the mere existence of an implicit cultural formation or particular content that distinguishes truth from falsehood but the *function* of any formation that becomes embodied in the actual use of that content or cultural formation that is decisive. This posed the dilemma for canonical criticism of how to defend itself against the charges of radical pluralism, whereby no truth is true; radical particularism, whereby only my truth is true; or radical transcendence, whereby what is true is ultimately so. The story-formed character of the canon proved to offer an alternative to this entrenched either/or dichotomy.

The rationality of the Torah (or Torah-Christ) story provided a clue to balancing the need for coherence (against radical pluralism) and the need for rigorous debate (against radical particularism) with the need for freedom (against radical transcendence). It is a story in which all its many stories—some with their own prophetic stamp—are relativized to the implied narrator of the whole "as" Scripture or canon. That narrator is God, literarily for some, literally for others. Canonical criticism suggests that this truth argues for a pluralism *limited* ultimately by the One God, implied or real. Here, a particular story provides space for many other stories but also absorbs them into its domain as canon. Canonical criticism advocates for this construal of reality based on the very real political gains from such a view. In other words, canonical criticism declares that true understanding includes practical application. To fail to relate truth to the body politic (ethos) is to misunderstand the power and politics of every claim to truth.

Canon Politics

What were the political gains advocated by the canonical-critical venture? The construal of reality imagined by the canonical-critical process insisted that all parties to a conversation be heard. At the same time, the need to voluntarily submit to self-imposed limits, even if temporarily, for the maintenance of communal identity was seen as essential. It recognized the need for prophetic critique (hermeneutic of suspicion) alongside that of constitutive support (hermeneutic of trust) under the domain of a meaningful (God-centered) reality. The advantages of such an imaginable construal were not a few.

Such a construct suggested that the shape of the conversation among prophets (and those who read them) haggling over truth must first happen within real live communities of conversation that provide limits of coherence and avenues for testing the claims being made. Such an argument diminishes the need to create flowcharts delineating how certain ideas work while others do not or hierarchies of truth claims based on propositional status or claims of universality. Rather, what is more crucial in the quest for truth is to define how the community itself functions, it being the final arbiter of all claims to truth.[90]

The prophet or the one who prophesies in a community serves as an "agent of direction."[91] He or she states or reinforces an imaginative construal of the place of the believing community in history. Indeed, the story of tradition being passed from one generation to the next, each tradent (prophet) adding his or her stamp to it or completely controverting its "original" use, argues for a position of conviction. To suggest that such a stance should be a humble one is not to argue against declaring one's conviction and advocating for it. Indeed, the canon models just that dynamic. Such real-life rhetorical battle is at the heart of the canonical sensibility. To avoid such commitment is to reject what is truly canonical about the Bible as canon, its canonical function. Within this political vision of the canon, the space for moral reasoning takes place. This vision is no less situational than that of some forms of modern existentialism, but it is less arbitrary since it finds itself confronted by the communal norms in which it voluntarily stands.

The community that forms itself in relation to the Torah (or Torah-Christ) story is provided with the moral authority of communal memory. As Joseph Blenkinsopp declared, "The canon does not contain its own self-justification but rather directs our attention to the tradition which it mediates."[92] Blenkinsopp rightly links the communal memory contained in the canon to that which was sufficient to sustain prophecy. As was argued in this chapter, such a memory bears with it a political or ethical mandate. Although a community's memory "will never make a decision for the present,"[93] it serves as a reservoir of meaning absent from other communities faced with the same dilemmas in moral reasoning. In distinguishing true prophets from false, elevating reading strategies, whether historical-critical, sociopolitical, or literary readings, above the common memory-pool provided by Scripture to its believing community is to forget the political force of memory at best and to be antipeople at worst.[94] Sanders rightly showed how just this tendency in "liberalism" and "neo-orthodoxy" effectively "decanonized the Bible or severed it from the ongoing believing communities."[95]

Canonical criticism insists that questions of true and false prophecy can be truly addressed only when there is a community in the present capable of remembering no less than it did in the past. The shared awareness of the believing community reading Scripture is a vision of the present community as being one with the community of antiquity and with the future community of believers as well. The readers now are the readers then, and the readers to come are the readers now. Far from rejecting the facts of history, or the significance of history's meaningfulness, such a shared reading stance claims the historic importance of the present time in the life of the believing community and, by implication, of every other present time in the life of the reading community. Such a claim justifies intense biblical study, here and now, since the canon of Scripture has contemporary, not merely ancient, political relevance.[96] Otherwise, the most sophisticated hermeneutic skills cannot make Scripture morally relevant in distinguishing the true prophet from the false, or in any other ethical claim.[97]

The politics of canon also insist that the canonical community be guided by order and due process. It was argued in this chapter that in order for hermeneutic power to be maximally effective, it must limit its claims and encourage its own contestation. The juxtaposition of various conflicting stories in the canon insists that every member in the body politic receive a hearing. Indeed, every member is summoned to advocate for his or her point of view, even while recognizing his or her own fallibility. In addition, the limited playing field that is marked out by the canon itself, even though multiple canons and canon as function preclude rigid boundaries, argues for the necessity of enough order to ensure identity and to provide due process for alternative voices to be heard. In the model of interpretation suggested by canonical criticism, such canonical "conversation" is a complex phenomenon composed of text, context, and hermeneutics, grounded in questioning itself. Such a conversation accords primacy to one largely forgotten notion of truth: "truth as manifestation."[98]

Certainly there are very real concerns about community provincialism. This fear is especially acute in seeking to distinguish true prophets from those with false claims. I have argued, however, that such fear is somewhat misplaced since there is truly no community, however wide, that is not provincial and whose truths are simply self-evident. It is somewhat more optimistic, and certainly more fruitful politically speaking (realpolitik), to affirm the marketplace of ideas at the edges and between communities rather than to suppose there is some hypothetical wider "public" to which we might appeal when embarrassed by our own particularity. Deep within canon-shaping communities lies a truth that liberates its adherents from a projected universality that, when studied more closely, is no less particular and often "full of empty meaning."[99]

Robert P. Carroll, in his study on several of Jeremiah's noncogent arguments, concludes, "Every attempt to delineate true and false criteria would render every prophet false."[100] Such a statement is the reverse equivalent of Nietzsche's rather famous line, "There is no truth, only an array of interpretations." Both of these statements can now be considered truthful only from the perspective of a horizon of understanding that assumes the possibility of propositional criteria beyond particular instances in time and space for judging true from false prophets or that assumes a particular truth is no truth at all. Canonical criticism admits to the contrariness of a variety of convictions, and recognizes that one prophet's truth may not be another's, but it refuses to theorize from there that there is no truth that is true.

Finally, canonical criticism holds up what it believes to be a model for discerning true and false prophets and the kind of community necessary to sustain that vision. Canonical criticism is aware that it remains in a contest for that reading over against the alternatives. As a method, it cannot delineate ahead of time criteria for true and false prophecy that do not take into account the reader, the text, and the community of interpretation, past and present. Having so concluded, it remains to show how it is still possible to move from a theoretical political model of canon to an analysis of specific conflicting prophetic texts and so provide a case study of canonical hermeneutics in true and false prophecy.

FIVE

Swords into Plowshares into Swords

T HE questions raised and addressed concerning conflicting canons now approach their denouement in the prophecies of Isaiah/Micah and Joel. Any study of true and false prophecy, such as the one under investigation, results from either the ambiguity of prophetic texts or the editorial activity that inevitably follows the collection and analysis of prophetic oracles in light of new contexts or the final juxtaposition of these "compressed texts" in the canon.[1] The prophecies of Isaiah/Micah and Joel in their historically compressed juxtaposition within the canon of sacred scripture are no exception. It remains for us to provide the reader with a critical example of how he or she may negotiate conflicting biblical texts now aided by a renewed understanding of the politics and hermeneutics at stake when negotiating canons and conflict. Diachronic (historical) readings and synchronic (literary) readings of the plowshare passages will provide a fully contextual exegesis enabling the reader-hermeneut, for the first time, to gain a more complete understanding of how these texts have been negotiated by believing communities prior to and beyond the texts' inclusion into the canon. The collapse of horizons between the first negotiators and all subsequent readers will be a matter for observation and analysis compelling us to finally ask and answer in the next chapter: In this day, at this time, in our reading context, can these conflicting plowshare passages both be true prophecies?

Negotiating Readings: Rationale and Method

Rationale

The plowshare texts (Isa. 2:4; Mic. 4:4; and Joel 4:10 [Eng. 3:10]) lend themselves to the study of canonical hermeneutics in true and false prophecy for several reasons. In the first place, all three passages employ common-tradition elements in which Isaiah and Micah are nearly identical in form, while Joel consciously inverts the language of both.

Second, the different contexts (literary and historical) make use of common traditions, providing well-defined and obvious parameters for comparison. Such a tradition history, which includes redactional layers, offers additional levels of comparative depth for clarifying canonical function.

No comprehensive comparison of the *hermeneutics* underlying these particular texts and contexts has been made to date,[2] offering a third reason for the timeliness of this analysis. A void stands ready to be filled that has implications for many similar intrabiblical/intertextual traditions.[3] These texts in fundamental conflict provide an excellent case study for discerning the hermeneutics between the lines of text to account for the shift in perspectives at both ends of the now three-dimensional hermeneutic triangle and at points in between. A review of the commentators of the twentieth century reveals that the range of opinion varies concerning the relationship between Isaiah 2:4/Micah 4:3 and Joel 4:10 (Eng. 3:10). Many do not even note a relationship;[4] others acknowledge the relationship but define it only in terms of genetic or causal dependence;[5] others recognize Joel's reversal of Isaiah/Micah but do not elaborate;[6] still others acknowledge the reversal but conclude, nevertheless, that the texts' meanings are in fundamental agreement;[7] finally, some maintain that a fundamental disagreement exists between Joel and Isaiah/Micah.[8] Our task is to clarify this somewhat confusing state of affairs by a multidimensional study of the hermeneutics of each text/ tradition *in relationship* to its several contexts (diachronically and synchronically).

Finally, these texts are canonically recognized as coming from so-called true prophets. Fundamental disagreement among them heightens the hermeneutics of true and false prophecy acutely. There are potentially real life-and-death issues involved in discerning how these texts are to be understood (visions of universal war versus those of universal peace). Since, as has been argued, all human thinking and speech proceed from within distinct sociopolitical situations, such social settings elicit ideological (political) stances that are inherently survivalist. In terms of rhetorical power, it is speech as "an assertion of power that seeks to override some other rhetorical proposal of reality."[9] In terms of social psychology, there is a mortal conflict between "immortality systems," a struggle for survival over death.[10] In essence, the Bible has incorporated multiple structures of reality such as these, issuing forth a life-and-death contest that cannot be avoided by a biblical scholarship opting for the "safe" results of historical-critical method.[11] A study of the plowshare passages offers one probe into this larger question of mutually exclusive hermeneutics. It proposes that canonical hermeneutics provide a prophetic role in all claims to truth and universal ideations. But such a proposal must now be demonstrated.

Method

The method employed in this comparative analysis is based on several assumptions. In the first instance, it is assumed that the prophets were not simply speaking what they believed to be true in a contextual vacuum. They were not simply compelled to speak for speaking's sake or from some sense of the revelatory nature of their utterances. Following the lead of those who have focused on the vox populi or the prophet's audience, it is further assumed that the prophet had something to say that his audience would understand. What was spoken by the prophet was different from what the audience already took for granted.[12]

The hermeneutic triangle described previously attempts to ask questions regarding the content of the tradition within the life of the listening (or reading) community (who, what, where, when) and the function of that tradition in the community (how). In effect, the tradition is imperiled, lost over and over, only to be recovered, remembered, and rewritten again and again.[13] The task for the reader is to attempt to recover as far as is possible the series of "original" contexts that would clarify the canonical function of these texts over time.

In each and every reconstruction of the various "original" contexts, the reader must be ready to compare his or her reconstruction with those various "original" readings forged by others. The truth of a particular reading is not determined by objective exegetical methods (your eisegesis against my exegesis) as much as by comparing and defending one's exegetical reconstruction against that of another. In telling the story of a tradition's path from beginning to end, we are actually telling the story of a limited number of possible readings usually delineated by sometimes narrowly defined discursive communities (e.g., the historical-critical reading community). Without caution, such a method, while heuristically necessary, can lead to epistemological myopia. Care will be taken in this study to allow for the widest range of possible reconstructed "contexts" that provides a representative sampling of readings. As we have argued in the preceding chapter, any negotiation between competing claims to truth must, in the end, factor in the politics of truth of the reader reconstructing those "original" contexts. The history of tradition is always also the story of the agents of reconstruction of that history. If concerns about the "historicity" of an "original" event have often overshadowed Israel's *interpretation* of that event,[14] those same concerns for the "facts" of history have often obliterated the contemporary reader's perception of Israel's interpretation of that "original" event.

Tradition-Gestalt *and the Reader*

The *Gestalt* psychology tradition in Europe that researched sensation and perception provides an important phenomenological backdrop to understanding tradition history in biblical studies.[15] To speak of a tradition-*Gestalt* is to argue for a unified configuration or portrait of a passage whose meaning as a whole is more than the sum of its parts. Another way of expressing the same idea is to argue that perception of a passage is more than single perception and that "a combination" of perceptions is more than additive. We perceive and think about texts in terms of integrated units that cannot always be analyzed into smaller units such that the relations between perceptual entities determine how we perceive those entities.[16]

In developing his phenomenology of reading, Wolfgang Iser speaks of the *Gestalt* of a literary text. The interaction between the text and the reader cannot be traced back exclusively to the written text or to the disposition of the reader. Apprehension is finally dependent on what he calls "gestalt groupings."[17] One never discovers the true meaning of a text per se but only a "configurative meaning" in one's "seeing-things-together." In turn, a "fixed" and definable outline emerges that is essential to one's understanding.[18] The *reader* unfolds the network of possible connections to form a *Gestalt* and then makes a selection from that network, guided by what is familiar to him or her. Any such selection immediately creates an overflow of possible alternative meanings requiring the reader to return to the text to question the original selection, which may, in turn, cause a change in the *Gestalten*.[19]

The phenomenon of reading so described provides two important assumptions to bear in mind when speaking of biblical tradition on the one hand and a history of those traditions on the other. In the first instance, to speak of *a* biblical tradition is in reality always to speak of a tradition-*Gestalt*. Using the criteria of Douglas Knight's "admittedly arbitrary" and "ideal" definition of a tradition, he reiterates its "malleable," "relatively stable," "cumulative and agglomerative" nature.[20] Knight insists on the necessity of what he calls *Literaturgeschichte* as a means of providing an "all-inclusive" way of bringing literary forms and their oral backgrounds into discussions about tradition.[21] I would expand Knight's notion of "history of literature" to include the "literary history" of Hans Robert Jauss and the "comparative midrash" of James A. Sanders, both argued earlier.

The Tradition-Gestalt *of the Plowshare Passages*

The literary context of the plowshare passages contains a complex of theological motifs clustered around ideas of varied origins. Such a complex of interconnected ideas might be called the "tradition-*Gestalt*" of these parallel passages. Reflected in this *Gestalt* are such motifs as the "day of Yahweh," the holy city, the cosmic mountain (here, of Zion), attacks by enemy nations, theophany, holy war, the power and efficacy of the Torah-word, the deliverance of God's people, the judgment of the nations, and the establishment of the kingdom. Limiting such a varied set of motifs exclusively to one *Gattung* would be asking too much of these texts. However, the question would be justified if one or two tradition-*Gestalten* provided a heuristic narrowing of the field to help explain the formal characteristics of these parallel passages.

In the texts under analysis here, there is a tradition-*Gestalt* that, when coupled with a second, comparable tradition-*Gestalt*, provides the reader with relative methodological control for determining what assumptions a given listening audience might have and what point the prophet was thereby scoring in his use of the tradition. The first tradition-*Gestalt* can be identified as the "Zion tradition." Its complement is that of the "Day of Yahweh."

Although no consensus has emerged regarding the date and origin of the Zion tradition, an early pre-exilic date is all but certain.[22] There is general consensus on the cluster of motifs, culled from various psalms usually equated with the Zion tradition. That cluster is summarized as follows:[23] (1) Zion is the peak of the highest mountain, Zaphon (Ps. 48:3–4); (2) the river of paradise flows from this mountain (Ps. 46:5); (3) Yahweh triumphs over the flood wreaking chaos there (Ps. 46:3); (4) Yahweh prevails over the kings and their nations (Pss. 46:7, 48:5–7, 76:4, 6–7) through theophanic terror (Ps. 48:6) or reproach (Pss. 46:7, 76:7), destroying the weapons of war, thus ending war forever (Ps. 76:4); and, though likely added later, (5) the nations make pilgrimage to the cosmic mountain.[24]

An original audience would likely have heard the recitation of this tradition-*Gestalt* in the annual cultic event in Jerusalem that celebrated Yahweh's victory over primordial chaos and his enthronement as king on Mount Zion. Still earlier audiences, perhaps at cultic centers such as Shiloh, had celebrated the exaltation of "Yahweh of Hosts" whose throne or footstool was the Ark (1 Sam. 4:4; 2 Sam. 6:2). This celebration was later adapted, its liturgies rewritten when the Ark was transferred to Jerusalem as reflected in the Enthronement Psalms (47, 93–99). At any event, the Zion symbolism of the Jerusalem cult reiterated Yahweh's "exclusive prerogative" as king on Zion.[25]

As the main actor in the drama, the human king would most likely functionally embody Yahweh's rule over his people. Such an endorsement could serve both to empower a king and to challenge his rule. As to which, much depended on the hermeneutic mind-set of those with the rhetorical power to persuade audiences (including competing individuals or coalitions of power) to criticize or support the king on Zion.

In addition to the Zion tradition's providing a stock of conceptual and formal elements from which the plowshare passages draw, it is also possible to isolate determinant factors from tradition(s) concerning the great and terrible "Day of Yahweh." Debate about the origin and *Sitz im Leben* of this tradition shifted between arguments relating the "Day of Yahweh" to the new year's ritual in monarchic Israel,[26] the ancient traditions about holy war in the tribal confederacy,[27] traditions about the covenant,[28] and theophanic disturbances.[29] Frank Cross provided a blended version suggesting that the new year's festival and the holy war tradition need not be seen in exclusivist terms. A combined tradition including both themes could be argued for from the perspective of myth and ritual patterns of later Israel.[30]

The stereotypical pattern of ancient holy wars was described formally by von Rad under the following scheme: (1) the theophanic entrance of Yahweh (Judg. 5:4–5); (2) the call to arms by Yahweh with Yahweh's entry into battle (Judg. 7:1–25); (3) sanctification of the army; (4) panic among the enemies (Exod. 15:14–16, 23:27; Josh. 2:9, 24, 5:1, 7:5, 24:12); (5) natural wonders and disasters (Judg. 5:4; 1 Sam. 7:10, 14:15; Josh. 24:7; Exod. 14:20); and (6) the total destruction of the enemy nations (*ḥerem*) (Josh. 6:18, 21, 7:12, 8:26, 10:28; 1 Sam. 15:3, 21).

Since in any religion's earliest stage of life everything is somehow incorporated into the religious sphere, war was no exception. "Holy war" was seen as an extension of the cultic act, a sort of "continuous, highly expanded sacrifice."[31] Although scholars recognized that every nation of the ancient Near East claimed that their gods participated in war, they also noted that only Israel seemed to understand this claim to mean that it was unnecessary for human warriors to fight. A major debate ensued over the degree of human participation in early Yahweh wars, most attributing this difference in Israel to "pietistic" history writing of a later period seeking to downplay any human action.[32]

What is clear is that the ambiguity of early Israelite tradition appears to have played itself out in the *modern reader's* reconstructions of these traditions. For example, Hermann Gunkel's reading of the Old Testament war stories emphasized the heroism and war piety in these stories. His major study of war in the Old Testament, not incidentally, was dedicated to his son in the German Army of World War I.[33] Gunkel believed a nation's existence depended on the fighting prowess of its youth: "As long as a nation preserves faith in itself and its future [youth] . . . it is, even under the most severe circumstances, invincible."[34] In effect, Israel's heroic use of the sword and heroic faith became, for Gunkel, the model for Germany's own guarantee of invincibility. At the other end of the continuum of modern readers on Old Testament war stories is Millard Lind's challenge of the conventional wisdom about biblical warfare.[35] Reading Exodus 15 and other early texts in a new light, he argued against the notion of a nonviolent pietistic reworking of earlier traditions by post-exilic redactors. Instead, Lind defended Israel's early experience of Yahweh war as that of Yahweh fighting on behalf of Israel by miraculous intervention. Only in time did Israel begin to participate in war like all her neighbors, as reflected in the biblical texts as currently shaped. For Lind, Israel's early theology continued to provide an inherent critique of human participation in war, even as it increasingly launched bloody battles under God's command. This is not the place to argue for or against Gunkel or Lind or other readers, but it is the place to note that Lind's reading, like Gunkel's before him, was no doubt influenced by his own reading context. Lind was a professor in one of the historic peace church seminaries. Again, the determining factor then and now seems to lie in the rhetorical power of the ancient *and* modern reader to convince his or her audience to accept one reading over another—in this case, whether to engage in militant action alongside Yahweh or to let Yahweh engage the battle on his own.

What can be said about the plowshare passages seems clear enough for our purposes: that any audience within hearing of Isaiah, Micah, and Joel would immediately recognize long-standing traditions, perhaps still recited in their religious observances (in Jerusalem or later in exile) by means of psalms and shared liturgical practice. Any rhetorical change in the well-established liturgical readings regarding the means and message of Yahweh's rule on Mount Zion would be immediately apparent. These original audiences heard the tradition-*Gestalt* as intoned by priests and elders as an annual message of hope in Yahweh's military prowess, protection, and sovereignty over Israel, indeed, over the whole cosmos. Their eventual emergence in the land of Canaan as a nation with their own king and capital city had ensured the near-inviolability of this central theolougomena of Zion, "the city of the great king." The hermeneutic of constitutive support would appear to be the foundational mode of understanding this tradition-*Gestalt* among its earliest readers.

Having noted the primary tradition-*Gestalt* regulating the use and understanding of the plowshare texts, we can now more completely develop the history of its use by Isaiah, Micah, and Joel. Arguments about who borrowed from whom or who was the "original" crafter of the plowshare scenario need not be limited to Isaiah, Micah, or Joel. By the ninth century B.C.E.,[36] the holy war/Zion/Day of Yahweh tradition-*Gestalten* might have already provided Isaiah, Micah, and Joel with a common conceptual fund from which to work and rework the tradition for their particular audiences. This is not to suggest that any one of them might not have had direct access to any other, as the various reconstructed scenarios arguing for such a possibility point out.[37] Rather, it is to relativize any discussion of genetic links to that of canonical hermeneutics. We turn then to the story of the tradition-*Gestalt* of the plowshare passages in the second sense of that term noted above: the story of their *perceived* use over time.

Canon as Function: Diachronic Readings of the Plowshare Passages

Reading Isaiah 2:2–4, 5

Adequate surveys exist on the critical problems related to the book of Isaiah.[38] For our purposes, it is sufficient to observe that there is almost unanimous consensus regarding Isaiah 2:2–4 as a well-defined unit, though less so on whether verse 5 is also to be included.[39] Following the arguments laid out by Wildberger following Vermeylen,[40] it is fitting to view verse 5 as a connecting verse to what follows. Verse 5 serves as a liturgical call to hearing (i.e., obeying) the oracle just preached. Because of the close correspondence between Isaiah 2:2–5 and Micah 4:1–5, verse 5 will be retained in this study for comparative purposes. Generically, these verses are designated a "salvation oracle" (vv. 2–4)[41] followed by an "invitation to Jacob to join Yahweh" (v. 5).[42] Overall, the pericope might be aptly titled, "The Pilgrimage of Nations to Zion."[43]

A survey of commentators indicates a variety of possible social contexts for Isaiah 2:2–4, 5. For the purposes of this study, four contexts—and there are more—will be highlighted, providing as they do a representative sampling of the hermeneutic range possible in the reuse of the tradition-*Gestalt* over time. The four reading options here described have the added advantage of coinciding with several redactional stages of the Isaiah book.[44] In each case, the social context will be described, suggesting how an audience in that particular context may have heard the tradition-*Gestalt*. Such a comparison will in turn suggest the hermeneutic stance of the prophet/editor in that setting, triangulating out, as it were, the meaning and function of the text for that context.

In each case, I will also assume a particular reading "as" a real option. It is here presupposed that reasonable arguments can be made, indeed have been made, for each particular period reconstructed. The task now is not to reargue each case but to compare reasonable readings with each other. Of course, those who argue for a late date for Isaiah 2:2–4, 5 will not be satisfied with any reconstruction prior to the exile. Those who argue for the early date may not appreciate arguments by their colleagues who posit "later hands" as "original" even if, as I claim, those later hands simply reworked the earlier "original." For those arguing for a post-exilic origin for Isaiah 2:2–4, 5, this would be a first hearing, not a new reading of an older tradition.[45] Chronologically, the reconstruction by late-daters at least allows for the possibility of an earlier manifestation and use of the tradition. I can only remind those proposing later dates that our task here is not to argue for the possibility of an earlier date over against their reconstruction; that, after all, has been done many times before. What is important for our purposes is that some readers *have* reconstructed earlier options, and our task is to allow their reading to stand in contrast to other readings. The politics of canon, indeed, canonical function, requires such a hearing. This is especially so if an earlier reading (as is the case with every option here outlined) provides its own internal logic and rationale for its reconstruction. In the end, the meaning derived from any reading (precritical, historical-critical, early or late reconstructions, canonical, typological, and so on) must be compared with others. However, in order to make such comparisons, the full range of options must be delineated.

The fact that I have chosen to recount the story of various historical-critical reconstructions does not mean that there are not many other options. The ones I have chosen are representative of several significant scholarly agreements, though they are sometimes in conflict with each other. I have chosen to compare these options chronologically for heuristic reasons and for the force of argument. I personally believe that the story here presented is one possible trajectory of how the plowshare passage of Isaiah was imperiled and saved in several different contexts over time. The reader will have to judge whether the force of this story sustains itself.

PRE-EXILIC READINGS OF ISAIAH 2:2–4, 5 It is fitting to reconstruct a situation whereby the plowshare passage might be understood within the social setting of Isaiah ben Amoz, the eighth-century prophet. At least two life-settings present themselves as options during Isaiah's tenure, both audiences of which would have been in a position to respond to Isaiah's oracle. The first setting has as its historical backdrop the Assyrian alliance made by King Ahaz of Judah; the second, that of Hezekiah's rebellion against Assyria. The two places in which the prophet Isaiah actually appears are in chapters 6–8, during the reign of Ahaz, and in chapters 36–39, during the reign of Hezekiah—clues to the argument here regarding the two social settings of Isaiah's early audiences.[46] The fact that in the first instance Isaiah's message was ignored and in the second it was heeded provides an important contrast in the Book of Isaiah itself.[47]

Early in the vocation of Isaiah, the politics of Israel and Judah stirred up Isaiah's ire. When Ahaz assumed the throne (742–727 B.C.E., 2 Kgs. 16; 2 Chron. 28), Judah still had strong vassal ties to Israel, the status of the Davidic family was somewhat in question, the land had suffered a severe earthquake, Syria and Israel were attempting to extort Ahaz to join their alliance against Assyria, the Edomites had invaded Judean territory and taken captives, and there was a growing lack of political support for Ahaz among Judean cities.[48] The realpolitik of Ahaz seemingly left him with only two options: join the rebellious alliance against Assyria or cut a deal with Assyria. He chose the latter, politically and religiously, but not without warning from Isaiah.

Ahaz's capitulation only prolonged a major onslaught by Assyrian forces.

Following the death of Ahaz, his heir Hezekiah (ca. 727–698 B.C.E.; 2 Kgs. 18–20; 2 Chron. 29–32) would also face intractable choices, heightened in their consequence by the decisions of his father. Hezekiah had expansionist desires that included controlling all of Israel once again (Isa. 9:1–7), thus aggravating an already strained foreign policy. He reversed his father's policies at every point, at first cautiously, then boldly, and unpried Judah from allegiance to Assyria—which was made possible by Assyria's own troubles with Babylon and Asia Minor and by the death of the powerful Sargon (703 B.C.E.). Hezekiah embarked on a military buildup and strengthened Jerusalem against prolonged conflict, as is apparent from the now-famous tunnel unearthed by archaeologists beneath Jerusalem built to bring water inside the city during a siege (2 Kgs. 20:20; Isa. 22:8b–11). As a religious reformer, motivated in part by Israel's ill-fated demise, Hezekiah eventually centralized worship in Jerusalem, closing competing centers of worship elsewhere, to the praise of Isaiah and the Temple hierarchy (2 Kgs. 18:3–6).[49]

Soon enough, owing to Sennacherib's preoccupation in the East, revolt spread throughout Palestine and Syria, allowing a number of coalitions to form in defiance of Assyria. Egypt, seeking to enhance its position, was a willing partner, offering military aid to Hezekiah, which he accepted against the harsh criticism of Isaiah (Isa. 30:1–7, 31:1–3). Later, in 701 B.C.E., Sennacherib struck (2 Kgs. 18:13–16), devastating much of Palestine, including forty-six of Judah's fortified cities.[50] Sennacherib sent his commanding general to Jerusalem to demand an unconditional surrender. Hezekiah, like Ahaz before him, was faced with two options: succumb to fate by surrendering to Assyria or defy the forces of Sennacherib. Hezekiah, supported by Isaiah (14:24–27, 17:12–14, 31:4–9), chose the latter.[51]

If one is to assume, methodologically, that Isaiah had something to say to his audiences in the historical context of the Syro-Ephraimite war and the Assyrian juggernaut of 701 B.C.E., then it is most likely that he would say something that was not only understandable by his contemporaries but also different from what they were already thinking. On the matter of commonly understood tradition, the Zion-Yahweh war *Gestalt* was a palatable one: exaltation of Zion, call to arms by Yahweh, gathering of peoples to Zion, and destruction of enemies' weapons by Yahweh, followed by the nations' surrender. All temple-goers had heard and perhaps recited that nationalistic liturgy before.

What would have struck their ears as unconventional would have been Isaiah's (2:2–4, 5) reinterpretation and transposition of these earlier traditions. Whereas the Zion psalms were militant in the extreme, Isaiah's oracle describes a reign of peace resulting from the nations voluntarily "flowing up" the side of Mount Zion and dismantling their weapons and transforming them into farm implements on their own—all this after submitting to Yahweh's *tôrâh* and learning his ways. There is no hint in Isaiah's reworking of this ancient tradition that the enemy nations were out to wreak havoc against Jerusalem. The crowd-silencing impact of Isaiah's rhetoric found its greatest force precisely because it was delivered in the face of the extortion attempts of the Israel/Syria coalition, on the one hand, and Assyria's equally ominous threat on the other. Indeed, Isaiah's reshaping of the older Zion tradition parallels his reworked image of the Davidic king who was out to shatter the nations like a piece of pottery (Ps. 2:9) and at whose throne the crushed heads and corpses of his enemies were thrown (Ps. 110:6). Instead, Isaiah's king would be a Prince of Peace whose birth would turn the raiment of war into kindling (Isa. 9:4–5) and whose reign would be marked by security on God's holy mountain (Isa. 11:9).[52]

In the ears of Ahaz and his retinue or Hezekiah and his foreign policy advisers, Isaiah's message offered a critical alternative to the realpolitik of the older tradition to which Ahaz would incline, as would Hezekiah in his treaty with Egypt. This would especially be the case insofar as the king was viewed as the embodiment of Yahweh's military actions. Millard Lind accurately summarizes Isaiah's own foreign policy alternative:

> As a successful policy of political self-interest must be guided realistically in the historical situation by power oriented wisemen, so successful political reliance upon Yahweh required a wisdom informed not only by Yahweh's past acts of justice but also by a knowledge of the present political situation. Isaiah's foreign policy based on trust in Yahweh was *the realistic* foreign policy rather than the misguided "realistic" power politics of Ahaz and [previously] Hezekiah. . . . Based in the first instance on religion (trust in Yahweh, excluding effective military armaments and coalitions), it was a trust *related* successfully *by the prophet* to the political situation of the times. The only alternative realistic foreign policy based on political realism would have been that of the later Manasseh, complete subjection to Assyrian domination.[53] (emphasis added)

Isaiah offered a prophetic challenge to both Ahaz and Hezekiah, demanding total trust in Yahweh, most especially in the wisdom of Yahweh's *tôrâh* and in the power of *dĕbar-yhwh* ("the word of Yahweh") to make peace with foreign nations, not least of whom was Assyria. Trust in *tôrâh,* especially as it appears here in the presentation of Yahweh as the king to whom nations come for instruction, fits well with the wisdom traditions of the day. The king in the ancient Near East enjoyed a special claim to wisdom and to being considered a source of wisdom. Yahweh is here seen as divine king to whom subject nations come for judgment and correction; the first is the function of the wise king, the second, of the wise teacher.[54] Never mind that Ahaz still refused to be persuaded by what was in effect Isaiah's call for nonalignment with either Assyria or the Syro-Ephraimite coalition, trusting in Yahweh's word and wisdom alone. Ahaz chose instead to side with Assyria against the Syro-Ephraimite coalition and paid a heavy political price. Ahaz had set into motion the process of cleansing, which would include Yahweh's warring against his own people and would not be concluded until after Hezekiah's lifetime. On the other hand, Hezekiah is shown to have heeded Isaiah's challenge to trust Yahweh completely over against reliance on his own military prowess or on outside coalitions. He is rewarded by a miraculous rout of Sennacherib's army (Isa. 37:36–37).[55]

Insofar as the Book of Isaiah in its present form shows Ahaz's failure as the result of refusing Isaiah's guidance, and insofar as Hezekiah's success could be linked to listening to Isaiah's political strategy of trust in Yahweh, then the force of Isaiah's vision in Isaiah 2:2–4, whether first drafted in the time of Uzziah[56] or that of Ahaz and heard again in Hezekiah's time, whether seen as an ideal future or a very realpolitik in its own right, would always stand as a counter-reading to the earlier militant traditions out of which it was reworked and reread. Yahweh had a way, and it was the way of his *tôrâh* and *dâbâr,* not the way of the militant Yahweh war of old. Later, the *tôrâh*-reform of Josiah would assist in establishing this reading as a legitimate alternative, a royal paradigm, a model of obedient trust for future generations under siege.[57]

POST-EXILIC READINGS OF ISAIAH 2:2–4, 5   The Babylonian invasion and destruction of Jerusalem and its Holy Temple on Mount Zion (598, 587 B.C.E.), along with the simultaneous mass deportation of the citizenry into exile, marked a decisive moment in the history of Israel on many fronts, not least of which was canon formation.

Formally, Torah and canon would function in new ways as the "vehicle of survival" par excellence.[58] Now, all reference to authority ("canon"), previously anchored in the power and prestige of the monarchy and Temple, was shifted to the preconquest, premonarchic period. Deuteronomy had begun to displace Joshua as the climax of the canonical period of authority after the events of 701 B.C.E. emphasized the role of obedience and sin in salvation and adversity, respectively. Josiah would aid in this shift, and the exile would permanently anchor this shift historically. Torah as wisdom also shifted to include increasingly formal notions of Torah as canon, at least with respect to the first five books. The persistent theologem that ran throughout Israel's history, that God alone was king, though relatively quiescent during the monarchy, resurfaced in force during the exile and thereafter.[59]

It was argued earlier that the designation of certain texts as canonical by a process of inclusion or exclusion has always been an ideological factor in religious (and secular) traditions. The goal in these ongoing canonical debates has always been to "fix and legitimate one form of self-understanding and by implication to exclude others."[60] In the exile, the most basic claim to religious authority was granted to the prophets, and to Moses in particular. This provided the reemphasis on early Torah traditions noted previously and provided the warranty for adding prophetic writings in their own right to this first canon.

A prophet's authority derived from personal experience on the one hand and his or her rhetorical power to mediate shared traditions on the other.[61] The two major referents to which the prophets appealed in their call was that of the "word of God" (classical prophets) or the "spirit of God" (preclassical prophets).[62] The transcendent sense of Yahweh's work in history compels Isaiah to elaborate on *dâbâr* ("word") and *ruaḥ* ("spirit") as important extensions of divine power in the world. For Isaiah, the most relevant active force in metahistory was the *dâbâr*. The word of God as *dâbâr* established Israel's destiny. Thus, in a real sense, for Isaiah, prophetic rhetoric *constructs* history, not merely predicts it.

Klaus Koch, in his study of Isaiah's view of Yahweh's rhetorical power, argues against a modern "positivist invention" that might contend that history is a "history of facts" and that the question of meaning can only be asked at a later stage after the "facts" are delineated. This, says Koch, may not be a true view of history at all. Speech events cannot be distinguished from history: "For Isaiah there was no such thing as history-in-itself, but only metahistory."[63] Koch's comments about Isaiah come very close to what was argued above as being a critical revival in the postmodern mind along with new efforts to speak to the functional nature of language (word as deed) over against language as content.

Both emphases (word and spirit) would now, during the exile and thereafter, provide a notional *Gestalt* for discerning God's will in a period when the material symbols of authority (land, Temple, monarchy) were no longer available. A heightened sense of the power of God's Torah-word would reemerge that would find (or *construct*) its historical genealogy in the premonarchic period, a time when Yahweh defeated Pharaoh by the word of the prophet par excellence, Moses. The Torah-word of Yahweh (with its emerging consciousness of "canon") became the realpolitik of defeated, powerless people in exile.

When the Babylonian empire fell to the Medes and Persians, Cyrus decreed permission for the exiled Jews to return to their homeland and reestablish their religion there. This, of course, was simply part of the foreign policy of Cyrus for governing his subject territories. However, as Isaiah had always done before them, new readers of the Isaianic traditions interpreted these historical events theologically.[64] Since chapters 2–4 of Isaiah nowhere made explicit reference to Sennacherib, Hezekiah, or the Assyrians, readers after Cyrus's decree were now able to read these texts as referring to the events they knew all too well: the Babylonian invasion and destruction of Jerusalem.

The returning exiles could now read the oracle in 2:2–4, 5 in a new light as well. With the rebuilding of the Temple at the end of the sixth century B.C.E., this oracle continues to presuppose the Zion tradition as reinterpreted by Isaiah. The idea of nations peacefully approaching Zion in search of Yahweh's Torah-word was now seen as a real possibility, given the magnanimous license the Persian rulers seemed to offer a reconstituted Israel. The post-exilic readers were now able to understand the Isaianic tradition in relation to the destruction and restoration of Jerusalem, proof in their minds that Yahweh was, indeed, king over the whole earth, the nations being but "a drop in the bucket" (Isa. 40:15) in God's universe. Indeed, the poet did not miss the chance to give a marvelous description of this gathering of nations. Sailing ships come from the western sea like flights of doves, caravans and camels on a *haj* from the east. They bring sheep for sacrifice, along with gold and incense for the Temple. Even more imaginatively wonderful is their carrying back to safety the refugees among God's people. Lawlessness and social oppression will then come to an end, and peace will be the overseer and righteousness the governor in God's holy city. The days of mourning will be gone forever (Isa. 56:7, 66:18, 23).[65]

In the language of canonical hermeneutics, what the "readers" in the days of Ahaz and Hezekiah heard as a prophetic challenge to their trust in alien powers now was read by alien Jews returning to their homeland as a word of constitutive support. What appeared to Ahaz's audience as a policy of capitulation and to Hezekiah's audience as a challenge to its foreign policy temptations was now read by returning Jews as a profound message of hope in their immediate futures.

A final post-exilic reading of Isaiah 2:2–4, 5 must also be noted in that it differs in audience from that described above and so illustrates a still more nuanced hermeneutic. As has been ably argued by Marvin Sweeney, the last major stage in the formation of Isaiah 1–4 is especially reflected in its first chapter.[66] Sweeney suggests that this redaction happened sometime toward the end of the fifth century B.C.E., about the time of Nehemiah and Ezra.

The sociopolitical differences of rival factions that had been largely overlooked during the heyday of the exodus from Babylon, when idealism ran high, began to splinter toward the end of the century. Conflicting ideologies began to surface as exaggerated hope gave way to realism, then outright pessimism.[67] There had been no pilgrimage of nations to Mount Zion, no universal acknowledgment of Yahweh's rule; the Temple was not even as grand as the first Temple had been, nor was Yahweh's Torah deemed by the world the final arbiter of justice. Even worse, the tide of assimilation was coming in, as more and more Jews intermarried with the local pagan population, going so far as to worship with them. Within this deteriorating situation, Ezra (Ezra 7–19; Neh. 8–10) and Nehemiah (Neh. 13) sought to stem the tide by instituting strict reforms: banning intermarriage, removing syncretistic worship elements, reaffirming the authority of the Torah, requiring Sabbath observance, and reinstituting the Jewish festivals.[68] There was a special interest in distinguishing a true Jew from a false one.[69] Such were the beginnings of post-exilic Judaism.

The Isaianic oracles of judgment in Isaiah 1 were now reread. No longer did they refer to Assyrian devastation and apostasy in the days of Ahaz or Hezekiah; now they were read by the reformers in Ezra's day against the nonobservant Jews among them. Sweeney suggests that the redactors organized the materials in chapters 1–4 in such a way that they now offered a Deuteronomistic-like choice to the people: accept Torah instruction (1:10) and be redeemed (1:19, 27); refuse and perish (1:20a, 28). Specifically, with regard to the universal peace proposal of Isaiah 2:2–4, since it was obvious no such peace was imminent, it too was now read using a prophetic critique, in keeping with its Deuteronomistic orientation.[70]

Now explanation could be given for why the promises of Yahweh (chaps. 2–4) had not yet materialized, as well for why those same promises were still in force. Such an explanation could occur by reading the tradition through the bifocals of a constitutive hermeneutic *and* a prophetic critique.[71] The promise of the realization of Isaiah 2:2–4 was now conditional, in keeping with the Deuteronomic ideology.[72] For the faithful, it would come to pass; for the wicked, it would be withheld. Readers in Ezra's day would be challenged to choose righteousness, which necessarily meant Yahweh's Torah (Isa. 2:3b). The liturgical invitation to "come . . . let us walk in the light of Yahweh" (2:5) held out in a new way the promise that the realization of Isaiah 2:2–4 was still a possibility: "What else can this mean than that the Israelite hearers already now should follow the instructions of Yahweh, which at a future time will lead all peoples to peace with one another? Thus, the eschatological promise for the peoples has become a word to help give direction for Israel for the present."[73]

Reading Micah 4:1–5

Brevard Childs correctly observes that "few books illustrate as well as does Micah the present crisis in exegetical method."[74] The obvious relationship between this unit and its counterpart in Isaiah has provoked a debate unresolved among commentators to this day.[75] The contrast of this passage, with its predictions of everlasting peace for Yahweh's house on Zion, with the immediately preceding caustic judgment oracle prophesying the utter destruction of Jerusalem on Mount Zion (3:9–12) has also contributed to the fervent discussion regarding its origin. Whether pre-exilic, exilic, or post-exilic (there are strong arguments all around),[76] the most important reading option for the present discussion is that defended by Adam Van der Woude in his several articles on Micah.[77] This is especially so, given the fact that most of the other readings of Micah as reconstructed by commentators would reflect the hermeneutic options already described in detail in the previous discussion of Isaiah. The contribution of Van der Woude is unique in the debate linking this unit to the broader argument regarding true and false prophecy. To better understand Van der Woude's contribution, it is important first to sketch briefly the context of Micah's prophecy.

Although critical prophecy had probably begun some years earlier with Isaiah, Micah, his younger contemporary, was the first prophet to predict the actual destruction of Jerusalem, most likely in the days of Hezekiah (Jer. 26).[78] Micah's harsh social criticism is directed primarily against the injustices perpetrated by "the heads of the house of Jacob and the rulers of the house of Israel, who abhor justice and pervert all equity" (3:9–10). He extrapolated a link between the social and economic abuses prevalent among his contemporaries and the Assyrian threat hovering over a decadent Jerusalem. His political instinct united with his theological insight to declare judgment against Mount Zion. Indeed, Jerusalem, the great city, would be destroyed (3:12). It has been suggested that Hezekiah's reformation was due to the unrelenting preaching of Micah.[79] Naturally, there would have been those within earshot of Micah's harsh judgment concerning the utter destruction of Jerusalem who would have viewed him as heretical in the extreme.

In Van der Woude's reading of Micah 4:1–5, he proposes a novel solution to the structural and interpretative problems of chapter 4 (and other sections of Micah), blaming the exegetical impasse on the "atomizing literary analysis" of traditional reading strategies (1969:249). The most obvious problem facing readers of Micah 4 is its kaleidoscopic alternation between "despair and triumph, calamity and salvation."[80] The question arises as to whether any prophet or redactor could juxtapose words of hope and criticism in such a seesaw fashion and expect the reader to take seriously those prophecies of resolute calamity.[81] Furthermore, when the Book of Micah does prophesy hope regarding the Davidic line, it promotes a more rural leader from Bethlehem Ephratha, not rulers in Jerusalem, which, as has been noted, are unequivocally condemned by Micah (1973:398). Rather than posit later postexilic hands for the expectant passages, a traditional explanation of these odd juxtapositions,[82] Van der Woude suggests that these alternating parts are best understood as instances of a disputation between the prophet and false prophets of Micah's day.[83] The argument is sustained, in part, because earlier in 2:6–11 Micah explicitly quotes those who try to prevent him and his supporters from prophesying oracles of doom. His antagonists' words there sound every bit like the positive-minded rejoinders oddly juxtaposed with Micah's doom-saying oracles in the present context.

Van der Woude argues persuasively, given his proposal and assumptions, that the theological thrust of the passages of weal, not least of which is that of the plowshare passage (Mic. 4:1–4) in its current literary setting, is typical of Micah's spiritual opponents, demonstrated in their words in 4:9, 11–13 (also 5:4–9, 2:12–13). Micah's adversaries try to argue that his prophecy of doom (3:12) blatantly contradicts the prophecy of hope uttered by his great contemporary (and perhaps teacher), Isaiah (1973:401).[84] Furthermore, the additional verse (4:4), which has as its main force Yahweh's very own pledge, "the mouth of Yahweh of hosts has spoken," underscores their rhetorical attempts at legitimating their claim.[85]

Finally, though its liturgical function closely parallels Isaiah 2:5, Micah 4:5 is adapted in its literary setting in a telling way. What was simply an appeal in Isaiah 2:5 ("Come, House of Jacob, let us walk in the light of Yahweh") becomes in Micah 4:5 a self-confident declaration of assurance by Micah's adversaries: "All people may walk, each in the name of his god, but *we* will walk in the name of Yahweh, our God, forever and ever" (1973:402).

If Van der Woude's arguments hold, and there are detractors,[86] then Micah 4:1–4, 5 provides an example of an audience using the hermeneutic of constitutive support to read the plowshare passage in such a way as to circumvent its earlier use by Isaiah to warn against the very mentality of those now wielding it against Micah. In particular, Micah's opponents, with their uncritical commitment to Zion and Jerusalem (i.e., to the status quo), are obliged to the very same realpolitik of Ahaz (with Assyria) and Hezekiah (with Egypt) in forming military coalitions as a means of warding off outside threat (5:4b–5). Ironically, Isaiah had reinterpreted the militant Zion theology to serve as a prophetic critique of just such dependence on military prowess, inside and outside Jerusalem. Now, Micah's opponents were using Isaiah's reinterpretation to defend just such a foreign policy, ignoring for the time being its inherent critique of its own use of the reinterpretation. As Van der Woude concludes: "This shows again that the difference between pseudo- and true prophecy is not to be found in pseudo-prophecy having or preaching another objective truth, but in its ideological use of truth with a complete disregard of the fact that truth has its own *kairos*, and is conditioned by it" (1973:402). His observation regarding a *kairos*-conditioned truth need only be augmented to include the conditioning power of one's interpretative community. The opponents of Micah defended their truth against Micah's falsehoods, and they could appeal to authoritative tradition (Isa. 2:2–4) as support.

Reading Joel 4:9–17 (Eng. 3:9–17)

Commentators have largely agreed on the overall literary structure of the Book of Joel, if not the dating of any of its major parts or the whole. Since B. Duhm's classical literary-critical reading of Joel, the book has largely been understood as balanced between two sections, its fulcrum text being 2:17, 18.[87] The first section (1:1–2:18) emphasizes disaster; the second section (2:19–4:21 [Eng. 2:19–3:21]) features a message of salvation.[88]

The text under discussion (4:9–17 [Eng. 3:9–17]) is part of a Yahweh speech "against all the nations" (4:1–21) gathered together in the Valley of Jehoshaphat (vv. 1, 12). The literary form that best illuminates the meaning and function of this chapter was described above as part of the tradition-*Gestalt* reflected in the divine warrior hymns celebrating Yahweh's victory over Israel's enemies on "the great and terrible day of Yahweh" (2:31). These very old hymns (Exod. 15:1–18; Judg. 5), along with their reuse during the monarchy (Pss. 2, 24, 29, 68, 89, 97), were revived by apocalyptic writers to describe Yahweh's final vindication of Judah and the defeat of its enemies (Isa. 59:15b–20, 66:14b–16, 22–23; Zech. 14:1–21; Ezek. 38–39).[89] Specifically, the formal description of Joel 4:9–17 is deemed a "summons to battle," originally associated with the inauguration of holy war.[90]

The parallels between Joel 4:9–17 (Eng. 3:9–17) and Isaiah 2:2–4 (Mic. 1:1–4) are striking. Yahweh, in Joel's account, summons the nations as enemies to battle, in direct contrast to their voluntary allegiance portrayed in Isaiah. The statement in 4:10a—"Beat your plowshares into swords, and your pruning hooks into spears"—except for the substitution of *r^emahim* for *h^anitotehem* (synonyms for "spears")—is an explicit reversal of Isaiah 2:4b.[91] Compare that command to what the nations do in Isaiah upon hearing the Torah of Yahweh. In Isaiah, they voluntarily undertake a "cease-fire" arrangement, transforming their war machinery into farm implements.

Other parallels between these two texts are equally noteworthy. The theme of judging the nations found in Isaiah 2:4a finds its counterpart in Joel 4:12b. Isaiah's version suggests Yahweh (as wise teacher and judge) arbitrates between the nations, whereas Joel has Yahweh (as holy warrior) judging every nation. In both accounts, Yahweh ends up on Mount Zion (Isa. 2:3; Joel 4:17): in Isaiah's account, as divine gravity wooing the nations up the mountainside; in Joel's account, as divine warrior slaughtering them in the valley. Since readaptation and reinterpretation of older prophetic materials seem to run rampant in Joel,[92] one cannot doubt that Joel also borrows his plowshare material from Isaiah or Micah or a common source.[93] He clearly uses what apparently by then was a well-known plowshare tradition-*Gestalt*, with its proclamation of universal peace, to declare its opposite: universal war on the nations.

It is necessary to extrapolate from Joel's message to the social context of his audience, a feat notoriously prone to varied results. Exegetes reading exactly the same data have dated Joel from the ninth century to the second century B.C.E. Willem W. Prinsloo has shown how these widely divergent findings have everything to do with the particular preconceptions—particularly as regards method—of the commentator reading Joel.[94] The text itself gives no unambiguous pointers as regards dating.

For purposes here, a date soon after Nehemiah and Ezra (late fourth century B.C.E.) will be assumed. This was an era when the political establishment of the post-exilic community was that of a "theocracy," and later forms of prophecy readily reinterpreted earlier traditions to new generations. Other factors include the condition of Judah in Joel 4:2–3 (Eng. 3:2–3), the condition of the Temple, the fact that the walls of Jerusalem had been rebuilt, the absence of reference to monarchy and king, the preeminence of the priests, the type of offering mentioned, language and style, and so on.[95]

It must be admitted that those who defend an earlier date have reasoned arguments on their side as well. Right up to the middle of the nineteenth century, virtually everyone assumed Joel to be associated with the earliest prophets on the basis of the position the book occupies in the canon. In addition, close parallels with the Zion theology of the Royal Psalms supported an early date. It was argued that Joel makes sense during the time of Joash, when the high priest Jehoida acted as regent (2 Kgs. 11–12), and the arguments go on from there.[96] Sundry other possible "origins" were still adduced.[97] The arguments are often all of one piece and somewhat circular. Notwithstanding, if Joel was early, one would assume that Isaiah borrowed from Joel in much the same way that he borrowed from the Zion tradition reflected in the early psalms; otherwise, Joel borrows from Isaiah or both from a common tradition-*Gestalt*.

What can be said is that, early or late, the audience listening to the thrust of the book would hear a very similar message. Joel's theocentric proclamation declares Yahweh the main protagonist (in speech and action).[98] Joel uses a calamitous situation in his day to declare a renewed confidence in the prophetic message (of the past?). The crisis situation (plague of locusts) instigated by Yahweh is interpreted by Joel theologically (chaps. 1–2) as the cause for the people's distress cry to Yahweh (2:17–18)—all so Yahweh could rescue those who call on his name (3:5). The calamity experienced by Judah and Jerusalem is then transformed into violent destruction and death for all the nations of the world in direct proportion to their heinous crimes against Judah (4:1–17). By contrast, Judah and Jerusalem will live on in perpetuity. Joel ends on a triumphal note not unlike the uncritical days when Zion theology was unfettered by the prophetic critique of prophets like Isaiah. Yahweh, once again the holy warrior, rules from Zion (4:17, 21).

Of course, the picture portraying this same eschatalogical assault by the nations on the largest scale is the prophecy of the coming of Gog and Magog and of their destruction "on the mountains of Israel" (Ezek. 38–39:20). Significantly, Ezekiel's prophecy appeals, as does Joel's, to earlier predictions (Ezek. 38:17) of such calamity. The prophecy regards itself as being based on prior prophetic tradition. Like Joel, these nations do not come voluntarily but are summoned, even compelled, by Yahweh to the battlefield (Ezek. 38:4, 39:2). Still later, these variations on a theme in Joel and Ezekiel find their full development in Zechariah 12 and 14. Here, the enemy nations are again summoned to battle by Yahweh but then actually force their way into the holy city and wreak all kinds of bloody havoc. Yahweh responds with even more gory force, leaving them all but annihilated. Out of this bloodbath Yahweh establishes the long-awaited eschatalogical peace.[99]

Joel's version of events was in good biblical company. His audience, whatever their specific situation,[100] would hear Joel's message as one of constitutive support. If the day of Yahweh once meant Israel's defeat (Amos 5:18–20), it now would be a day of everlasting bliss for Judah and Jerusalem. If Israel once anticipated a peaceful and inclusive resolution to its foreign policy (Isa. 2:4; Mic. 4:3), it now could anticipate a violent resolution to those international relationships and an exclusive claim to salvation.[101] The mood that Joel sought to relay to his audience was surely "one of confidence in the inviolability of its own salvation and in Jerusalem's election as the throne of Yahweh's kingdom."[102]

Summary of Readings of the Plowshare Passages

It has been our task to provide a reasonable sampling of the alternative uses of the tradition-*Gestalt* by different reading audiences. Such a history of the use of these traditions over time has also provided an example of reading the Bible intertextually. As was described earlier, five levels of intertextuality provide ample room for a text's adaptability.[103] A diachronic reading highlights the level of intertextuality and the process of reuse of a text over time.

The history of use of the plowshare traditions over time reveals a dynamic intertextual process. The interplay between texts in such a process demonstrates how a new text reflects on an earlier text or tradition through citation, allusion, and use of phrases and paraphrases echoing and sometimes completely reformulating the earlier text. Isaiah echoed the *Gattung* of an earlier Zion tradition, reworking it for his own use, while still later Isaianic disciples would also find the tradition useful for their particular settings. Apparently, another group countered Micah's harsh prophecy by citing Isaiah almost verbatim to score their own points, only to be followed later by Joel, who also quoted Isaiah to score a radically opposing viewpoint. Those alternatives are provided in table 5.1.

The summary of possible contexts listed in table 5.1 highlights several things. Given the militant nationalism of Joel 4:9–17 ("plowshares to swords"), whether in its pre-exilic efforts to affirm the monarchy or to fan the flames of renewed hope in Zion's inviolability or its post-exilic apocalyptic-

TABLE 5.1. Reading the Plowshare Passages: A Summary

Tradition-*Gestalt*	Social Context	Hermeneutic
Plowshares to swords (Royal Psalms; Joel 4:9–17[1])	Early pre-exilic ninth century B.C.E.	Constitutive support
Swords to plowshares (Isa. 2:2–4, 5[1])	Uzziah/postearthquake (747–735 B.C.E.)	Prophetic critique
Swords to plowshares (Isa. 2:2–4, 5[2])	Ahaz/Syro-Ephraimite threat (734–732 B.C.E.)	Prophetic critique (unheeded)
Swords to plowshares (Mic. 4:1–4, 5[1])	Hezekiah (732–722 B.C.E.)	Constitutive support ("false" prophets)
Swords to plowshares (Isa. 2:2–4, 5[3])	Hezekiah/siege of Assyria (701 B.C.E.)	Prophetic critique (heeded)
Plowshares to swords (Joel 4:9–17[2])	Assyria demise/Babylon threat (612–600 B.C.E.)	Constitutive support
Swords to plowshares (Isa. 2:2–4, 5[4]; Mic. 4:1–4, 5[2])	Early post-exilic (515–500 B.C.E.)	Constitutive support
Plowshares to swords (Joel 4:9–17[3])	Post-exilic after 500 B.C.E.	Constitutive support
Swords to plowshares (Isa. 2:2–4, 5[5])	Post-Ezra/Nehemiah	Constitutive support (remnant) Prophetic critique (impious)

Note: The superscripted numbers reflect the possible contexts in which a particular tradition *may* have appeared across time, depending on the argument of the scholar-reader reconstructing that context. Five contexts are suggested for Isaiah, three for Joel, and two for Micah.

like foreign policy, the militant Zion theology evoked by Joel 4:9–17 (and its predecessor, the Zion Psalms) was always read using the hermeneutic of constitutive support.

Not so the nonmilitant rendering of the Zion theology in Isaiah 2:2–4 (Mic. 4:1–4) ("swords to plowshares"). Depending on its audience, this tradition-*Gestalt* was read either as prophetic criticism or as constitutive support or both. In the main, the only time the nonmilitant version of the plowshares passages was read using a hermeneutic of constitutive support *before* the exile was when those reading it were "false prophets" arguing against Micah (and, by extension, Isaiah). In turn, *after* the exile, the nonmilitant versions were more easily seen as visions of a glorious future, not as accommodation-politics threatening Zion's ultimate invincibility. For some, sobered by the exile, hope in the future could only come by way of Yahweh's Torah-word; for others, the militant option would remain the only true vision of how Zion would again become the center of the world.[104]

At all times, the two alternative options as argued here were known by competing parties; sometimes one alternative had the rhetorical upper hand, sometimes the other. As we have shown, it *did* matter which one was used when. Most notably, those times when Israel might have enjoyed enough political and military strength to be swayed to respond to the old Zion militant theology, as explicitly reclaimed by Joel against Isaiah, proved to be disastrous for Israel. On the other hand, in times of relative political weakness, the militant Zion theology could provoke hope, even if such hope was still in the future and largely rhetorical.

Canon as Context: Synchronic Reading of the Plowshare Passages

Canonical process may go a long way in explaining the use of contradictory texts over time as indicated in the story of the function of the plowshare passages above. However, even if scholarly agreement regarding the historical-critical process (diachronic history of traditions) were unequivocal, the narrative problem emerging from a synchronic reading in canonical context remains. People who read the narratives read them as they are, not as historical critics would prefer them to be read. What is in front of the contemporary reader is not the process of a story's use but its compressed history. As has been demonstrated, unpacking the canonical process takes some very critical effort. Unfortunately, the force of a story in juxtaposition with the force of its opposite still leaves the average reader at a loss for understanding what to do in his or her own context. Michael Fishbane defines the dilemma acutely: "Just how the exegetically disclosed fragments should be diachronically evaluated and aligned is of obvious hermeneutical concern—particularly so with the Bible, since its evaluation has been historicized, and its varieties and contradictions *cannot be resolved synchronically*" (emphasis added).[105]

The contradictions between Joel and Isaiah are indeed unresolvable through a synchronic reading. The force of canon has sponsored mutually exclusive constructions of reality. Joel 4:9–17 (Eng. 3:9–17) and Isaiah 2:2–4 (Mic. 4:1–4) contain two competing views, the ethical and moral implications of which are distinctly and dangerously provocative. If one lives by Isaiah's foreign policy of utter dependence on Yahweh, he or she risks everything on a Torah-word promise in a historical hour that may prove to be suicidal. On the other hand, if one lives by Joel's militant exclusivism, wars might never cease. The Bible as canon when read synchronically sponsors these divergent views in a "concordant discord."[106]

Reading Isaiah 2:2–4 and Joel 4:9–17 illuminates the notion of intertextuality at the level of literary context. The potency between them never collapses at this intertextual level. Each scores its own theological point without yielding to the other. On the one hand, Joel emphasizes God as Redeemer, advocate of Israel alone. Joel's image of God is very much worldly, a God personal enough to fight a bloody war in the trenches of the Jehoshaphat Valley against the nations. On the other hand, Isaiah, influenced in part by the wisdom traditions of the surrounding culture, concerns himself with an international, ecumenical vision. Isaiah's perception of Yahweh is that of Creator of all nations. Yahweh's involvement in the affairs of the nations is somewhat more distant; Yahweh is the dispenser of Torah wisdom, a hands-off speaker of sorts more than an immanent actor. Theologically, it would be a disservice to both Isaiah and Joel to attempt to harmonize them or to merge the two into one story by trying to speak of a "redemptive creator God, or a creative redeemer God."[107] Nor would it be appropriate to mellow the harshness of their differences by positing a temporal "gap" between them, as if to say Joel's bloody account prepares the world for Isaiah's peaceable vision. We noted how that argument fails on its own logic. These texts in all their intertextual difference provide a powerful hermeneutic of lasting duration that can be seen throughout the biblical canon and that must not be muted.[108] Ethically, however, their juxtaposition requires a response. But first, a few general conclusions are in order.

Conclusions: Canon Hermeneutics

Diachronic Readings and the Hermeneutic Continuum

It has been shown how a tradition-*Gestalt* can be (and was) manipulated rhetorically both to provide a check on Israel's uncritical self-reliance and to encourage trust in Yahweh's providential hand in history. The ethical force of the argument for universal war and exclusive claims to salvation (Joel 4:9–17) was largely diminished by historical shifts in Israel's fate and by the counterargument for universal peaceful coexistence with all nations under Yahweh's reign of Torah (Isa. 2:2–4). In this sense, by making explicit the function of the conflicting views in their context, canonical process was able to clarify the hermeneutics being used in each case. It was shown how explicitly contradictory texts that are false in one setting (as read by one audience) might be true in another.

Such a reading across time and space said something as well about canonical function. Each time an authoritative tradition was cited, it was proclaimed with conviction. Each prophet believed his point of view and operated under the burden of being accused of uttering falsehoods. The ethic of personal responsibility cannot be underestimated, even if that responsibility was sometimes shuffled into the heavens with the rhetorical claim that this word was Yahweh's word. In anthropological terms, terms most of us can identify with at least some of the time, the prophet's rhetoric of persuasion was his own. He had to make his case and risk the consequences. Canon as function requires such risk of all who might appeal to its content.

In general, by dynamic analogy, a reader of these contradictory passages now has available to him or her a hermeneutic continuum by which to help determine how she or he might read these passages in the new setting. Important to such a reading is the matter of *how* a text is read. Indeed, to read a text asking *how* a particular audience heard it in their particular setting and risking its application to the new context may be the truly canonical act, more than simply exegeting the *what* of a text or tradition for its canonical content. To ask *how* a text is read is more than a hermeneutical question, it is also a question of ethics—a question to which a tentative answer remains to be provided.

The Comfort and Challenge of Canon

The internal shape of the canon as context recognizes that whereas the Bible was the original sponsor of raging differences, these differences have been compressed into a canonical-literary whole and as such now serve a critical function of checks and balances upon each other. The canon serves as its own self-correcting apparatus. Something happens to each reading option in its placement alongside the other within the canonical context, not least of which is the relativizing of any exclusive claim of being *the* truth. As such, the canon is the maker and breaker of exclusive views.[109] This is its comfort.

Such a blessed rage for disorder also poses its challenges. The implications of canon as a compressed text of many contexts, when it comes to choosing to live by Isaiah 2:2–4 or Joel 4:9–12, are disquieting for anyone who prefers the one over the other. Indeed, from the perspective of one reading, the other can rightly be deemed "false." In principle, Yahweh can return to Zion, in accordance with Joel's reconstruction, as a violent and exclusive God, *or* Yahweh can return to Zion with Torah and an invitation of inclusion to all nations to join Yahweh there, as Isaiah envisions. Yahweh cannot do both, though Yahweh may do neither. In other words, Yahweh alone is the final arbiter between Joel and Isaiah with regard to their truth or falsehood.

But having defended neither, both may suffer. The politics of canon insist, Yahweh's exclusive prerogative notwithstanding, that it is ethically essential here and now, insofar as these texts construct mutually exclusive realities, to advocate one reading over the other or read neither. Here and now, we cannot choose both. We are obligated in any single point in time when reading Joel 4:9–17 or Isaiah 2:2–4 to deem one "false," the other "true." As Joel and Isaiah and their many readers along the way have reminded us, such advocacy, when chastened by our own fallibility, conserves the ethical force of canon.

It remains to gather up the defining assumptions, interests, and aims of this work in a final chapter. In so doing, can it be canonically sustained that in the closing years of the second millennium c.e., we *must* read Isaiah 2:2–4, 5 as true prophecy over against Joel 4:9–12 as false? That question provokes a needed rejoinder, to which we now turn.

SIX

A Final Reading: Which Prophet?
Whose Truth?

A STUDY of true and false prophecy must account for its own stance in relation to the field of inquiry that it attempts to describe. Does it claim freedom from presuppositions? Is it free from its own inherently contestable beliefs? For example, is its elevation of interpretative conflict to all but ontological status free from its own parochial reading stance? Can it provide universally valid criteria for its own claims to truth over against falsehood?

By maintaining a theory of conflicting readings as central to its quest for truth, canonical criticism, as the critical ground for discussions of true and false prophecy, must confess its own assumptions, interests, and aims. It does so acknowledging that its presuppositions may be at irreconcilable odds with assumptions embraced by others. Insofar as such assumptions are "testable responses to otherness,"[1] what I offer here invites criticism even as I attempt to persuade all challengers to surrender their assumptions to the force of my argument. Such public confession need no longer be seen as an embarrassment or a deficiency. Rather, in this historical hour, it is an essential condition for all would be "truth-tellers."

What follows, then, is a postscript of sorts outlining the basic assumptions with regard to the central theses of this study—in effect, a confession of belief in and a recapitulation of many of the conclusions offered in the foregoing chapters. This chapter will then conclude by arguing specifically for a particular reading of a particular plowshare passage against its challengers.

Postscript: Instead of a Conclusion

Canonical criticism denies the existence of a single logic or rationality that can claim universal authority for negotiating between conflicting readings. In part, this assumption emerges out of an inductive study of language (texts), history (contexts), and the human psyche (readers). What has been defined as the intertextual nature of reality supports an anarchic ambiguity to all claims to truth.

The implication of such an inductive reading of reality means that the meaning of a particular text is known only *in contra dictus* to other possible meanings. Stories that contain the same basic events, characters, and settings may be told in ways that produce radically different narrative meanings, including those stories often described in less narrative terms, such as scientific "truth," ethics, law, and history. What emerged from such observations was a shift in focus from what a text *means* to what it *does*. A text's content was relativized by its use, its function in certain settings.

Appeals to textual determinacy or, in its broader version, to the authority of *the* canon as having constraint on the pluralism of meaning were found wanting. The story of the fall and rise of canons, biblical and otherwise, showed again that the location of textual stability and meaning could not be found in the text or in a collection of sacred texts (*the* canon). Rather, texts and canons were products of particular interpretative communities, each with their own autonomous authority. Again, canonical criticism, emerging at the horizon between the modern and postmodern eras, refocused discussions of canon away from content to canonical function: *how* a community interpreted a tradition for its own particular setting.

The clash of canons and their canon-making communities was shown to be *functionally* equivalent to the clash of prophetic ideologies between true and false prophets. In effect, by necessarily placing the discussion of prophetic conflict in its larger canonical context, the question of who a true prophet was in contradistinction to a false one was shown to be a function of the interpretative community of a particular prophet in a particular setting. Furthermore, the criteria for judging between the two was also shown to be a function of the particular reading context of the reader establishing the criteria in the first place. Insofar as discussions of true and false prophecy thus pivoted on *how* prophecy was understood in particular contexts (ethos), a politics of canon was articulated.

The politics of truth associated with prophecy was seen as the claim and counterclaim between communities across time or space or both, each arguing for its own transcendent norming center. It was argued that this center not only boasts wings to transcend all limited projections of humankind but also must wear shoe leather that treads in the very real world in which all readers find themselves. A theologizing hermeneutic will always be subsumed in an integrity beyond our comprehension (mythos), but such a hermeneutic must always also be vulnerable to comings and goings in time and space (ethos).

To highlight the function of language, what a text does *over* its content suggests that what may be truly canonical about Scripture is not so much its profound reservoir of doctrine, propositions, or for that matter even its stories. Rather, canon as function models a working together, a living under the same rubric (canon) of people and cultures and theologies, some very different and often conflicting. The implication of such a paradigm suggests that it may be a more realistic and hopeful approach when living with disagreeing others to negotiate those differences at the level of ethics (the *how* of our living) than to try to find common ground at the level of our belief.

James Kugel and Jon Levenson on the question of Jewish/Christian dialogue, for example, insist that to find agreement at the level of our identities (our story-dependent selves) is almost impossible. Even the generic belief in one God has not necessarily been all that helpful in uniting us. Kugel and Levenson go on to suggest a provocative alternative to trying to find common-denominator themes in our differing stories, instead finding them at the level of common ethics. Even then, Kugel and Levenson despair that their alternative can only be considered as "procedural," based as it is on "trivial matters" common to Western cultural academic premises.[2] While agreeing with Kugel and Levenson as to the proper locale to begin discussions seeking common ground, I cannot disagree more with their assessment as to the importance of such a quest. In a world in which people of faith have been killing each other for centuries over the *content* (mythos) of their belief, to negotiate common rules for living together on this planet (ethos) seems like anything *but* a trivial matter. Rather, I would argue it is precisely to this alternative that the ethic of canonical function would lead us.

A recent hopeful sign of progress in the direction of living out the ethic of canon is the Parliament of the World's Religions.[3] Some 130 religious groups reached common ground on upward of thirty *ethical* principles, not least of which was a call to all people "to live by a rule that respects all life, individuality and diversity so that every person is treated humanely." This, by a group who could never agree among themselves on the existence of God, much less a supramoral category such as the "monotheizing process." Of course, the fact that they could not agree on such a theologem (content) does not make the confession in God ("monotheizing process") untrue; it merely relativizes this belief to questions of function, that is, to its ethical implications.

Such a stance does not discount the importance of story at all. By positing a rationality to the Torah story as story, canonical criticism provides a clue to balancing the need for coherence (against radical pluralism) with the need for rigorous debate (against radical particularism) and the need for freedom (against radical transcendence). Canon as a story of many stories forcefully relativizes them all. Additionally, in that the narrator of the biblical story is God, literarily for some, literally for others, canonical criticism suggested that this truth argued for a pluralism *limited* ultimately by the one God, implied or real. Here, a particular story provided space for many other stories but also absorbed them into its domain as canon.

God alone is the unifying reality. All else is contradiction. When chastened by a nonviolent praxis, this confession becomes the better belief system because it is arguably the better sociopolitical model for living. It could even be argued ethically that such a model is no longer an illusion or utopia. Indeed, it may be the only realism in life left to us, given the violent apocalyptic alternatives.[4] The biblical canon, then, becomes a realist paradigm of life. Canonical criticism advocated for this construal of reality based on the very real *political* gains from such a view. In other words, canonical criticism acknowledged that failing to realize that true understanding includes practical application is to misunderstand the power and politics of every claim to truth.

The political gains offered by a canonical reading of the text can be summarized as follows: in principle, all parties in a conversation are to be heard; there is an epistemological advantage to any claim that encourages its own contestation; conversations that happen within living communities provide limits of coherence and avenues for testing prophetic claims (i.e., order and due process); voluntary commitment to the community, even temporarily, provides the necessary context for discerning truth in relationship to an articulated politics of truth; communal memory of a canonically shaped community serves as a reservoir of meaning not available to individuals or communities not so self-consciously identified; and the prophet is an "agent of direction" who constructs visions of reality which *when advocated for* may become adapted and finally accepted (or rejected) by the community.

The community of interpretation bears the responsibility for creating and transmitting traditions it deems authoritative and so wields not a little power over texts and readers. The making of canons, biblical and otherwise, has been described as an act of power that can easily become coercive and oppressive. Any canon authorized as such by its community of interpreters has the potential to demand conformity and silence debate. Any canon that does not contain within it the seeds of its own deconstruction will become a tool of ideological and political brutality. This is especially the case when the canonmakers have access to social, political, military, material, and ecclesial power.

In the case of Israel, it was shown that the periods of "intense canonical formation" were always periods of intense social, political, military, and ecclesial *vulnerability*. The exile (and the post–second Temple period) provided the crucible out of which the biblical canon as we know it was given its relative shaping, including the excising of the conquest tradition (Joshua) from its first Torah and attaching it as introduction to a failed history of power politics (Joshua–2 Kings) ending in exile. For Israel to survive, it relied on the only indestructible element left to it: a story. This story, a book of words reconstituted as canon by a disarmed, dispossessed community in exile, became the paradigm judging all forms of coercive power, including those described by its own content. Of great canonical significance for any reader of the Bible is that the canon as it stands functions as "mere" literature. But as literature, it has its own power, which functions to deconstruct every word "between its covers." The biblical canon is a canon whose authority derives from its ethical *performance* as a "democracy of words." Its very form and function as canon dominate its own violent content. The implication of such an observation insists on nonviolence as a first principle (rule of order) in any canonical dispute. This is not simply a confession of faith but the literary achievement of canon as function. These assumptions must now be applied one last time to a reading of the plowshare passages submitted here to the judgment of other readers.

"Here I Stand": Under the Authority of the Community

Coming full circle, I argue here by personal example for the priority of the interpretative community over the text and its reader(s).[5] The fact that I confess an evangelical commitment to the Bible's authority over me in matters of faith and practice confirms the influence my community of interpretation holds in making such a confession. This communally inspired conviction in no way relieves me of the difficult task of adjudicating conflicts such as those between Joel and Isaiah. Indeed, the more sacred one claims these texts to be, that is, "the Word of God," the greater the problem one encounters in negotiating such vastly different and mutually exclusive canonical claims. The problem simply and gravely shifts from a literary one to a theological one, making the ethical choice even more serious.

Reading the plowshare passages and comparing their use across time does offer a range of possible interpretations for relating these oracles to our own situation by dynamic analogy. It was shown how the universal war elements in Joel's recapitulation of Isaiah's reading of the Zion tradition was somewhat relativized over time. However, reading both versions juxtaposed in their final canonical form still confronts the modern reader who seeks in these prophets some guidance for living with a reading dilemma of moral severity.

If these were simply two versions sharing a common tradition-*Gestalt* (which they in large measure do), or two versions sharing a similar theology (which they also do, relatively speaking), or a common hermeneutic stance (which they have at times), then reading them as has been illustrated in the last chapter would be sufficient. However, reading them with an eye to their ethical force, one cannot avoid what each text recommends to its readers. Joel offers a violent exclusive portrayal of Yahweh's elevation on Mount Zion, whereas Isaiah offers a more inclusive nonviolent portrayal of Yahweh's rule from Zion. Does Scripture wish for us to imagine, with the prophet Joel and all subsequent readers persuaded by his prophetic vision, that the "last days" are provoked by the bloody mother of all final battles? Or does Scripture want us to imagine with Isaiah that the nations will voluntarily "flow up" to the mountain of Yahweh, enroll in the *beit midrash,* sit under the tutelage of Rabbi Yahweh as Yahweh exegetes and lectures on the Torah, then submit their differences to Yahweh for mediation such that they melt down their F-16 fighters into tools of agriculture and close down their war colleges?

The two imaginative construals cannot be more radically different. They demand a choice. If actions follow images, as they most certainly do, what might the practical consequence in real-life terms be of choosing one over the other? Without even resorting to complicated theological discernment, on purely human ethical terms, trusting our own intuitive sensibility as to which construal is more in keeping with our imaginative portrayal of who God is (or who we hope God is), which version strikes us as the better reading option? Which version is more humane? Since, as has been previously argued, the truth of any reading must be discerned within the politics of truth of one's reading community, and since the canon itself requires commitment to a particular reading at a particular time for particular reasons, even while acknowledging the limits of doing so under God, such a commitment must now be made and defended. I reject Joel 4:9–17 as true prophecy and would argue that in time, if not yet, its voice will become, in functional terms, as canonically marginalized as other "texts of terror" are increasingly becoming (on women) or have already become (on slavery). Could it be that future generations will consider the question of sacred violence in the name of Yahweh as canonically closed, functionally if not formally?

I have tried to argue that the canon as function over content provides a sufficient model for discounting any reading (or text) that advocates violence as the means of preserving one's identity as a community or otherwise. It can reasonably be argued that, if the Zion theology as understood by Joel and his forerunners were given canonical force in every way, all voices contrary to his reading would have been silenced. Given Joel's unequivocally violent historico-political stance, insofar as others of like mind might have had the means and will to completely quiet all opposition, Isaiah's version would not have been available for Joel to use to score his opposing point of view. The reverse scenario would never be the case. That is, insofar as Isaiah's account allows for nations coming to Yahweh voluntarily, insofar as the Torah/Word of Yahweh is the only means of arbitrating between the nations, insofar as any ethical stance might allow for this form of persuasion (and opposition) to occur in lieu of violent suppression, Joel's voice would at least always be allowed a hearing, if not advocated. The canon does not silence Joel's voice. This appears to be a privilege that Joel would not have extended to Isaiah if his imaginative construal were actually carried out.

I have claimed that the canon contains within it the seeds of its own deconstruction. This has been described as the canon having its own "self-correcting apparatus." Said differently, and perhaps more politically, the biblical canon, a reservoir of authoritative traditions, is ultimately anarchistic in relation to questions of authority. Concomitant with such a view is the belief that a nonviolent political stance best incarnates the anarchistic paradigm of the biblical canon. It is time to correct the great misunderstanding for which Christianity bears much blame, namely, that the church has transformed the *free and liberating Word* into an intolerable form of power.[6] For evangelical reasons and out of obligation to its canon, if not for the sheer morality of it, the church must now decide against any negotiating stance, including that belonging to the prophet Joel, that defends its claims to truth coercively.

I have argued that the Bible's ultimate authority lies not in its content per se but in the canonical community that accepts and receives its message as authoritative. Such a community incorporates the author and the text and its many readers. It is the canonical community that provides the language, the images, the metaphors in order to create tradition-*Gestalten* that can construct, if but for a moment in time, a new picture of the world for the many "original" audiences that may encounter its vision. The success of that construal of reality will depend on whether that vision leads new readers into new ways of perceiving the world of their own experience. Actions follow images. Could it be that if we imagine that plowshares and pruning hooks are to be converted into nuclear warheads under Yahweh's aegis for some final cataclysmic war, such a scenario may surely come to pass? Such a living-out of that vision could well become our judgment day. If, however, we imagine that bombs and missiles and other instruments of war are to be beaten into agricultural appliances and knitting needles, could such a construal alternatively become our final blessing? It is my conviction that Isaiah's construal of reality regarding the peaceful dominion of Yahweh comes closer to a truly biblical hermeneutic than does Joel's exclusive and violent portrayal.

Of course, and finally, the choice of Isaiah's account of the plowshare episode over that of Joel's version rests on the hermeneutical question: "What does the text mean to *us*?"[7] More carefully put, What are the politics of truth of the believing community to which I owe my primary identity as a follower of God (in Christ)? I am part of the Christian tradition that finds its communal memory running deep into the radical reformation of the sixteenth century. In theological thought, the process of deconstruction has been going on under different names since that time and was radicalized under these early Anabaptists.[8]

Early followers of Menno Simons (1525) considered themselves neither Catholic nor Protestant, undergoing martyrdom at the hands of both.[9] This communal memory of martyrdom is important to the discussion of true and false prophecy, not least of which is the rhetorical force of the word *martyr* itself. It is a well-worn fact that the term *martyr* contains the semiotic union of two important concepts: "bearing witness" and, of course, "to give one's life in that effort." Such a metaphor raises to the supreme limit Stanley Fish's belief in rhetorical persuasion as the only means a community ultimately has for determining and validating meaning. Every community must argue its case before the dictums of history.

The art of persuasion as practiced by the Anabaptists grew out of a conviction that every person should be free to choose to believe or, more important, to disbelieve. In other words, having been accused and killed by the magisterial powers as *false* prophets (heretics), these martyred believers had nothing but the rhetorical power of their interpretative community to sustain them. They died for a truth—the right to choose to disbelieve in the face of the *Corpus Christianum* that demanded belief—that only later became so apparent a truth as to be regarded as an inalienable right of all people and enshrined in constitutions of many democracies. The accusation of being false prophets and the communal memory of martyrdom gave rise to a healthy suspicion among Anabaptists of all coercive measures to ensure belief, Joel's apocalyptic war notwithstanding. Insofar as Isaiah's construal portrays *voluntary* submission to Yahweh's rule, it is for my believing community a truer picture of God's sovereignty.

An Anabaptist Christian is perhaps more closely aligned with his or her Jewish counterparts, who view a person's moral and ethical stance toward the world as a more telling indicator of the spiritual state of that person than the language used by that person to communicate his or her spiritual state.[10] Dogma is relativized by ethics.[11] In other words, the criterion for judging among prophets is not the content of their confession so much as the conduct of their character. On this very point, Jesus provided a similar criterion for judging between true and false prophets of his day (Matt. 7:15–20). In point of fact, such a stance is the only way to make political judgments in a pragmatic, rationally accountable way. It may be helpful in arguing for the integrity of reality to posit a theocentric worldview wherein God is the "coincidence of opposites." This, as we have noted, provides a course correction for all unyielding construals of reality. However, in political terms, one cannot fail his or her responsibility to choose between the ethical force of one story over another, even if both can be ultimately relativized by claims of a monotheizing process. Again, the Bible as canon demands such a choice in any given historical hour insofar as canonical function truly matters. Having said this, arguably Isaiah's version of the plowshare passage *constructs* a more humane vision of the world from almost any believing community's account of morally suitable ethical behavior. It is not insignificant that the Parliament of the World's Religions *unanimously agreed* to call on all religions in whose name wars and atrocities have been committed to forsake violence as a means of settling differences.[12] One might argue that the canon of world religious opinion is fast coming to closure on the question of beating swords into plowshares, even as Christians continue to debate its practical validity.[13]

Again, the Anabaptist tradition, in which I am embedded, would argue for a Christocentric hermeneutic over against a more comprehensive and generic theocentrism. This is as much a sociopolitical stance as it is a theological confession. Insofar as God is a construal of the ultimate, it can be argued that a God "out there" (beyond history) is more easily manipulated than a God fully incarnate in Christ, construed in very human terms and subject to the judgment of ethics as we understand them.[14] Such a construal might be termed a "disciple's theology" oriented to a particular time and place rather than to some universal declaration about God.[15] A particularism that envisions God in Christ (as a slain lamb) on the throne in Zion (Rev. 14:1, 21:2), in good midrashic fashion, is no more particular than that of Yahweh construed as Judge, King, or Teacher on Mount Zion. I have argued that canon as process insists that all truth is so particular.

If central to the construction of meaning and purpose is the construction of an image of God by the canon's final shape, an image that stands "ahead of us, calling us to acts of justice and reconciliation,"[16] then we must accept the canon of Scripture as a whole piece. For Christians, this means reading both testaments together as Scripture. Of course, for others, reading both testaments together as a whole could offer similar political force as literature. For Christians, the image of God *begins* with God in Christ insofar as they call themselves by this incarnational title. From such a reading stance, the canon itself can be taken up into the image of God in Christ such that it still serves as a paradigm of the Integrity of reality. This reading might claim not so much that Christianity is a subset of history itself as that history has become one of the great things of a truly Christian worldview. Such a confession must fend for itself in the arena of conflicting claims of truthfulness. Further, it must do so in part because the politics of canon functionally require it.

For Anabaptists, the integrity of Christ as Lord offers a vision of reality *not* in accordance with traditional Protestant orthodoxy, which from the beginning interpreted the cross in a way that justifies religious imperialism and the use of violence to establish God's peaceful rule on earth as it is in heaven. By contrast, the Isaianic plowshare vision was understood at first to be an earthly social peace, not a transcendent one. Such an understanding was later accepted by a powerless, peaceful community in the New Testament (Luke 24 and Acts 1) and by pre-Constantinian patristic writers. Even among the post-Constantinian Christians, Isaiah's construal was initially viewed as an earthly social peace, though reread to imply the *imperium Pax Romanum* of the day as its fulfillment. Only later was the same plowshare text fatefully reread so that the peace advocated was assumed to be secured only by means of force! It would not take much to transition from such a viewpoint to accepting Joel's vision without reservation when the times so dictated.[17]

If it is accepted, however, that God in Christ is "our peace" (Eph. 2:14), literarily or literally, and if canon as paradigm functions to illustrate this truth, it can no longer mean challenging a few key interpretations here and there. Instead, it must mean that fundamental definitions of love and justice, the nature of the biblical witness and authority, claims of canonical guidance, the history of establishment exegesis, and the meaning of the incarnation itself are all subject to a thoroughgoing rereading.[18]

The canon thus becomes illustrative of the peace-making force of the Word made flesh. Here, incarnation as Torah (Oral and Written, for the Jew) and incarnation as the Word of God (Christ, for the Christian) come so close as almost to intersect. The biblical canon "as" Scripture is a book of words whose center is the one Word. This is not the place to develop such a notion fully, but, as I have suggested, central to the Isaianic imaginative construction is the power of Yahweh's Torah/Word to render judicial arbitration and educative instruction to all the nations of the earth. Indeed, the prophets, especially Isaiah (and Ezekiel and Jeremiah), direct their efforts to persuade skeptical hearers of Yahweh's efficacious Word. It was, after all, during this time that the latent problem of authority of the prophetic word was rearing its head in dramatic acuity. Jeremiah, in the context of a surprisingly abstract and theoretical consideration of the value placed on different modes of revelation, opts for the "Word of God" as the better option (Jer. 23:28–40). For Isaiah, all else was transient; only the word of Yahweh maintained its creative force in the end (Isa. 40:6–8, 45:10–25). For the first time in the prophetic movement, these prophets offer an axiomatic definition and explanation of the phenomenon of the word of Yahweh. Of course, as bearers of this word, they occupied an absolutely key position between Yahweh and Yahweh's governance of the world and sought to legitimate their prophetic authority by appeal to Yahweh's word.[19] It was a rhetorical move every bit as constructive as we ourselves are faced with in our own historical hour, with its real sociopolitical alternatives and real potentially false prophetic visions.

Should we be at all surprised that the literary canon, borne as it is by the community of believers across time and space, would incorporate in its "final chapters" stories of cosmic battles and warfare with all the force of having to choose between alternative readings? The great end-of-days battle scenes of the Book of Revelation (chaps. 12, 19) initially appear to be more akin to Joel's imaginative construal. However, a closer look reveals that the name of the commander-in-chief at the head of the army is "the Word of God" (19:13) whose only weapon, in good prophetic fashion, comes from his mouth. Not to be semiotically outdone, the writer imagines the Word as a double-edged sword (19:11, 15; cf. 1:16, 2:12, 16; Heb. 4:12). Any smiting of the nations appears to be a verbal slash from a "sword coming from his mouth" (19:15). In the earlier heavenly battle (chap. 12), Satan and his minions are conquered by "the blood of the Lamb" and the "word" of the "testimony" of the martyrs (12:11). The final canonical battle(s) appears to end, as the world began, with words, better, *the* Word.[20] Such a recapitulation is reminiscent of the ancient Near Eastern mythic battle scenes fought in the heavens as explanation for the origins of creation. There, as here, the biblical writer's reworked tradition gives prominence to the efficacy of the Word of God in creation of a new reality (Gen. 1; John 1:1).[21] Literarily, the Word of God as a powerful sociopolitical force forms a semiotic canonical *inclusio* of profound ethical imagination. The question remains: Do we, as readers of the sacred canon, accept this powerful imaginative construct as our own?

The story of God in Scripture as canon is ultimately the story of the one politically all-powerful Word undivided. I am not suggesting here the modernist's foundational logocentrism but rather a postmodern belief in a rhetorical nonfoundationalism that is constructed by faith with no guarantees of its truth claim that is not also subject to the need for persuading others to believe in the political efficacy of Yahweh's Word. There may be and are many conflicting words, a fact that is inevitable in the world of many cultured nations. As has been defended, there is no other way for human beings to communicate except *in contra dictus*. Any belief in a single tongue for humanity is to *the* one Word what belief in an idol is to the one God.[22] As creatures, we can never fuse the verbs and nouns of life into one common tongue. We are many; God alone is one. Our tongues will always be many; God's alone is undivided. The modern search for a common tongue (Esperanto?)[23] is ultimately a search for the *One Word,* undivided, who spoke the world into being and whose speech is able to woo nations to the top of Mount Zion, to arbitrate and educate wisely such that the nations will voluntarily beat their swords into plowshares and their spears into pruning hooks.

Micah's "revolutionary coda" to the plowshare tradition is telling. In his version, each nation will go in the name of its own God (4:5). Fishbane has correctly observed that here, in modern terms, Micah "saw the multiple visions of peace of all peoples as converging synergistically towards a truth which Israel knows through its God. No symbolic construction would exclude any other in this vision of 'concordant discord.'"[24] Such a vision hints again at the relativization of dogma to an ethic of inclusion of voices in the journey up the mountain. Of course, Micah, Isaiah, and Joel are all three finally committed to the construal of *Yahweh* as the ultimate ruler on Zion, the deconstructive coda (4:5) notwithstanding. From a postmodern reader's perspective, the universal visions of Isaiah, Micah, and Joel remain embedded in their particular story, as they must. Theirs is a communally situated truth claim seeking assent. For the Christian, the semiotic equivalent of the prophetic pilgrimage of nations is that of "a great multitude that no one could count, from every nation, from all tribes and peoples and languages, standing before the Lamb" (Rev. 7:9) who sits on the throne on Mount Zion. In terms of biblical theology, such a reading offers critical support to acceptance of Isaiah's own vision of the end as being the more truthful one.

Clearly, the goal of canon "as" Scripture has never been to remove crisis or conflict from reality, as evidenced by the canonical inclusion within it of Isaiah and Joel and their contradictory constructs. It does appear, however, that the canon of sacred Scripture demonstrates that the inevitable crises of a multipeopled life must be negotiated in and between canon-making communities in a nonlethal, noncoercive manner in which the only weapon is word against word; the only battle, persuasion. For me, standing under the authority of the believing community of which I am a part, I have become persuaded by the hermeneutic of prophetic critique to read Isaiah over against Joel as that construal of reality to which I myself am being wooed. I only hope that other readers will also be so persuaded.

Surely, the Torah/Word of God, as canon, requires that any such advocacy position can never be the last word. Joel's voice cannot be silenced. However, having the power over this text in this particular situation, I will grant Isaiah, through the pen of another reader, the last word for now:

I have beaten my sword
till the sweat of my back
Wet the ground at my feet,
and my veins boiled with
the throbbing pulse within.

Now my soldier's hands
are calloused and cracked
with the Earth lines,
and the sword that slayed
a mother's child
brings forth wheat
for its belly.[25]

Notes

Introduction

1. Grace Halsell, *Prophecy and Politics: Militant Evangelists on the Road to Nuclear War* (Westport, Conn.: Lawrence Hill, 1986).

2. Vaclav Havel, "From Arrogance to Humility: The Ambiguous Power of Words," *Media Development* 1 (1990): 44.

3. Hos. 6:5; Jer. 1:9f., 5:14, 23:28, 29; Ezek. 11:13, 22:24, 28; Isa. 11:4, 49:2; Ps. 56 [57]:5, 33:6; Prov. 5:4. In early Christianity: Heb. 4:12; Eph. 6:17; Rev. 1:16, 2:12, 19:11–21. In early Judaism: Pss. of Sol. 17f., 23–27, 39; Wisd. of Sol. 18:14; 4 Ezra 13:26, 32; 1 Enoch 62:2; 2 Baruch 39:7–40:4; Testament of Daniel 5:13; Sibylline Oracles 5:108–10. Cf. F. Moriarty, "Word as power in the Ancient Near East." in *A Light unto My Path: Old Testament Studies in Honor of Jacob M. Meyers,* ed. H. Bream, R. Heim, and C. Moore (Philadelphia: Temple University Press, 1974), 345–362.

4. James Sanders, *Torah and Canon* (Philadelphia: Fortress Press, 1972).

5. Jan Gorak, *The Making of the Modern Canon: Genesis and Crisis of a Literary Idea,* Athlone Series on Canons (London: Athlone, 1991), 40.

6. Jonathan Z. Smith, "The Influence of Symbols on Social Change," in *Map Is Not Territory: Studies in the History of Religions* (Leiden: Brill, 1978), 129–146.

Chapter 1

1. Daniel Boyarin, *Intertextuality and the Reading of Midrash* (Bloomington: Indiana University Press, 1990), 39. See also the classic discussion in Meir Sternberg, *The Poetics of Biblical Narrative: Ideological Literature and the Drama of Reading* (Bloomington: Indiana University Press, 1986), 186–229.

2. James A. Sanders, "The Integrity of Biblical Pluralism," in *"Not in Heaven": Coherence and Complexity in Biblical Narrative*, ed. Jason P. Rosenblatt and Joseph C. Sitterson, Jr. (Bloomington: Indiana University Press, 1991), 162–163. One only wishes Sanders had enclosed the words "orthodox" and "orthodoxy" in quotes, since their meanings must be carefully circumscribed if not by the "original" context, then by what Sanders himself means by those terms.

3. See Robert L. Thomas, ed., *The NIV Harmony of the Gospels, with Explanations and Essays Using the Text of the NIV* (San Francisco: Harper & Row, 1988), and Gleason Archer, *Encyclopedia of Bible Difficulties* (Grand Rapids: Zondervan, 1982).

4. See Robert Polzin's discussion of this in *Moses and the Deuteronomist: A Literary Study of the Deuteronomic History* (New York: Seabury Press, 1980), 17. Of course, Polzin relies on the formulations of literary master M. M. Bakhtin in Bakhtin's "Discourse in the Novel," in *The Dialogic Imagination: Four Essays,* trans. and ed. Michael Holquist (Austin: University of Texas Press, 1981), 259–423.

5. Gerald T. Sheppard, "True and False Prophecy within Scripture," in *Canon, Theology, and Old Testament Interpretation,* ed. Gene Tucker, David Petersen, and Robert Wilson (Philadelphia: Fortress Press, 1988), 262.

6. For example, see the prototypical case of Hananiah against Jeremiah in Jeremiah 28, in which Hananiah is called the "pseudoprophetes" by the Septuagint (see also Zech. 13:2 and Jer. 6:13, 26:7, 8, 11, 16, 27:9, 29:1, 8).

7. Jer. 8:10, 14:14, 23:11, 14, 16, 25f., 26:7ff.; Ezek. 13:1f., 22:28, 13:3; Mic. 3:5; 1 Kings 22:24; Zeph. 3:4; and so on.

8. See Edgar Krentz, *The Historical-Critical Method,* Old Testament Series: Guides to Biblical Scholarship (Philadelphia: Fortress Press, 1978), 9–10.

9. Brevard Childs, *Biblical Theology in Crisis* (Philadelphia: Westminster Press, 1970), offers one perspective of the current debate to which his canon studies are considered the antidote. In his 1977 review of the state of biblical criticism, James Sanders suggested that biblical criticism was in crisis, having "locked the Bible in the past" (Hans Frei). Furthermore, no synthesis had yet been reached that could shield biblical criticism from Walter Wink's censure that it was "bankrupt." Sanders acknowledged that his purpose in writing this review article was to offer a "way out" of this impasse. See James Sanders, "Biblical Criticism and the Bible as Canon," *USQR* 32 (1977): 157–165, reprinted in *From Sacred Story to Sacred Text* (Philadelphia: Fortress Press, 1987), 78–79.

10. The first call for the engagement of biblical scholarship in canonical criticism can be found in Sanders's introduction to his *Torah and Canon* (Philadelphia: Fortress Press, 1972), translated into French as *Identité de la Bible* (Paris: Cerf, 1975) and into Japanese in 1984. The term *canonical criticism* hereafter will refer to the distinct discipline as articulated by James Sanders. Brevard Childs consciously does not use the term for his version of "reading the Bible in canonical context." See James Sanders, "Canon as Shape and Function," in *The Promise and Practice of Biblical Theology,* ed. John Reumann (Minneapolis: Fortress Press, 1991), 88, and Brevard Childs, *Introduction to the Old Testament as Scripture* (Philadelphia: Fortress Press, 1979).

11. A distinction can be made here between the canonical-critical approach of James Sanders and that of Brevard Childs. Sanders emphasizes (but not to exclusion)

the canonical process whereas Childs emphasizes the final form of a particular canonical text (for him, the Masoretic form). Further distinctions in approach and terminology are outlined in the dialogue between Sanders and Childs, among others, in *HBT* 2 (1980): 113–211. See also James Sanders, *Canon and Community: A Guide to Canonical Criticism,* Old Testament Series: Guides to Biblical Scholarship (Philadelphia: Fortress Press, 1984), 2; Stephen Delamarter, "Concepts in Canonical Criticism" (master's thesis, Claremont Graduate School, 1984); and the recent helpful comparisons in Donn F. Morgan, *Between Text and Community* (Minneapolis: Fortress Press, 1990), esp. 11–29.

12. For Sanders, canon as *function* precedes canon as *shape*. See "Canon (Hebrew Bible), *ABD,* 1:847.

13. The method James Sanders uses for discerning these distinctives is the triangle of interpretation. See his "Hermeneutics in True and False Prophecy," in *Canon and Authority: Essays in Old Testament Religion and Theology,* ed. George W. Coats and Burke O. Long (Philadelphia: Fortress Press, 1977), 21–41, reprinted in *God Has a Story Too* (Philadelphia: Fortress Press, 1979), 5–17; the appendix of *Canon and Community* (Philadelphia: Fortress Press, 1984), 77–78; and as "Canonical Hermeneutics: True and False Prophecy," in *From Sacred Story to Sacred Text* (Philadelphia: Fortress Press, 1987), 87–105. The current study will extend the use of the triangle of interpretation to *explicitly* include not only the implied reader (at every historical juncture) but also the actual reader (at hand, reconstructing every historical reading), thus transforming Sanders's two-dimensional triangle into a pyramid of three dimensions.

14. The self-conscious, metacritical concern with the nature of signifying and validating systems in the sciences and humanities is reaching a crescendo—what Thomas S. Kuhn described as a "paradigm shift" in *The Structure of Scientific Revolutions,* 2d ed. (Chicago: University of Chicago Press, 1970); compare Karl Jasper's "axial age" conceptualization in *Vom Ursprung und Zeil der Geschichte* (Munich: Piper Verlag, 1949), 15–106. Influencing this shift are such works as Roland Barthes, *Elements of Semiology* (1967); Jacques Derrida, *Of Grammatology* (1974); Michel Foucault, *The Archaeology of Knowledge* (1972); Louis Althusser, "Ideology and Ideological State Apparatuses," in *Lenin and Philosophy* (1971); Jacques Lacan, *The Four Fundamental Concepts of Psychoanalysis* (1979); Hayden White, *Metahistory: The Historical Imagination in Nineteenth-Century Europe* (1975); Fritjof Capra, *The Turning Point* (1982); and Clifford Geertz, *The Interpretation of Cultures* (1973). One could list more. As will be elaborated below, biblical, theological, and literary studies have not been unaffected by this "revolution." The program outlined in James Sanders's canonical criticism represents one such adaptation.

15. In a 1992 lecture, New Testament scholar Tom Boomershine made note of the "five media revolutions" that have impacted the history of Bible and religious mission, the fifth and most recent being from book culture to screen culture. (Unpublished lecture given to Mennonite Board of Missions, Elkhart, Indiana, October 1992.)

16. For a good overview of the crisis from the literary point of view, see Terry Eagleton, *Literary Theory: An Introduction* (Minneapolis: University of Minnesota Press, 1983), and Frank Lentricchia, *After the New Criticism* (Chicago: University of

Chicago Press, 1980). For a review of current social splinterings and their effect, see, for example, Mary Douglas and Aaron Wildavsky, *Risk and Culture* (Berkeley: University of California Press, 1982); J. Habermas, *Knowledge and Human Interest* (Boston: Beacon Press, 1968); and Michael Harrington, *The Politics at God's Funeral: The Spiritual Crisis of Western Civilization* (New York: Holt, Rinehart and Winston, 1983).

17. See Childs, *Biblical Theology in Crisis*, and Sanders, *From Sacred Story*, 78–79.

18. On the interface between text criticism and canonical criticism, see, among others, James Sanders, "Stability and Fluidity in Text and Canon," in *Tradition of the Text: Studies Offered to D. Barthelemy*, ed. G. J. Norton and S. Pisano (Göttingen: Vandenhoeck & Ruprecht, 1991), 207. On the impact of the Dead Sea scrolls on the launching of canonical criticism, see especially James Sanders, "Cave 11 Surprises and the Question of Canon," in *New Directions in Biblical Archaeology*, ed. David Noel Freedman and Jonas C. Greenfield (Garden City, N.Y.: Doubleday, 1969), 101–116, also in *The Canon and Masorah of the Hebrew Bible: An Introductory Reader*, ed. Sid Z. Leiman (New York: KTAV Publishing House, 1974), 37–51, and, more recently, his "The Dead Sea Scrolls and Biblical Studies," in *"Sha'arei Talmon": Studies in the Bible, Qumran, and the Ancient Near East Presented to Shemaryahu Talmon*, ed. Michael Fishbane and Emanuel Tov (Winona Lake, Ind.: Eisenbrauns, 1992), 334.

19. Sanders, "Canon (Hebrew Bible)," 1:837–852.

20. Ibid.

21. See Julia Kristeva, *Semeiotike: Recherches pour une Semanalyse* (Paris: Editions du Seuil, 1969).

22. See Richard Rorty, ed., *The Linguistic Turn* (Chicago: University of Chicago Press, 1967); David Tracey, *Plurality and Ambiguity: Hermeneutics, Religion, and Hope* (San Francisco: Harper & Row, 1987), esp. chaps. 2, 3; and Noam Chomsky's acknowledgment of the symbiotic overlap of methodologies in *Language and Mind* (New York: Harcourt Brace Jovanovich, 1972), 161.

23. James Sanders describes three "basic relationships" to which this term applies. See his "Hermeneutics" in *The Concise Encyclopedia of Preaching*, ed. William H. Willimon and Richard Lischer (Louisville: Westminster/John Knox Press), 178. He does not mention the intertextual dynamic at the levels of grammar or reality at large; no doubt both are presupposed by him.

24. René Girard first articulated his thought in *Deceit, Desire, and the Novel: Self and Other in Literary Structure*, 2d ed., trans. Yvonne Freccero (Baltimore: Johns Hopkins University Press, 1976); he expanded it anthropologically in *Violence and the Sacred* (Baltimore: Johns Hopkins University Press, 1977). See also his *Things Hidden since the Foundation of the World* (Stanford: Stanford University Press, 1987); *To Double Business Bound* (Baltimore: Johns Hopkins University Press, 1988); *The Scapegoat* (Baltimore: Johns Hopkins University Press, 1986); and *A Theater of Envy* (New York: Oxford University Press, 1991).

In her recent book, *The Fall to Violence: Original Sin in Relational Theology* (New York: Continuum, 1995), Marjorie Suchocki connects the "human bent toward aggression that easily tends toward violence" with primal relationships gone amok and offers a relational model for breaking the chain of violence.

25. John H. Yoder, *The Priestly Kingdom: Social Ethics as Gospel* (Notre Dame: University of Notre Dame Press, 1984), 7.

26. Kristeva, *Semeiotike*.

27. In the opening paragraphs of his article "Differance," in *Speech and Phenomena,* trans. David Allison (Evanston, Ill.: Northwestern University Press, 1973), Jacques Derrida playfully illustrates this point by using the letter "a" in the word *différance*. See also, Derrida, *Margins of Philosophy,* trans. Alan Bass (Chicago: University of Chicago Press, 1982), 1–27.

28. For what follows on de Saussure, see his *Course in General Linguistics,* trans. Wade Bashin, ed. Charles Bally and Albert Sechehaye (New York: McGraw-Hill, 1966), and David Tracey, *Plurality and Ambiguity,* 47–65.

29. Saussure, *Course,* 120. Here I follow Tracey in translating Saussure's *langue* as "linguistic system" to distinguish it from *parole,* which could be translated "language" but which for Saussure describes the more limited notion of historically conditioned "speech" (as in "speech-event").

30. Tracey, *Plurality and Ambiguity,* 47–65.

31. Ibid., 67–70.

32. Indeed, a major criticism Sanders makes of Childs hinges precisely on this point: that one must take seriously the plurality of biblical canons. Also, as I will discuss further, even if we could agree on the particular biblical canon to use for a particular understanding, the question of *how we read* that canon ("compressed text") as giving shape to the parts within it remains. Here are hints of why I find myself moving ever more comfortably to the more radical reader-response criticism of literary critics such as Stanley Fish as his work interfaces with canonical criticism.

33. Derrida, *On Grammatology,* 35–71; Tracey, *Plurality and Ambiguity,* 56.

34. Tracey, *Plurality and Ambiguity,* 56.

35. Derrida does just that in "Structure, Sign, and Play in the Discourse of the Human Sciences," in *The Structuralist Controversy: The Languages of Criticism and the Sciences of Man,* ed. Richard Macksey and Eugenio Donato (Baltimore: Johns Hopkins University Press, 1972), 247–248.

36. Northrop Frye, *The Anatomy of Criticism: Four Essays* (New York: Atheneum, 1967), 117–118.

37. See Derrida, "Abysses of Truth," in *Spurs: Nietzsche's Styles,* trans. Barbara Harlow (Chicago: University of Chicago Press, 1978), 119–123. Frank Lentricchia suggests that Derrida's center is "the abyss," though with this proviso: "Derrida believes in a center as function not as a being or as a reality." See Frank Lentricchia, *After the New Criticism* (Chicago: University of Chicago Press, 1980), 174.

38. Boyarin, *Intertextuality,* 94.

39. Michael Fishbane, *Biblical Interpretation in Ancient Israel* (Oxford: Clarendon Press, 1985).

40. Michael Fishbane, "Inner Biblical Exegesis: Types and Strategies of Interpretation in Ancient Israel," in *Midrash and Literature,* ed. Geoffrey Hartman and Sanford Budick (New Haven: Yale University Press, 1986), 36. See also Fishbane, *Biblical Interpretation,* 10–13.

41. See Douglas Knight, *Rediscovering the Traditions of Israel: The Development of the*

Traditio-historical Research of the Old Testament, with Special Consideration of Scandinavian Contributions (Missoula, Mont.: Society of Biblical Literature Press, 1973), and Walter E. Rast, *Tradition History and the Old Testament* (Philadelphia: Fortress Press, 1972).

42. Renée Bloch inaugurated the comparative midrash method in a series of short articles in which she argued for the similarities between Rabbinic midrash and its biblical and early Jewish precursors. See "Midrash," *IDBSup* 5, cols. 1263–1280; "Midrash," trans. Mary Howard, in *Approaches to Ancient Judaism: Theory and Practice*, ed. William S. Green, Brown Judaic Studies no. 1 (Missoula, Mont.: Scholars Press, 1978), 29–50.

43. See Bloch, "Midrash." For the best current work outlining the history of scholarship on comparative midrash as a discipline and its precursors, see the introduction to David M. Carr, "Royal Ideology and the Technology of Faith: A Comparative Midrash Study of I Kings 3: 2–15" (Ph.D. diss., Claremont Graduate School, 1988), 1–37.

44. Geza Vermes, "The Bible and Midrash: Early Old Testament Exegesis," in *The Cambridge History of the Bible: From the Beginnings to Jerome*, ed. P. R. Ackroyd and C. F. Evans (Cambridge: Cambridge University Press, 1970), 199.

45. Boyarin, *Intertextuality*, x, 16.

46. Ibid., 15. For a very similar view, see Gerald Bruns, "Midrash and Allegory," in *The Literary Guide to the Bible,* ed. Frank Kermode and Robert Alter (Cambridge, Mass.: Belnap Press of Harvard University Press, 1987), 626–627, and "The Hermeneutics of Midrash," in *The Book and the Text: The Bible and Literary Theory,* ed. Regina Schwartz (Cambridge, Mass.: Basil Blackwell, 1990), 189–213.

47. Boyarin, *Intertextuality,* 16.

48. Carr, "Royal Ideology," 4. See James Sanders, "Adaptable for Life: The Nature and Function of Canon," in *Magnalia Dei, the Mighty Acts of God: Essays on the Bible and Archaeology in Memory of G. Ernest Wright,* ed. Frank Moore Cross, Werner E. Lemke and Patrick D. Miller (Garden City, N.Y.: Doubleday, 1976), 541, 556, n. 47, and reprinted in *From Sacred Story to Sacred Text,* 9–39.

49. Sanders, "Hermeneutics," 5.

50. See Hans Robert Jauss's programmatic lecture, "Literary History as a Challenge to Literary Theory," in the journal it spawned *NLH* 2 (1970): 7–37; it was later included in his book *Toward an Aesthetic of Reception,* Theory and History of Literature, no. 2, trans. Timothy Bahti (Minneapolis: University of Minnesota Press, 1982), 3–45. Jauss is viewed as the sometime "founding member" of the *Rezeptionsästhetik* school, otherwise known as "reader-response criticism" or, more controversially, "affective stylistics."

51. Roland Barthes, *Image, Music, Text* (New York: Hill and Wang, 1977), 146–147.

52. Sanders, "Hermeneutics," 1.

53. This brief overview depends on Severino Coratto, *Biblical Hermeneutics: Toward a Theory of Reading as the Production of Meaning* Eng. ed.; (Marynoll, N.Y.: Orbis Books, 1987), 3.

54. Sanders, "Hermeneutics," 4.

55. A foundational *logoumenon* in canonical criticism as articulated by James Sanders. in "Adaptable for Life," 541, 556.

56. M. H. Abrams in "The Deconstructive Angel," *CI* 3:3 (Spring 1977): 431, and E. D. Hirsch, in *Validity in Interpretation* (New Haven: Yale University Press, 1967), esp. 217–219, are two of the most ardent critics of the notion of "indeterminacy" of meaning in texts here described.

57. What Mark Powell says of narrative criticism applies equally well here. See Powell, *The Bible and Modern Literary Criticism: A Critical Assessment and Annotated Bibliography* (New York: Greenwood Press, 1992), 9.

58. Tracey, *Plurality and Ambiguity,* 61. Compare Paul Ricoeur, *Interpretation Theory: Discourse and the Surplus of Meaning* (Fort Worth: Texas Christian University Press, 1976).

Chapter 2

1. James Barr, *The Scope and Authority of the Bible* (Philadelphia: Westminster Press, 1981), 11; see also his "Reading the Bible as Literature," *BJRL* 56 (1973): 10–33.

Although James Sanders recognizes the shift in ontology of canon that gave rise to new kinds of hermeneutics in first-century Judaism suggesting that few tradents read Scripture primarily as story, reading it instead as oracle, he still argues that biblical authority finally rests on the Torah *story* over against other elements of the OT. See Sanders, "Text and Canon: Concepts and Method," *JBL* 98 (1979): 5–29 (esp. 23–26). On his defense of story, see his review of Michael Fishbane, *Garments of Torah: Essays in Biblical Hermeneutics,* in *TToday* 47: (January 1991): 433–445. Again, in *From Sacred Story to Sacred Text* (Philadelphia: Fortress Press, 1987), Sanders embraces the whole Torah-Christ *story* authoritatively (41–60).

2. For excellent introductions to literary theory, see Terry Eagleton, *Literary Theory: An Introduction* (Minneapolis: University of Minnesota Press, 1983), and Frank Lentricchia, *After the New Criticism* (Chicago: University of Chicago Press, 1980).

3. Elie Wiesel, *Messengers of God* (New York: Random House, 1976).

4. James Muilenburg, "Form Criticism and Beyond," *JBL* 88 (1969): 1–18. Even then, heeding Muilenburg's call to move "beyond" the earlier, largely historical interests took some getting used to, as a brief review of the Guides to Biblical Scholarship Series shows. Norman Habel's *Literary Criticism of the Old Testament* (Philadelphia: Fortress Press, 1971) might more accurately have been described as an exercise in "source criticism." Six years later, David Robertson's *The Old Testament and the Literary Critic* (Philadelphia: Fortress Press, 1977) had begun to broaden the assumptions, methods, implications of a literary critical study of the OT, so that by 1990 Mark A. Powell's *What Is Narrative Criticism?* (Philadelphia: Fortress Press, 1990) included a comprehensive survey of options for the literary critic.

After the first few halting steps, the astonishing rate at which Muilenburg's call was being heard became clear—so much so that one might wonder whether this was a critical watershed in biblical studies. It was, and is, no small shift. As if to declare this new approach permanent, in 1992 Powell gathered some 1,472 works intersecting the fields of biblical studies and modern literary criticism in his *The Bible and Modern Literary Criticism: A Critical Assessment and Annotated Bibliography* (New York: Greenwood Press, 1992).

5. Barr, "Reading the Bible as Literature," 11.

6. H. W. Frei, in *The Eclipse of the Biblical Narrative* (New Haven: Yale University Press, 1974), has shown how the narrative portions of Scripture were usually eclipsed by the historical-critical reading strategies of English and German scholars who seemed more concerned with quests for historical *truths* behind the text and/or in *ideas* communicated by the texts than in the narrative itself.

7. For general introductions to reader-response criticism, see Robert C. Holub, *Reception Theory: A Critical Introduction* (London: Methuen, 1984); Jane P. Tompkins, ed., *Reader Response Criticism: From Formalism to Post Structuralism* (Baltimore: Johns Hopkins University Press, 1980); and Susan Suleiman and Inge Crosman, eds., *The Reader in the Text: Essays on Audience and Interpretation* (Princeton: Princeton University Press, 1980). To survey the changing face of biblical criticism under the influence of literary critical method, see John Barton, *Reading the Old Testament: Method in Biblical Study* (London: Darton, Longman and Todd, 1984), and Edgar V. McKnight, *The Bible and the Reader: An Introduction to Literary Criticism* (Philadelphia: Fortress Press, 1985); for a work with a slightly different focus, see Edgar V. McKnight, *Post Modern Use of the Bible: The Emergence of Reader-Oriented Criticism* (Nashville: Abingdon Press, 1988). And, finally, David Clines, *What Does Eve Do to Help? and Other Readerly Questions, JSOTSup* 94 (Sheffield: JSOT Press, 1990), 9–12, offers an excellent if brief review of the shift from author to text to reader that has transpired in biblical studies. Clines divides the approaches by decades (1960s, 1970s, and 1980s), showing the not atypical drag time between biblical disciplines and their literary counterparts.

8. Bernard C. Lategan, "Hermeneutics," *ABD*, 3:151.

9. James A. Sanders, *Canon and Community: A Guide to Canonical Criticism,* Old Testament Series: Guides to Biblical Scholarship (Philadelphia: Fortress Press, 1984), 19. In defense of naming this new approach "canonical criticism" instead of "canon criticism," Sanders accents the ongoing process in contrast to static notions of canon. See his "Canonical Context and Canonical Criticism," *HBT* 2 (1980): 187.

10. McKnight, *Post Modern Use of the Bible,* 78.

11. The canon studies of Brevard Childs have been censured for this tendency; see James Barr, *Holy Scripture: Canon, Authority, Criticism* (Philadelphia: Westminster Press, 1983), 77, 158, 159; also see John Barton, "Classifying Biblical Criticism," *JSOT* 29 (1984): 25, 27–28, as well as Sanders's review of Childs in *HBT* 2 (1980): 187—but not without reading Childs's denial in *HBT* 2 (1980): 204. On the other hand, as McKnight's question implies, Sanders has been accused of trying to have it both ways—that is, of trying to maintain a historical mooring *and* formalist interest in the final text itself. See also Childs's review of *Torah and Canon* (Philadelphia: Fortress Press, 1972), in *Int* 27:1 (January 1973): 88–91.

12. Hans Robert Jauss, "Literary History as a Challenge to Literary Theory," first appeared in English in *NLH* 2 (1970): 7–37 (it was reprinted as the opening essay in

his collected essays; see below) as a programmatic invitation to return to literature its historical dimension. Jauss became known as the founding member of the "Konstanz School," whose methodology was termed *Rezeptionsästhetik* and emphasized the reader/audience role in meaning production. For an excellent introduction to Jauss's thought, see Holub, *Reception Theory,* and Paul de Man's introduction to the English edition of Jauss's collection of originally German essays, *Toward an Aesthetic of Reception,* Theory and History of Literature no. 2, trans. Timothy Bahti (Minneapolis: University of Minnesota Press, 1982). Further references to Jauss's theory as described in this work will be noted parenthetically within the text.

13. Jauss, like Fish (an American member of the Konstanz school), would not agree with Krister Stendahl's "descriptive" task of differentiating so cleanly between what the text "meant" and what it "means"; see n. 41.

14. See Krister Stendahl, "Biblical Theology," in *IDB,* 1:418–432 (esp. 430–431).

15. E. D. Hirsch, *Validity in Interpretation* (New Haven: Yale University Press, 1967).

16. Holub, *Reception Theory,* 63–65.

17. Michel Foucault, in *The Archaeology of Knowledge* (New York: Pantheon Books, 1972), generates his own historiography on just this notion of "what can be known" (or not known) when speaking of history.

18. James A. Sanders, "Canon (Hebrew Bible)," *ABD,* 1:847.

19. James A. Sanders, "Canon as Shape and Function," in *The Promise of Biblical Theology,* ed. John Reumann (Minneapolis: Fortress Press, 1991), 92, and Sanders, "Deuteronomy," in *The Books of the Bible,* vol. 1, ed. B. W. Anderson (New York: Scribner's, 1989), 89–102.

20. Jauss, "Literary History," 23.

21. Sanders, "Canon as Shape and Function," 92.

22. Jauss, "Literary History," 23.

23. What Holub says of Jauss also applies to much of Sanders as well. For a more extensive review, see Holub, *Reception Theory,* 60–82.

24. Sanders, *Canon and Community,* 19.

25. In his article titled "Paradigmawechsel in der Literaturwissenschaft," *Linguistische Berichte* 3 (1969): 44–56, Jauss borrows from Kuhn's notion of "paradigms" and "scientific revolutions" and reviews literary scholarship as having undergone three paradigm shifts—classical-humanist, historicist-positivist, and aesthetic-formalist—and is currently undergoing a fourth. He modestly refrains from naming *Rezeptionästhetik* as the leading contender, but given his criteria for recognizing the new paradigm, that is, a mediation between the previous two paradigms in a new "historical aestheticism," it is clear that the reader should draw this conclusion.

One should also bear in mind the broad classification of critical theories proposed by M. H. Abrams in *The Mirror and the Lamp: Romantic Theory and Critical Tradition* (New York: Oxford University Press, 1953), esp. 3–29: mimetic, expressive, objective, and pragmatic. Mimetic theories assume that texts mirror reality; expressive theories associate meaning with authorial intent; objective theories elevate the text as essential producer of meaning; and pragmatic theories believe the reader to be the primary source for meaning production. For use of these classifications in biblical studies, see Barton, *Reading the Old Testament,* 198–207, and "Classifying Biblical Criticism," *JSOT* 29 (1984): 19–35.

Whether one sees reception theory as a change in paradigm or, more modestly, as a shift in emphasis, it is appropriate to ask whether Jauss has fully made the qualitative jump from the "old" to the "new" paradigm. By the same token, although Barton describes Sanders's approach as "essentially expressive," to the degree that he over-looks Sanders's explicit references to the synchronic plane of the final form and Gadamer-like appeals to the collapse of horizons, he fails to appreciate the objectivist and pragmatic parallels. Indeed, Sanders himself fails to appreciate fully the "pragmatic" dimension in his own work. One might suggest that Sanders, like Jauss, sits on the horizon between two paradigms, unable to make the leap across. We will return to this matter in the following chapter.

26. Wolfgang Iser's two major works—*The Implied Reader: Patterns of Communication in Prose Fiction from Bunyan to Beckett,* 2d ed. (Baltimore: Johns Hopkins University Press, 1975), German original, *Der implizite Leser* (Munich, 1974?); and *The Act of Reading: A Theory of Aesthetic Response* (Baltimore: Johns Hopkins University Press, 1978), German original, *Der Akt des Lesens: Theorie ästhetischer Wirkung* (Munich: Wilhelm Fink, 1976)—in their American debuts outsold all other books on the prestigious list of Johns Hopkins University Press, with the exception of Derrida's *Of Grammatology.*

27. In this section, page references to Iser's *Act of Reading* will be included parenthetically in the text.

28. Brevard Childs, *Introduction to the Old Testament as Scripture* (Philadelphia: Fortress Press, 1979), 9.

29. Sanders, *Torah and Canon,* 50–53.

30. See James Barr's critique of Sanders on just this issue in his *Holy Scripture,* 156–157.

31. What follows anticipates the arguments of Stanley Fish, to be outlined in the next section. I have extended his observations of Iser to include Sanders insofar as points of intersection between the two warrant comment. See especially the spirited dialogue between Fish and Iser that begins with Fish's provoking review, "Why No One's Afraid of Wolfgang Iser," *Diacritics* 11:1 (1981): 2–13, and is followed by Iser's reply, "Talk Like Whales," *Diacritics* 11:3 (1981): 82–87.

32. See Sanders, "Stability and Fluidity in Text and Canon," in *Tradition and Text: Studies Offered to D. Barthelema,* ed. G. J. Norton and S. Pisano (Göttingen: Vandenhoeck & Ruprecht, 1991), 203–217; *Canon and Community,* 22–24; "Adaptable for Life: The Nature and Function of Canon," in *Magnalia Dei, the Mighty Acts of God: Essays on the Bible and Archaeology in Memory of G. Ernest Wright,* ed. Frank Moore Cross, Werner E. Lemke, and Patrick D. Miller (Garden City, N.Y.: Doubleday, 1976), reprinted in *From Sacred Story to Sacred Text,* 9–39; "Canon (Hebrew Bible)," *ABD,* 1:843, 847–884; to name just a few examples of many.

33. For what follows, see Sanders, "Communities and Canon," in *The Oxford Study Bible: REB with the Apocrypha,* ed. M. Jack Suggs, Katharine D. Sakenfeld, and James E. Mueller (New York: Oxford University Press, 1992), 91–10.

34. Ibid., 99.

35. See David Clines, *What Does Eve Do to Help?*, 9–12.

36. Fish, "Why No One's Afraid," 6.

37. Sanders, "Communities and Canon," 96.

38. Stanley Fish *Is There a Text in This Class?: The Authority of Interpretative Communities* (Cambridge, Mass.: Harvard University Press, 1980). All references to this work in this section will be identified in the text in parentheses.

39. He confronted head-on the influential arguments of William Wimsatt and Monroe Beardsley, who had made a successful case for the New Critical notion of a text's autonomy by arguing that the intentions of the author were unavailable and the response of readers too variable. See their essays "The Intentional Fallacy" and "The Affective Fallacy" collected in William Wimsatt, *The Verbal Icon: Studies in the Meaning of Poetry* (Lexington: University of Kentucky Press, 1954), 3–20, 21–40.

40. James L. Kugel, "On the Bible and Literary Criticism," *Prooftexts: A Journal of Jewish History* 1 (September 1981): 230.

41. Harold Bloom, *The Western Canon: The Books and School of the Ages* (New York: Harcourt Brace, 1994), 23.

42. Ibid., 23, 24.

43. Edward Said, *Orientalism* (New York: Pantheon Books, 1978).

44. Earlier, Fish had tried to distinguish between description and interpretation, as had the New Testament scholar Krister Stendahl.

45. David Bleich, "The Subjective Paradigm in Science, Psychology and Criticism," *NLH* 7 (1976): 313–334.

46. Bleich, "The Subjective Paradigm," 327 (citing Jean Piaget, *Biology and Knowledge*, trans. Beatrix Walsh [Chicago: University of Chicago Press, 1971], 368).

47. See Edgar W. Conrad, "Changing Context: The Bible and the Study of Religion," in *Perspectives on Language and Text: Essays in Honor of Francis I. Andersen's Sixtieth Birthday, July 28, 1985,* ed. E. W. Conrad and E. G. Newing (Winona Lake, Ind.: Eisenbrauns, 1987), 393–402.

48. Stephen Moore, *Literary Criticism and the Gospels: The Theoretical Challenge* (New Haven: Yale University Press, 1989), 176.

49. See also Michel Foucault, *Language, Counter-memory, Practice: Selected Essays and Interviews* (Ithaca, N.Y.: Cornell University Press, 1977).

50. Foucault, *Archaeology of Knowledge,* 138.

51. Ibid., 140.

52. Ibid., 144.

53. See Frank Lentricchia's analysis of Foucault's "history" as the poststructuralist answer to Derrida's "abyss" and traditional historical approaches in "History or the Abyss: Poststructualism," *After the New Criticism* (Chicago: University of Chicago Press), 156–210 (esp. 188–210).

54. Sanders, *Canon and Community,* 32. On the question of history, truth, and truth in fiction, see James Mays, "Historical and Canonical: Recent Discussions about the Old Testament and Christian Faith," in Cross et al., *Magnalia Dei,* 510–528; Robert Alter, *The World of Biblical Literature* (New York: Basic Books, 1992), esp. "Scripture and Culture," 191–210; Hans Frei, *The Eclipse of the Biblical Narrative* (New Haven: Yale University Press, 1974); Leo G. Perdue, *The Collapse of History:*

Reconstructing Old Testament Theology, OBT (Minneapolis: Fortress Press, 1994); Meir Sternberg, "Fiction and History," in *The Poetics of Biblical Narrative: Ideological Literature and the Drama of Reading*, 23–34; see also, and by comparison, V. Philips Long, *The Art of Biblical History* (Grand Rapids: Zondervan, 1994).

55. Sanders, *Torah and Canon*, 25–26, 48.

56. Sanders, *Canon and Community*, 19.

57. Schuyler Brown, "Reader Response: Demythologizing the Text," *NTS* 34 (1988): 232–237. See also Robert Detweiler, "Speaking of Believing in Gen. 2–3," *Semeia 41: Speech Act Theory and Biblical Criticism*, ed. Hugh C. White (Decatur, Ga.: Scholars Press, 1988), 135–142.

58. Brown, "Reader Response," 232. Compare Richard Hayes, *Echoes of Scripture in the Letters of Paul* (New Haven: Yale University Press, 1989). For Wittgenstein, "every sign by itself seems dead . . . [but] in its use it is alive" (*Philosophical Investigations*, paragraph 432); again, Norman Holland, *Poems in Persons: An Introduction to the Psychoanalysis of Literature* (New York: Norton, 1973), says it thus: "Meaning— whether we are talking simply of putting black marks together to form words or the much more complex process of putting words together to form themes—does not inhere in the words-on-the-page, but like beauty, in the eye of the beholder" (98).

59. Daniel Patte, *Ethics of Biblical Interpretation: A Reevaluation* (Louisville: Westminster John Knox Press, 1995), 99.

60. Stanley Hauerwas, *Unleashing the Scripture: Freeing the Bible from Captivity to America* (Nashville: Abingdon, 1993), 28.

61. Fish, *Is There a Text?*, 312.

62. Ibid., 163. See preceding argument.

63. Fish, "Why No One's Afraid," 7.

64. David Steinmetz, "The Superiority of Pre-critical Exegesis," *TToday* 37:1 (April 1980): 27–38.

65. For these questions and a more fully developed response by an admittedly "modern" reader at the horizon of postmodernity, see Patte, *Ethics of Biblical Interpretation*, 117–25.

66. John H. Yoder, "The Hermeneutics of Peoplehood," in *The Priestly Kingdom: Social Ethics as Gospel* (Notre Dame: University of Notre Dame Press, 1984), 15–45. See also Willard M. Swartley, *Slavery, Sabbath, War, and Women: Case Issues in Biblical Interpretation* (Scottdale, Pa.: Herald Press, 1982), 216–217.

67. Yoder, "The Hermeneutics of Peoplehood," 22–23.

68. Nathan O. Hatch, "Sola Scriptura," in *The Bible in America: Essays in Cultural History*, ed. Nathan O. Hatch and Mark A. Noll (New York: Oxford University Press, 1982), 61–62.

69. Hauerwas, "The Politics of the Bible: *Sola Scriptura* as Heresy," in *Unleashing the Scripture*, 27.

70. Wilfred Cantwell Smith, *What Is Scripture?: A Comparative Approach* (Minneapolis: Fortress Press, 1993), 18.

71. Smith, *What Is Scripture?*, 19.

72. Jacob Neusner, *Death and Birth of Judaism* (New York: Basic Books, 1987).

73. Jacob Neusner, *Self-Fulfilling Prophecy: Exile and Return in the History of Judaism* (Boston: Beacon Press, 1987), 6.

74. Hauerwas, *Unleashing the Scripture,* 23.

Chapter 3

1. Regina Schwartz, *The Book and the Text: The Bible and Literary Theory* (Cambridge, Mass.: Basil Blackwell, 1990), 14. Michel Foucault asks similar questions in "What Is an Author?," in *Language, Counter-memory, Practice: Selected Essays and Interviews,* (Ithaca, N.Y.: Cornell University Press, 1977), 113–138.

2. Peter Ackroyd, "The Open Canon," *Colloquium: The Australian and New Zealand Theological Review* 3 (May 1970): 286.

3. For an excellent review of the early history of canon that is more broadly situated than discussions to date regarding the Bible as canon, see especially Jan Gorak's "More Than Just a Rule: The Early History of the Canon," in his *The Making of the Modern Canon: Genesis and Crisis of a Literary Idea,* Athlone Series on Canons (London: Athlone, 1991), 9–48.

4. Harold Bloom, *The Western Canon: The Books and School of the Ages* (New York: Harcourt Brace, 1994), 19.

5. For eight essays by sociologists and cultural historians marking the parameters of much of the recent discussion on "canon" concerning fears of endlessly bickering victims versus continued domination of one canon over another, see E. Digby Baltzell, Amitai Etzioni, Lewis S. Feuer, Irving L. Horowitz, Dorothy Ross, Warren J. Samuels, Thomas Sowell, and Aaron Wildavsky, *Cracking the Cultural Consensus,* special edition of *Society* 29:1 (November/December 1991): 5–44; similarly six essays by literary critics in *Canons,* ed. Robert Von Hallberg, special edition of *CI,* 10:1 (September 1983); in comparative religions, Jacob Neusner et al., *Religious Writings and Religious Systems,* vols. 1 and 2 (Atlanta: Scholars Press, 1989); see also Miriam Levering, ed. *Rethinking Scripture: Essays from a Comparative Perspective* (Albany, N.Y.: State University of New York Press, 1989), and Jonathan Z. Smith, *Imagining Religion: From Babylon to Jonestown* (Chicago: University of Chicago Press, 1982); for a religio-political perspective, see Helmut Martin *Cult and Canon: The Origins and Development of State Maoism* (New York: M. E. Sharpe, 1982); and in higher education, Allan Bloom, *The Closing of the American Mind* (New York: Simon & Schuster, 1987), and William Bennett, *To Reclaim a Legacy: A Report on the Humanities in Higher Education* (Washington, D.C.: National Endowment for the Humanities, 1984).

6. James A. Sanders, "Canon (Hebrew Bible)," *ABD,* 1:838.

7. Historian of philosophy Stanley Rosen makes the point that categories such as "ancient" and "modern" define differences among people that are highly contingent. In other words, there are "ancients" and "moderns" in every period. He cites interesting examples of the "postmodern" repudiation of Platonism as being an odd version of the very thing of which it imagines itself the antithesis. On the other hand, "ancients" like Plato were well aware that knowledge was a play of powers—an idea heretofore

thought to be a postmodern, Nietzsche-induced "revelation." And so it goes. See Stanley Rosen, *The Ancients and the Moderns* (New Haven: Yale University Press, 1989), 20; compare Michel Foucault on history in "Nietzsche, Genealogy, History," in *Language, Counter-Memory, Practice: Selected Essays and Interviews* (Ithaca, N.Y.: Cornell University Press, 1977), 139–164, and Foucault, *The Archaeology of Knowledge* (New York: Pantheon Books, 1972).

8. For this phrase, see *Theology at the End of Modernity (Essays in Honor of Gordon D. Kaufman)*, ed. Sheila Greeve Davaney (Philadelphia: Trinity Press International, 1991). In the preface, Kaufman notes that judgments about the "end of modernity" depend heavily upon one's own interpretation of what has been important about the modern period (ix). What can be said is that in the last thirty to forty years, we have begun to witness the reevaluation of the assumptions that commenced with the Enlightenment, the questioning of which has allowed us to speak openly about approaching the "end of modernity" if not yet to unabashedly use "postmodern" to designate a "new age" altogether.

9. There is some debate over who first invented or used the term "postmodern." Martin Marty suggests three contenders: Canon Bernard Iddings Bell, in his *Postmodernism and Other Essays* (1926); Laura Riding and Robert Graves, who applied the term to literature in *A Survey of Modernist Poetry* (1927); and Arnold Toynbee, who in *A Study of History* (1947) said that the "postmodern" was a "new cycle of history which started in 1875." See Martin Marty, in *Context* 25:9 (1 May 1993): 3.

For a more nuanced discussion that acknowledges these forerunners but demarcates the modern/postmodern horizon as being more recent (ca. 1950–1960) based on the three shifts outlined here, see Nancey Murphy, *Theology in the Age of Scientific Reasoning* (Ithaca, N.Y.: Cornell University Press, 1990), 199–208. A fully developed argument appears in Nancey Murphy and James W. McClendon, Jr., "Distinguishing Modern and Postmodern Theologies," *Modern Theology* 5:3 (April 1989): 191–214. For a concurring recent introduction and bibliography on postmodernism, see the collection of otherwise widely scattered formative essays on the subject in Patricia Waugh, ed., *Postmodernism: A Reader* (London: Edward Arnold of Hodder & Stoughton, 1992).

10. That the language of crisis accompanies all paradigm revolutions is central to Thomas Kuhn's proposals in *The Structure of Scientific Revolutions,* 2d ed. (Chicago: University of Chicago Press, 1970), 66–91.

11. What follows is instigated in part (especially the first two points) by Walter Brueggemann's "Canon and Contextualization" in his *Interpretation and Obedience: From Faithful Reading to Faithful Living* (Minneapolis: Fortress Press, 1991), 117–132.

12. See Rebecca Chopp, *The Praxis of Suffering* (Maryknoll, N.Y.: Orbis Books, 1986), and Francis Fiorenza, who borrows from Foucault's notion of "local knowledge" as knowledge rooted in the "bedrock of existence" and suggests that suffering is a "source of 'local knowledge' that points out the inadequacies of ideological, social and economic systems" ("The Crisis of Hermeneutics and Christian Theology," in Davaney, *Theology at the End of Modernity,* 134–135).

13. For a sobering attack on the ideal of scientific unity wherein our choices deter-

mine not only what kinds of order we observe in nature but also what kinds of order we impose on the world we observe, see Stanford philosopher John Dupre's *The Disorder of Things: Metaphysical Foundations of the Disunity of Science* (Cambridge, Mass.: Harvard University Press, 1993).

Einstein's relativity (the variability of previously invariable parameters of space, time, and mass), Bohr's complementarity (that the essential experiential character of light is not the same as its essential ontological character), and Heisenberg's uncertainty principle (an "object" is something our perception renders permanent) are three formulations in modern physics that forced the reevaluation of our epistemological assumptions from an objectivist paradigm to the subjective. See David Bleich, "The Subjective Paradigm in Science, Psychology and Criticism," *NLH* 7 (1976): 313–334.

14. Brueggemann, *Interpretation and Obedience,* 124. See also Mary Douglas and Aaron Wildavsky's anthropological sociology of centers and margins in their *Risk and Culture* (Berkeley: University of California Press, 1982).

15. Reprinted in Murphy and McClendon, "Distinguishing Modern and Postmodern Theologies," 200.

16. Kuhn, *The Structure of Scientific Revolutions.*

17. Friedrich Nietzsche, *The Will to Power,* trans. R. J. Hollindale and W. Kaufmann, ed. Walter Kaufmann (New York: Random House, 1967), esp. 261–456; Foucault's dependence on Nietzsche in *The Archaeology of Knowledge* and "Nietzsche, Genealogy, History" see also J. Habermas, *Knowledge and Human Interest* (Boston: Beacon Press, 1968).

18. Fish, "Consequences," *CI* 11 (1985): 439.

19. For what follows, see Fiorenza, "Crisis of Hermeneutics." Specific page references are noted within the text.

20. Francis Fiorenza, "The Crisis of Scriptural Authority: Interpretation and Reception," *Int* 44:4 (October 1990): 353–368.

21. Fiorenza, "Crisis of Scriptural Authority," 362–363.

22. Hans Robert Jauss, *Question and Answer: Forms of Dialogic Understanding* (Minneapolis: University of Minnesota Press, 1989), 220, as cited in ibid., 366.

23. His triangle represents the interconnection between the readers' life-relation (situation), background theories (Kuhn's paradigms?), and understanding (hermeneutics?). One might just as well apply Sanders's triangle to the reader in the latest setting.

24. In his essay, "Paradigmawechsel in der Literaturwissenschaft," *Linguistische Berichte* 3 (1969): 44–56, Hans Robert Jauss, arguing from Kuhn's notion of paradigm revolutions, describes the waning of the literary paradigm (the fourth such literary revolution for Jauss) since the end of the Second World War culminating in the present crisis, to which his *Rezeptionästhetik* is poised in response. See Robert C. Holub, *Reception Theory: A Critical Introduction* (London: Methuen, 1984), 1–12.

25. See Paul Lauter's commissioned lecture at the Modern Language Association's centennial meeting, "Society and the Profession, 1958–1983," *PMLA* 99 (May 1984): 414–426, and printed in slightly different form in his *Canons and Contexts* (Oxford: Oxford University Press, 1991), 3–21.

26. See M. H. Abrams, "Modern Theories of Literature and Criticism," in his *A*

Glossary of Literary Terms, 5th ed. (New York: Holt, Rinehart, and Winston, 1985), 201–247; Terry Eagleton, *Literary Theory: An Introduction* (Minneapolis: University of Minnesota Press, 1983); Frank Lentricchia, *After New Criticism* (Chicago: University of Chicago Press, 1980); Mark Taylor, *Deconstruction in Context: Literarily and Philosophically* (Chicago: University of Chicago Press, 1986); Mark Powell, *The Bible and Modern Literary Criticism: A Critical Assessment and Annotated Bibliography* (New York: Greenwood Press, 1992); Ann Jefferson and David Robey, *Modern Literary Theory: A Comparative Introduction* (Jamesbury, N.J.: Barnes & Noble Books, 1982); and so on.

27. Terry Eagleton, a Marxist literary critic, not only frames the larger debate around the question "What is literature?" but concludes that the criteria of what counts as literature have always been (admittedly or not) ideological in thrust: "Writing which embodied the values and tastes of a particular social class qualified as literature"; see Eagleton, *Literary Theory: An Introduction,* 17; Frank Kermode, "The Argument about Canons," in his *An Appetite for Poetry* (Cambridge, Mass.: Harvard University Press, 1989), 189.

28. Bloom, *The Western Canon,* 17.

29. Brevard S. Childs, *Biblical Theology in Crisis* (Philadelphia: Westminister Press, 1970). Two responses of note include George M. Landes, "Biblical Exegesis in Crisis: What Is the Exegetical Task in a Theological Context?," *USQR* 26 (1971): 274–298 and Bernhard W. Anderson, "Crisis in Biblical Theology," *TToday* 28 (1971): 321–327.

Even more antagonistic (albeit unadmittedly) toward biblical theology as a discipline are the following "biblical theologians": James Barr, whose *The Bible in the Modern World* (London: SCM Press, 1973); *Old and New in Interpretation* (New York: Harper & Row, 1966); and *The Semantics of Biblical Language* (London: Oxford University Press, 1961) carry on a long-running debate with other "biblical theologians" and their attempts at doing "biblical theologies"; and G. Ernest Wright, whose *God Who Acts: Biblical Theology as Recital* (Chicago: Henry Regnery, 1952), which was followed seventeen years later by his *The Old Testament and Theology* (San Francisco: Harper & Row, 1969), had little good to say about the direction of the discipline.

James Smart also gives some perspective to the current "crisis" by showing how the history of biblical science suggests that theological interest waxes and wanes at regular intervals. Fears of the ultimate demise of biblical theology are, for Smart, unfounded. See Smart, *The Past, Present, and Future of Biblical Theology* (Philadelphia: Westminster Press, 1979), 10–11.

30. Ben C. Ollenburger, "From Timeless Ideas to the Essence of Religion: Method in Old Testament Theology before 1930," in *The Flowering of Old Testament Theology,* Sources for Biblical and Theological Study no. 1, ed. Gerhard F. Hasel, Ben C. Ollenburger, and Elmer A. Martens (Winona Lake, Ind.: Eisenbrauns, 1992), 3–19.

31. On this last point, see esp. Langdon Gilkey, *Naming the Whirlwind: The Renewal of God-Language* (Indianapolis: Bobbs-Merrill, 1969), 73–106.

32. John H. Hayes and Frederick Prussner, *Old Testament Theology: Its History and Development* (Atlanta: John Knox Press, 1985); Gerhard Hasel, *Old Testament The-*

ology: Basic Issues in the Current Debate (Grand Rapids: Eerdmans, 1972); Henning Graf Reventlow, *Problems of Biblical Theology in the Twentieth Century* (Philadelphia: Fortress Press, 1986).

33. For a sampling of new approaches, see Hayes and Prussner, "Recent Developments in Old Testament Theology," in *Old Testament Theology* 219–279, and John Barton, *Reading the Old Testament: Method in Biblical Study* (London: Darton, Longman and Todd, 1984).

34. James Sanders, *Torah and Canon* (Philadelphia: Fortress Press, 1972), and "Adaptable for Life: The Nature and Function of Canon," in *Magnalia Dei, the Mighty Acts of God: Essays on the Bible and Archaeology in Memory of G. Ernest Wright,* ed. Frank Moore Cross, Warner E. Lemke, and Patrick D. Miller (Garden City, N.Y.: Doubleday, 1976); Brevard Childs, *Biblical Theology in Crisis* (Philadelphia: Westminster Press, 1970), *The Book of Exodus* (London: SCM Press, 1974), *Introduction to the Old Testament as Scripture* (Philadelphia: Fortress Press, 1979), and *Biblical Theology of the Old and New Testaments: Theological Reflection on the Christian Bible* (Minneapolis: Fortress Press, 1993); John Bright's canonical exegesis in *The Authority of the Old Testament* (Nashville: Abingdon Press, 1967).

35. James Barr rightly describes the situation by arguing that all past discussions of biblical authority seem irrelevant because today all authority is seriously questioned. In citing Barr, Sanders suggests that such a pronouncement obliges us to address the question of the "nature and authority of the Bible, its *function* as canon, because if we do not we will have provided the answer in our failure to do so" (emphasis added); see Sanders, *Torah and Canon,* 117. Of course, Barr's answer has been to do away with the notion of canon altogether wherever he can in favor of "history" as norm.

36. See, P. R. Ackroyd and C. F. Evans, eds., *The Cambridge History of the Bible: From the Beginnings to Jerome* vol. 1 (Cambridge: Cambridge University Press, 1970); G. W. H. Lampe, ed., *The Cambridge History of the Bible: The West from the Fathers to the Reformation,* vol. 2 (Cambridge: Cambridge University Press, 1975); and A. L. Greenslade, ed., *The Cambridge History of the Bible: The West from the Reformation to the Present Day* vol. 3 (Cambridge: Cambridge University Press, 1963).

37. Most notably, Harold Bloom, *The Western Canon;* see also Henry Gates, *Loose Canons: Notes on the Cultural Wars* (New York: Oxford University Press, 1992), 34.

38. For a brief summary, see Bruce M. Metzger, "History of the Word *kanon,*" in *The Canon of the New Testament: Its Origins, Development, and Significance* (Oxford: Oxford University Press, 1987), 289–293, and Childs, *Introduction,* 49–50.

39. For a succinct review of that history, see Childs, *Introduction,* 50. In literary circles, the term was also variously applied as (1) works accepted by experts as "genuinely written by a particular author, such as "the Chaucer canon" or "the Shakespeare canon"; or (2) those authors whose works, by cumulative consensus of authoritative critics, have come to be viewed as "major" works, often appearing in anthologies of "the great American writers," and so forth. See Abrams, *Glossary of Literary Terms,* 19–21; Bloom, *The Western Canon.*

40. Jan Gorak describes four added dimensions of sacred canon to the classical understanding: (1) the divine source of a canon's authority; (2) the notion of total narrative in sacred book as constitutive over against mere collections of rules; (3) that

the narrative was "closed" and contained a retrospectively binding plot; and (4) that the plot served to govern the life of the community. See Gorak, *The Making of the Modern Canon,* 19–20.

41. Ibid., 21.

42. For a more extended account of this erosion of the traditional view of canon, see Childs, *Introduction,* 51–57. He fails to mention the Qumran discoveries as effecting this trend, one of the factors most significant in undermining the traditional views up to 1947. He corrects this oversight in *Biblical Theology of the Old and New Testaments* 56.

43. Frank Kermode, "The Canon," ed. Robert Alter and Frank Kermode, *The Literary Guide to the Bible* (Cambridge, Mass.: Harvard University Press, 1984), 601.

44. Sanders, *Torah and Canon,* xvii.

45. H. E. Ryle, *The Canon of the Old Testament,* 2d ed. (London: Macmillan, 1909) (1st ed. published in 1892). See also Roger Beckwith, *The Old Testament Canon of the New Testament Church* (Grand Rapids: Eerdmans, 1985), 4.

46. James A. Sanders, "Cave 11 Surprises and the Question of Canon," in *The Canon and Masorah of the Hebrew Bible,* ed. Sid Z. Leiman (New York: KTAV, 1974), 37–51 (originally published in *McCormick Quarterly Review* 21 [1968]: 284–298).

47. For other examples, see James A. Sanders, "Hebrew Bible *and* Old Testament: Textual Criticism in Service of Biblical Studies," in *Hebrew Bible or Old Testament?: Studying the Bible in Judaism and Christianity,* ed. Roger Brooks and John J. Collins (Notre Dame: University of Notre Dame Press, 1990), 62–65, and Eugene Ulrich, "Double Literary Editions of Biblical Narratives and Reflections on Determining the Form to Be Translated," *Pers* 15 (1988): 101–116.

48. Three papers summarizing the Jewish, Roman Catholic, and Protestant rethinking of canon in light of the recovery of the Qumran finds were presented at the Society of Biblical Literature meetings of 1965 and summarized in "A Symposium on the Canon of Scripture: Samuel Sandmel, Albert Sundberg, Jr., and Roland E. Murphy," in *Old Testament Issues,* ed. Samuel Sandmel (New York: Harper & Row, 1968). Sundberg argued for Protestants' accepting the early Christian canon (with Apocrypha) in light of the fact of their authoritative functioning at Qumran. Sandmel also confessed that the closed canon of the Jewish tradition was no longer a necessity for him, though he did not recommend abolishing it altogether, as did Sundberg.

49. See Barton, *Reading the Old Testament,* 91–92; William Hallo, "Assyriology and the Canon," *American Scholar* 59:1 (Winter 1990): 105–108; and Sean P. Kealy, "The Canon: An African Contribution," *BTB* 9:1 (January 1979): 13–26.

50. Wilfred Cantwell Smith, *What Is Scripture?: A Comparative Approach* (Minneapolis: Fortress Press, 1993), 13; cf. Greenslade, *Cambridge History of the Bible* vol. 3, 199–237, 339–346.

51. See Sanders, "Hebrew Bible *and* Old Testament," 65–68.

52. For an anticanon perspective, see James Barr, *Holy Scripture: Canon, Authority, Criticism* (Philadelphia: Westminster Press, 1983); for another perspective, see Ackroyd, "The Open Canon," 279–291; Sandmel, Sundberg, and Murphy, "A Symposium on the Canon of Scripture"; and Roger Beckwith, *The Old Testament Canon,* 7. Beckwith notes the inadequacy of previous studies on canon. A survey of books on

"canon" published since 1970, contrasted to the relative silence prior to that time (except mentions of canon as afterthoughts in various introductions), suggests how influential the Dead Sea scrolls became in invoking a crisis of canon that called for response. See the bibliographies in Jan Martin Mulder, ed., *Mikra* (Philadelphia: Fortress Press, 1988), 797–852, and James Sanders, *From Sacred Story to Sacred Text* (Philadelphia: Fortress Press, 1987), 195–200.

53. James A. Sanders led the way in this "revolution" in his groundbreaking introduction, "A Call to Canonical Criticism," in *Torah and Canon,* ix–xx; see also Sanders, "Canon (Hebrew Bible)," 837–852.

54. From the literary side of the aisle, see Robert Alter and Frank Kermode, eds., *The Literary Guide to the Bible* (Cambridge, Mass.: Harvard University Press, 1987); Robert Alter, "A Literary Approach to the Bible," *Commentary* 60 (December 1975): 70–77, reprinted in Alter *The Art of Biblical Narrative;* Alter, *The World of Biblical Literature;* Schwartz, *The Book and the Text;* Meir Sternberg, *The Poetics of Biblical Narrative: Ideological Literature and the Drama of Reading* (Bloomington: Indiana University Press, 1986); Mieke Bal, "The Bible as Literature: A Critical Escape," *Diacritics* 16:4 (1986): 71–79; Geoffrey Hartman and Sanford Budick, eds., *Midrash and Literature* (New Haven: Yale University Press, 1986); and Northrop Frye, *The Great Code: The Bible and Literature* (San Diego: Harcourt Brace Jovanovich, 1983). From the biblical studies side, see Mark Allan Powell's chronicle, *The Bible and Modern Literary Criticism: A Critical Assessment and Annotated Bibliography* (New York: Greenwood Press, 1992); David M. Gunn and Danna Nolan Fewell, *Narrative in the Hebrew Bible* (New York: Oxford University Press, 1993); J. Cheryl Exum and David J. A. Clines, *The New Literary Criticism and the Hebrew Bible* (Valley Forge: Trinity Press International, 1993). More recently, see the cross-disciplinary team of John Gabel, Charles Wheeler and Anthony D. York, *The Bible as Literature,* 3d ed. (New York: Oxford University Press, 1996).

55. Schwartz, "Introduction: On Biblical Criticism," in *The Book and the Text,* 14.

56. Ibid.,

57. Lauter, *in Canons and Contexts,* closely links discussions of canon with those of "the university" and "the republic"; in one essay, "Whose Culture? Whose Literacy?" (256–271) he notes that the question of canon is only one focus of a complex debate (x); compare Harold Bloom, *The Western Canon,* which is not to be confused with Allan Bloom's *The Closing of the American Mind,* although both scholars set forth their defense of the canons of Western society. See also E. D. Hirsch, Jr., *Cultural Literacy: What Every American Needs to Know* (Boston: Houghton Mifflin, 1987) and Bennett, *To Reclaim a Legacy.*

58. Exposure of a "patriarchal" bias in the literary canon can be observed in Elaine Showalter, ed., *The New Feminist Criticism: Essays on Women, Literature, and Theory* (New York: Pantheon Books, 1985); Carey Kaplan and Ellen Cronan Rose, eds., *The Canon and the Common Reader* (Knoxville: University of Tennessee Press, 1990); and James Winders, *Gender, Theory, and the Canon* (Madison: University of Wisconsin Press, 1991). On the fight to include African-American contributions, see Henry Gates, *Loose Canons: Notes on the Cultural Wars* (New York: Oxford University Press, 1992); Houston A. Baker, Jr., ed., *Reading Black: Essays in the Criticism of African,*

Caribbean, and Black American Literature (Chicago: University of Chicago Press, 1976); and Leslie A. Fielder and Houston A. Baker, Jr., eds., *English Literature: Opening Up the Canon* (Baltimore: Johns Hopkins University Press, 1981). A Native American appeal is made by Arnold Kruput, "Native American Literature and the Canon," in *Canons*, ed. Robert von Hallberg, special edition of *CI* 10:1 (September 1983): 145–172. Broadening the discussion a bit is Peter Hyland, ed., *Discharging the Canon: Cross-cultural Readings in Literature* (Singapore: Singapore University Press, 1986).

59. Wilfred Cantwell Smith, "The Study of Religion and the Study of the Bible," in *Rethinking Scripture: Essays from a Comparative Perspective,* ed. Miriam Levering (New York: State University of New York Press, 1989), 18–28, and "Scripture as Form and Concept: Their Emergence for the Western World," in Levering, *Rethinking Scripture,* 45. See also Smith, *What Is Scripture?,* ix. In the same vein, Smith suggests that there was a historic shift at the turn of the century in the use of the term *scripture* away from a singular use referring to the Bible to a more generic use for sacred texts of many religions (6).

60. Smith, "Scripture as Form and Concept," 40.

61. Ibid., 41.

62. Smith's observation about the relatively late entrance of canonical tendencies by Greek-speaking Jews does not take into account the fact that canon as function antedated canon as shape. As James Sanders has observed, "The function of a written canon has antecedents in the very process by which the concept arose, that is, in the function of authoritative traditions when there was as yet no written literature deemed canonical in the sense of *norma normata* or shape." See Sanders, "Canon (Hebrew Bible)," 847. Smith is here arguing from the traditional approach to canon that emphasized form over function, though his comparative observations ultimately shift the focus away from form to function. Indeed, Smith notes in *What Is Scripture?* several recent dissertations written under his tutelage that are almost exact models of Sanders's comparative midrash approach, only this time of the Bhagadvad Gita, Qur'an, and Lotus Sutra (5–6).

63. Smith, *What Is Scripture?,* examines the history of scripture in the world's major religious traditions.

Jacob Neusner and his students have begun a study titled "Systemic Analysis of Holy Books in Christianity, Islam, Buddhism, Greco-Roman Religions, Ancient Israel, and Judaism" that is now available in the Brown Studies of Religion series in two volumes: Jacob Neusner, Ernest S. Fredrichs, and A. J. Levine, eds., *Religious Writings and Religious Systems,* vols. 1 and 2 (Atlanta, Ga.: Scholars Press, 1989). Neusner's "system" incorporates a triangular relationship among text/context/matrix, wherein the social group frames the system, then defines its canon within that system (xii). For Neusner et al., once this "system" is put in place it seems to take on a life of its own. He places the survival of religious writings in the up-and-running "system" without fully appreciating that the primary power to redefine, recapitulate, and rewrite the system belongs to the interpretative community. For our purposes here, Neusner et al. do show the broadening of the canonical process, as process, to a variety of religious traditions.

In *Rethinking Scripture,* Miriam Levering cautions against trying to comparatively define a single category called "scripture" using lists of characterizing features. However, she goes on to argue that "if we instead attend principally to the dynamics of the relations that people have had with texts, their ways of receiving texts in the context of their religious projects," then comparisons are more hopeful (11). The comparative essays in the book underscore functional similarities where formal ones are lacking. On the matter of canon and the classic, she finds the polarity between normativity and resignification at the heart of her criteria for defining "scripture" comparatively. This relation between authority and reinterpretation depends on her reading of James Sanders and David Tracey (13).

Jonathan Z. Smith argues for redescribing canon in functional terms as the process of "sacred persistence" over against traditional formal stress on the "persistence of the sacred"; see Smith, "Sacred Persistence: Toward a Redescription of Canon," in *Imagining Religion: From Babylon to Jonestown* (Chicago: University of Chicago Press, 1982), 36–52.

Finally, from a political, quasi-religious perspective, Helmut Martin in *Cult and Canon* describes in detail the *process* involved in the "canonical" rise and resignification of Maoist writings from 1935 to 1981.

64. Brueggemann, "Canon and Contextualization," 124.

65. Von Hallberg, "Introduction," in *Canons,* v. As will be outlined below, this idea of "periods of intense canonical formation" and communal identity is central to Sanders's theses as well.

66. Stanley Fish, *Is There a Text in This Class?: The Authority of Interpretative Communities* (Cambridge, Mass.: Harvard University Press, 1980), in speaking of the relativism demanded by our new context, recognizes that "while relativism is a position one can entertain, it is not a position one can occupy" (319). In other words, in any one historical moment, decisions have to be made for psychological and social reasons of identity and survival that foreclose on other real options. These decisions are embedded in the communal norms of one's identity group, not in bedrock foundations per se.

67. For the structure of the following argument, I have found Frank Kermode's "The Argument about Canons," in his *Appetite for Poetry* (189–207) quite useful. My dependence on him will be obvious, though we finally part company in how we view the text's relationship to the community reading it. In questions of canon formation, his argument appears to stop short of its own logic, as he opts for a quasi draw between the text's power over the community and vice versa. I, on the other hand, opt for communal priority in canon formation.

68. Childs, *Introduction.* For a sampling of reviews, along with a response by Childs, see *HBT* 2 (1980): 113–211; John Barton, chaps. 6, 7, 10, 11, and appendix, in *Reading the Old Testament,* 77–103, 140–154, 170–177, 208–211; and Walter Brueggemann's description in "Canonization and Contextualization," 119–142, countered by Childs in his newest work, *Biblical Theology of the Old and New Testaments: Theological Reflection on the Christian Bible* (Minneapolis: Fortress Press, 1993), 71–73. The most ardent critic remains James Barr; see Barr, "Childs' Introduction to the Old Testament as Scripture," *JSOT* 16 (1980): 12–23, and *Holy Scripture.*

69. In contrast to Brueggemann, Childs defends against a purely formal reading in his *Biblical Theology of the Old and New Testaments,* 72.

70. See especially, Childs's three charges against the traditional historical-critical approach to canon in his *Introduction:* (1) that an enormous gulf between the description of the reconstructed literature and the actual canonical text emerges (40); (2) that a whole dimension is lost when the dynamic that issues from a collection with fixed parameters and affects both the language and imagery of the parts is ignored (40); and (3) that the historian assumes the determining force of every biblical text to be political, social, or economic, disregarding the religious dynamic of the canon (41).

71. Childs, *Biblical Theology of the Old and New Testaments,* 70–71.

72. Kermode, "The Argument about Canons," 194. in *What Is Scripture?,* Wilfred Cantwell Smith suggests that scholars such as Barr, who argue the irrelevance of "scripture" and "canon" for understanding the Bible as literature, are "teasingly" called "antiquarian" or "academic fundamentalists" and fail to accept the very real phenomenon increasingly apparent in religious cultures of many varieties (15). Indeed, his book is an attempt to persuade the academic world, secular and religious alike, to take this issue ever more seriously (214).

73. Kermode, "The Argument about Canons," 200.

74. Kermode terms this stance an "occult assumption that might for short be called magical" (Ibid., 202).

75. Murphy, *Theology in the Age of Scientific Reasoning.*

76. This phrase was first used by Jan Gorak, *The Making of the Modern Canon,* 153 to describe Frank Kermode's canonical stance. Insofar as Sanders's approach is as much a hermeneutic stance as it is a method, the phrase applies equally well. On the matter of the *via media,* both Sanders and Kermode appear to be the Erasmuses of the canonists and anticanonists, preferring compromise and reinterpretation over schism. Other such comparisons will be noted in the following comments.

77. Gorak, *The Making of the Modern Canon,* 152, on Kermode; what follows is a weaving of Gorak's analysis of Kermode (153–185) with my own analysis of Sanders.

78. Kermode, "The Argument about Canons," 202–203.

79. Sanders, *Torah and Canon,* 116.

80. Gorak, *The Making of the Modern Canon,* 156.

81. Kermode, "The Argument about Canons," 203.

82. Sanders, *From Sacred Story,* 4.

83. As his paradigm for the world, Kermode posits "fictions" (complex stories that explain phenomena only provisionally) over against Frye's "myths" (simple stories explaining everything). See Frank Kermode, *Sense of an Ending: Studies in the Theory of Fiction* (New York: Oxford University Press, 1967), 43. Sanders's paradigm is, of course, the canon (see *From Sacred Story,* 5–6). To suggest that these are "fictions" of discourse does not address the question of truth per se.

84. Frank Kermode, *Shakespeare, Spenser, Donne: Renaissance Essays* (New York: Viking Press, 1971), 180, cited in Gorak, *The Making of the Modern Canon,* 169.

85 Gorak, *The Making of the Modern Canon,* 170.

86. Gates, *Loose Canons,* 35.

87. Bloom, *The Western Canon,* 9, 19.

88. Richard Ohmann, "The Shaping of a Canon: U.S. Fiction, 1960–1975," *CI* 10:1 (September 1983): 199–223. The relationship between political power and interpretation is not lost to literary critic Jane P. Tompkins, in "The Reader in History: The Changing Shape of Literary Response," in Jane P. Tompkins, ed., *Reader-Response Criticism: From Formalism to Post Structuralism* (Baltimore: Johns Hopkins University Press, 1980), 201–232.

89. Robert B. Coote and Mary P. Coote, *Power, Politics, and the Making of the Bible* (Minneapolis: Fortress Press, 1990); Gerald L. Bruns, "Canon and Power in the Hebrew Scriptures," *CI* 10:3 (March 1984): 462–480; Ellis Rivkin, *The Shaping of Jewish History: A Radical New Interpretation* (New York: Scribner's, 1971).

90. Max Weber, *Wirtschaft und Gesellschaft* (1922; reprint, Tübingen: J. C. B. Mohr, 1975), 28: "Macht bedeutet jede Chance, innerhalb einer sozialen Beziehung den eigenen Willen auch gegen Widerstreben durchzusetzen, gleichviel worauf diese Chance beruht." See Gustavo Benavides, "Religious Articulations of Power," in *Religion and Political Power,* ed. Gustavo Benavides and M. W. Daly (New York: State University of New York Press, 1989), 1–12.

91. Joseph Blenkinsopp, *Prophecy and Canon: A Contribution to the Study of Jewish Origins* (Notre Dame: University of Notre Dame Press, 1977), 96.

92. Here one thinks especially of the historicist stance of Foucault, Lacan, Derrida, et al., whose radical historicism nearly handicaps their ability to sustain a vision of anything not subject to ubiquitous differential power plays, appealing, as it were, to Darwin's famous half-quote, "nature, red in tooth and claw," as a likely motto. Microbiologist Wayne Meeks has also suggested that Sanders's canonical process is a form of survival-of-the-fittest text or tradition.

93. This phrase comes from the subtitle of Charles Altieri's *Canons and Consequences: The Ethical Force of Imaginative Ideals* (Evanston, Ill.: Northwestern University Press, 1990), to which we will refer extensively below.

94. Coote and Coote, *Power, Politics, and the Making of the Bible,* 3. Hereafter, page references are given in the text. See also R. P. Carroll, "Rebellion and Dissent in Ancient Israelite Society," *ZAW* 89 (1977): 176–204, and M. Smith, *Palestinian Parties and Politics That Shaped the Old Testament,* 2d ed. (London: SCM Press, 1987).

95. For a historical overview less centered on the question of power and politics but no less thorough, see Sanders, *Torah and Canon.*

96. Bruns, "Canon and Power in the Hebrew Scriptures," 462–480.

97. For these expressions, see Altieri, *Canons and Consequences,* and Hazard Adams, "Canons: Literary Criteria/Power Criteria," *CI* 14 (Summer 1988): 748–764, respectively.

98. Vaclav Havel, ed., *The Power of the Powerless: Citizens against the State in Central-Eastern Europe* (New York: M. E. Sharpe, 1985).

99. Adams, "Canons: Literary Criteria/Power Criteria." Hereafter, page references are given in the text.

100. Altieri, *Canons and Consequences.* Hereafter, page references are given in the text.

101. David Miller, *The New Polytheism: Rebirth of the Gods and Goddesses* (New York: Harper & Row, 1974).

102. See Gordon Kaufman, "The Christian World-Picture (I): The Monotheistic Categorical Scheme," in *In Face of Mystery: A Constructive Theology* (Cambridge, Mass.: Harvard University Press, 1993), 70–82, for much of what follows, including his description of the polytheistic frame of orientation found in the ancient Near East, which I have applied here (72).

103. Gorak, *The Making of the Modern Canon*, 40–41.

104. In his argument about "theologizing" (reading the Bible theologically) *before* "moralizing" (reading the Bible morally), Sanders seems to stand under the modernist assumptions that "foundations"-doctrine-ethics is the *logical* hermeneutic order; see *From Sacred Story*, 69–70. In this sense, he seems to be arguing from an ahistorical aesthetic with regard to what the monotheizing process, for him, *necessarily* implies. I will argue in the following chapter for the logic of ethics-doctrine-"foundations," following from the postmodern narrative ethics of James W. McClendon, Jr., *Ethics*, vol. 1 of *Systematic Theology* (Nashville: Abingdon Press, 1991), and *Doctrine*, vol. 2 of *Systematic Theology* (Nashville: Abingdon Press, 1994), as ultimately more in keeping with Sanders's own emphasis on the Bible as story. See also Stanley Hauerwas, *A Community of Character: Toward a Constructive Christian Social Ethic* (Notre Dame: University of Notre Dame Press, 1981), and *The Peaceable Kingdom: A Primer in Christian Ethics* (Notre Dame: University of Notre Dame Press, 1983); John Howard Yoder, *The Politics of Jesus* (Grand Rapids: Eerdmans, 1972), and *The Priestly Kingdom: Social Ethics as Gospel* (Notre Dame: University of Notre Dame Press, 1984); and Alasdair MacIntyre, *After Virtue*, 2d ed. (Notre Dame: University of Notre Dame Press, 1984).

105. Sanders, *Canon and Community*, 56–60; H. R. Niebuhr, *Radical Monotheism and Western Culture* (New York: Harper & Brothers, 1960); Kaufman, *In Face of Mystery*, 70–82, and *The Theological Imagination: Constructing the Concept of God* (Philadelphia: Westminster Press, 1981).

106. Sanders, *Canon and Community*, 42, 56.

107. For Smith, in *What Is Scripture?*, "scripture" is precisely that human activity that constructs or mediates meaning between the cosmos and human beings, giving to one's life a "transcendent significance" (217, 221, 228). There is no "ontology of Scripture" per se. Rather, there is only the human propensity and potentiality to scripturalize—in short, Smith argues in his own way for process (that is, performance) over form (237). On Israel's attempts to orient its communal life, see also Mieke Bal, *Death and Dissymmetry: The Politics of Coherence in the Book of Judges* (Chicago: University of Chicago Press, 1988).

108. Kaufman, *In Face of Mystery*, 81.

109. What Kaufman says of his "monotheistic categorical scheme" I repeat here for Sanders's monotheizing hermeneutic. Kaufman refers also to the highly anthropocentric character of this world-picture as another disadvantage for all non-human creatures, including nature itself (*In Face of Mystery*, 75–78). For the best philosophical treatment of the ethical implications of such a totalizing hermeneutic and use of the image of the face as an "irreducible relation," see Emmanuel Levinas, *Totality and Infinity: An Essay on Exteriority*, trans. Alphonso Lingis, Duquesne Studies Philosophical Series no. 24 (Pittsburgh: Duquesne University Press, 1969), and *Ethics and*

Infinity: Conversations with Philippe Nemo, trans. Richard A. Cohen (Pittsburgh: Duquesne University Press, 1985).

110. Søren Kierkegaard, *Fear and Trembling* (Princeton: Princeton University Press, 1945); Kaufman, *In Face of Mystery,* 77. I guess one could argue that it is not our role to do ethics for God (so John Howard Yoder on this story).

111. Michael Fishbane, in "Saving Scripture and Our Mortal Souls," *Explorations* 7:2 (1993): 6, also seems to recognize some peril in the schemata of Sanders's monotheizing approach, even as he compliments him for his version of it. In a parenthetical but highly suggestive comment, Fishbane says: "I'm glad it is James Sanders speaking; for he speaks with great integrity. But others could find another center [i.e., not the wisdom core within prophecy, which Fishbane sees as Sanders's laudable theological kernel]. What do we say to them?" In other words, Fishbane admits—but only indirectly, because he happens to agree with Sanders's *Kern*—that what is in fact fundamental to Sanders's scheme is not his theological kernel per se but rather the ethical character of Sanders himself. Said differently, it is *how* Sanders might wield his "center" that apparently becomes the critical matter for Fishbane, less than, the content of that center!

112. Sanders, *From Sacred Story,* 67, and *Torah and Canon,* 73–90.

113. Sanders, *From Sacred Story,* 4.

114. Michael Fishbane, *Garments of Torah: Essays in Biblical Hermeneutics* (Bloomington: Indiana University Press, 1989), 130–131.

115. John H. Yoder, "The Authority of the Canon," in *Essays on Biblical Interpretation: Anabaptist-Mennonite Perspectives,* ed. Willard M. Swartley, Text-Reader Series no. 1 (Elkhart, Ind.: Institute of Mennonite Studies, 1984), 290.

116. Sanders, "Adaptable for Life," in *From Sacred Story,* 19. see Sanders, "The Shape of the Torah," in *Torah and Canon,* 1–30. and J. Neusner, *Self-Fulfilling Prophecy: Exile and Return in the History of Judaism* (Boston: Beacon Press, 1987), 5–17, 31–61.

117. Gil Bailie, *Violence Unveiled: Humanity at the Crossroads* (New York: Crossroad, 1995), 44, 45.

118. Stanley Rosen, *The Ancients and the Moderns,* ix. In a similar vein, Edward Said, in "Opponents, Audiences, Constituencies, and Community," *CI* 9 (1982): 1–26, following Fish, cites the political force in the art of persuasion as a "civil conquest," an attempt to "displace, win out over others" (11). See also James A. Sanders, "Intertextuality and Dialogue," *Explorations* 7:2 (1993): 4–5, and, finally, J. William Whedbee, "Why Read the Bible in a Post-Modern World: Difficulties, Dilemmas, and Dialogues" (speech delivered in Claremont, California, 1993), TMs photocopy.

Chapter 4

1. "Validation" is a concern central to literary discussions of late. For example, a primary objective of the literary journal *Critical Inquiry* since 1978 has been to study the question of adjudication and validation of diverse literary texts. For an excellent account of the history and state of affairs regarding the criteria for evaluation in literary

criticism, see Barbara Herrnstein Smith, "Contingencies of Value," 10:1 (1983): 1–35. See also E. D. Hirsch, *The Aims of Interpretation* (Chicago: University of Chicago Press, 1976), and *Validity in Interpretation* (New Haven: Yale University Press, 1967). In the realm of general hermeneutics, see Paul Ricoeur, *The Conflict of Interpretations: Essays in Hermeneutics,* ed. Don Ihde (Evanston, Ill.: Northwestern University Press, 1974), and the paper by Tat-Sing Benny Liew, "Adjudication: Deciding to Decide" (SBL annual meeting, 1992), TMs.

2. Rolf Rendtorff, "Reflections on the Early History of Prophecy in Israel," trans. Paul J. Achtemeier, in *History and Hermeneutic: Journal for Theology and the Church,* no. 4 (1967): 14–34 (original German *ZThK* 59 [1962]: 145–167); James Limburg, "The Prophets in Recent Study, 1967–1977," *Int* 32 (1978): 56–68; Hans Walter Wolf, "Prophecy from the Eighth through the Fifth Century," trans. Sibley Towner with Joy Heebink, *Int* 32 (1978): 17–30.

3. James Crenshaw, *Prophetic Conflict: Its Effect upon Israelite Religion* (Berlin: de Gruyter, 1971), 13–14, asks these and other more traditional questions.

4. See ibid., 5–22, and on this last point, Roff Rendtorff, *Men of God,* trans. Frank Clarke (London: SCM Press, 1968), 71.

5. Emphasis on the individual personality and profile of the prophet, reinforced by B. Duhm's programmatic approach, was typical of this early stage. J. G. Herder and H. Ewald would soon follow suit in the late nineteenth century. Gustav Holscher's emphasis on the psychological aspects of the prophetic experience—namely, ecstasy—in his *Die Profeten: Untersuchungen zur Religongeschichte* (Leipzig: J. C. Hinrich's Buchhandlung, 1914) added to the emphasis on the personality of the prophet. For the next twenty-five years, prophetic *experience* dominated the field, pressed to the limit by G. Widengren's *The Literary and Psychological Aspects of the Hebrew Prophets* (Uppsala: Lundequistska Bokhandeln, 1948). For a detailed discussion of this period, see W. Zimmerli, *The Law and the Prophets,* trans. R. E. Clements (Oxford: Basil Blackwell, 1965), 17–30. Subsequent studies have addressed this matter as well.

6. Gottfried Quell, *Wahre und falsche Propheten* (Gutersloh: Bertelsmann, 1952). Even though M. Buber, "Falsche Propheten," *Die Wandlung* 2 (1947): 279, defended Hananiah as a "principled man," he blamed Hananiah for his blindness to the politics of the hour. As late as 1963, Zimmerli argued that Hananiah's rejection as a false prophet (Jer. 28) was due primarily to Jeremiah's psychological experience; see his "Der Wahrheitserweis Jahwes nach der Botschaft der beiden Exilspropheten," *Tradition und Situation: Festschrift A. Weiser,* ed. E. Wurthwein and W. Kaiser (Göttingen: Vandenhoeck & Ruprecht, 1963), 133–151. For the matter of *pseudoprophetes,* see J. Reiling, "The Use of 'Pseudoprophetes' in LXX, Philo and Josephus," *NT* 13 (1971): 147–156.

7. On "criteria focusing on the man," see Crenshaw, *Prophetic Conflict,* 56–60.

8. See C. Westermann's treatment in *Basic Forms of Prophetic Speech,* trans. Hugh C. White (Philadelphia: Westminster Press, 1967) as a familiar example.

9. Sigmund Mowinckel, "The 'Spirit' and the 'Word' in the Pre-Exilic Reforming Prophets," *JBL* 53 (1934): 199–227.

10. For a modern example, see L. Festinger, H. Riechen, and H. and S. Schachter, *When Prophecy Fails: A Social and Psychological Study of a Modern Group That Predicted the Destruction of the World* (New York: Harper & Row, 1956).

11. Gerhard von Rad, "Die falschen Propheten," *ZAW* 51 (1933): 109–120. See also Eva Osswald's summarization in her *Falsche Prophtie im Alten Testament* (Tübingen: J. C. B. Mohr [Paul Siebeck], 1962).

12. Ironically, von Rad's helpful insights depended on the rather exclusivist argument that false prophets deliver messages of weal. Von Rad suggests that Deuteronomy's dogma of weal toward institutional prophets is the product of "falsehood." His willingness to categorize Deuteronomy's message on this score as false shows his bias toward historical fulfillment as the final arbitrator in this rhetorical war. History showed Hananiah and the 400 cult prophets of Ahab to be wrong; therefore Deuteronomy's support of the cult and its prophets must have also been the product of the same mistaken philosophy. What von Rad doesn't do is argue on Deuteronomy's behalf from a post-exilic perspective in which the canonical process saw Deuteronomy as anything but "false" and central to its editorial stance. History may be the final arbiter but only in its *telos,* not any particular moment in between. With that caveat, von Rad's thesis can be retained.

13. Buber and Osswald advocated such a stance, focusing on the "historical hour," though each had narrower criteria: fanatic patriotism (Buber) and judgment (Osswald).

14. Klaus Koch, *The Growth of the Biblical Tradition* (New York: Scribner's, 1969), 200–210.

15. Adam S. Van der Woude, "Micah in Dispute with the Pseudo-Prophets," *VT* 19 (1969): 244–260; "Micah IV 1–5: An Instance of the Pseudo-Prophets Quoting Isaiah," in *Symbolae Biblicae et Mespotamicae Francisco Mario Theodoro de Liagre Boehl Dedicatae* ed. M. A. Beek et al. (Leiden: Brill, 1973), 369–402; Crenshaw, *Prophetic Conflict,* 1971. A number of studies in true and false prophecy emphasize the struggle of "true" prophets against *public* opposition, necessitating efforts at legitimation by reinterpretation of the lack of fulfillment. See Robert Carroll, *When Prophecy Failed: Cognitive Dissonances in the Prophetic Traditions of the Old Testament* (London: SCM Press, 1979). On prophetic rhetoric against extreme vilification, see Martin Cohen, "The Prophets as Revolutionaries," *BAR* 5:3 (1979): 12–19, and D. F. Murray, "The Rhetoric of Disputation: Re-examination of a Prophetic Genre," *JSOT* 38 (1987): 95–121. On saying what the popular sentiment wanted to hear, see Ronald Manahan, "A Theology of Pseudoprophets: A Study in Jeremiah," *GTJ* 1 (1980): 77–96.

16. James Crenshaw, *Old Testament Wisdom: An Introduction* (Atlanta: John Knox Press, 1981), 202.

17. See Robert Carroll, *From Chaos to Covenant* (New York: Crossroad, 1981), 183–189, and B. Long, "Social Dimensions of Prophetic Conflict," *Semeia* 21 (1981): 31–53.

18. Crenshaw, *Old Testament Wisdom,* 110–111. Crenshaw failed to appreciate that long after classical forms of prophecy ended, other types of prophetic activity thrived in post-exilic Judaism and even in later Judaism. See David E. Aune, *Prophecy in Early Christianity and the Ancient Mediterranean World* (Grand Rapids: Eerdmans, 1983), 103–106. For other criticisms, see the reviews of Crenshaw, *Prophetic Conflict,* by Georg Fohrer, *ZAW* 83 (1971): 419; J. G. Williams, *JBL* 91 (1972): 402–404; Walter Brueggemann, *Int* 27 (1973): 220–221; M. Bic, *ThLZ* 97 (1972): 653–656; F. Dreyfus, *RB* 80 (1973): 443–444; and E. Jacob, *Bib* 54 (1973): 135–138.

19. Although von Rad and Quell had appropriately called into question any purely "objective" means of identifying the authority of a true prophet, they incorrectly assumed by extension that the effort was simply not subject to scientific analysis, as if such analysis itself was altogether "objective." L. Ramlot, "Les faux prophetes," *DBSup* 8 (Fasc. 47, 1971): cols. 1044, 1047–48, would sidestep the matter by appealing to the "mystery" of it all, as if to say that Crenshaw was right after all.

20. James A. Sanders, *Canon and Authority: Essays in Old Testament Religion and Theology,* ed. George W. Coats and Burke O. Long (Philadelphia: Fortress Press, 1977), 21–41, reprinted with an introduction in his *From Sacred Story to Sacred Text* (Philadelphia: Fortress Press, 1987), 87–105. References to the 1987 reprint will be noted parenthetically in the text.

21. Sanders, *From Sacred Story,* 89, 103, *God Has a Story Too* (Philadelphia: Fortress Press, 1979), 17, and "Hermeneutics," *IDBSup,* 402–407.

22. Brevard S. Childs, *Old Testament Theology in a Canonical Context* (Philadelphia: Fortress Press, 1985), 133–144. Hereafter, references to this work will be cited parenthetically in the text.

23. H. W. Frei, *The Eclipse of the Biblical Narrative* (New Haven: Yale University Press, 1974).

24. Gerald T. Sheppart, "True and False Prophecy within Scripture," in *Canon, Theology, and Old Testament Interpretation: Essays in Honor of Brevard S. Childs,* ed. Gene M. Tucker, David L. Petersen, and Robert R. Wilson (Philadelphia: Fortress Press, 1988), 262–282. Hereafter, references to this work will be cited parenthetically in the text.

25. See Robert R. Wilson, *Prophecy and Society in Ancient Israel* (Philadelphia: Fortress Press, 1980), 300, I. M. Lewis, *Ecstatic Religion* (Baltimore: Penguin Books, 1971), 122; and David Petersen, *The Roles of Israel's Prophets* (Sheffield: JSOT Press, 1981), 97.

26. Fish, *Is There a Text in this Class?: The Authority of Interpretative Communities* (Cambridge, Mass.: Harvard University Press, 1980), 367.

27. Paul B. Armstrong, "The Conflict of Interpretations and the Limits of Pluralism," *Profession,* special edition of *PMLA* 98 (1983): 349. See also Daniel Patte, *Ethics of Biblical Interpretation: A Reevaluation* (Louisville: Westminster John Knox Press, 1995).

28. E. Levinas, *Ethics and Infinity: Conversations with Philippe Nemo,* trans. Richard A. Cohen (Pittsburgh: Duquesne University Press, 1985), 2.

29. Rolf Knierim, "The Task of Old Testament Theology," *HBT* 6:1 (June 1984): 25–57, and "On the Task of Old Testament Theology: A Response to W. Harrelson, S. Towner, and R. E. Murphy," *HBT* 6:2 (December 1984): 91–128.

30. As this goes to press, a dissertation has just been completed by a Knierim student that attempts to address some of these questions about Knierim's claims of universality head-on. I have yet to see it and therefore cannot respond to his arguments here. See Wonil Kim, "Toward a Substance-Critical Task of Old Testament Theology" (Ph.D. diss., Claremont Graduate School, 1996).

31. For the phrase "transtribal validation," see John H. Yoder, "On Not Being Ashamed of the Gospel: Particularity, Pluralism, and Validation," *Faith and Philosophy* 9:3 (July 1992): 285–300.

32. Knierim, "The Task of Old Testament Theology," 25–27.

33. Foucault notes this danger in *Power/Knowledge: Selected Interviews and Other Writings, 1992–1977,* trans. and ed. Colin Gordon (New York: Pantheon Books, 1980), 1–36, 86–87.

34. Gerald L. Bruns, "The Hermeneutics of Midrash," in *The Book and the Text: The Bible and Literary Theory,* ed. Regina Schwartz (Cambridge, Mass.: Basil Blackwell, 1990), 203.; Bruns also notes that in the foreground of midrash, interpretation is inseparable from application to a situation that calls for action (the ethos of mythos!).

35. Simone Weil, "The Iliad, or the Poem of Force," in *Revisions: Changing Perspectives in Moral Philosophy,* ed. Stanley Hauerwas and Alasdair MacIntyre (Notre Dame: University of Notre Dame Press, 1983), 222–248.

36. Patricia Waugh's introduction in *Postmodernism: A Reader,* ed. Patricia Waugh (London: Edward Arnold of Hodder & Stoughton, 1992), 1.

37. James W. McClendon, Jr., *Doctrine,* vol. 2 of *Systematic Theology* (Nashville: Abingdon Press, 1993), 20.

38. F. E. Deist, *Witnesses to the Old Testament: Introducing Old Testament Textual Criticism,* Literature of the Old Testament no. 5 (Pretoria: NG Kerkboekhandel, 1988), 160–163.

39. What follows is an example of what Foucault calls creating a genealogy, something each period of history has done. In the case of the Enlightenment's version of history, it has become the standard account of how things "surely are."

40. For what follows, see also Stanley Hauerwas, *Truthfulness and Tragedy: Further Investigations in Christian Ethics* (Notre Dame: University of Notre Dame Press, 1977), 16–27.

41. For the complete argument, see ibid., 28–34, and Thomas Farrel, *Norms of Rhetorical Culture* (New Haven: Yale University Press, 1993).

42. Sanders, *God Has a Story Too.*

43. Hans Frei, in *The Eclipse of the Biblical Narrative,* notes the detour such a reading of the Bible took in the modern period. It has taken almost a quarter of a century since Frei for a setting that increasingly allows a narrative reading of the Bible that does not simply seek to "get behind" the story to the "real" history that matters. In truth, the Bible is an accumulation of stories and other material (see Sanders's review of Michael Fishbane's *The Garments of Torah: Essays in Biblical Hermeneutics,* in *TToday* 47 (January 1991): 433–435, for one example of the ongoing debate about the ingredient mix of the Bible, here between story and law). One can defend, at any rate, a narrative reading of the Bible. Indeed, Jack Miles's *God: A Biography* (New York: Knopf, 1995) is a shining example of just such a reading. See also Robert Alter, *The Art of Biblical Narrative* (New York: Basic Books, 1981).

44. Yale-educated Garrett Green (student of Hans Frei, George Lindbeck, and Brevard Childs), in his *Imagining God: Theology and Religious Imagination* (San Francisco: Harper & Row, 1989), maintains that the canon of Scripture provides the paradigm through which the faithful practice imagination (see esp. chap. 6). He identifies "as" as the "copula of imagination" (73, 137–145), not to be confused with the "as if" of older models of thinking that saw faith as contrary to fact. Thus, faithful people were asked to live "as if" life was different than it really was instead of living "as" life really is according to their construal. In other words, in an age of probable

reasoning, wherein all forms of knowledge are "construals" of reality "as it really is," one no longer needs to argue one's construal from an "as if" stance, any more than any other construal might need to do so in view of the alternatives presented to it. Such a stance is especially important in instances in which hegemonic assertions about life "as it really is" preclude alternative acts of imagination that argue for a different claim to life "as it really is."

Walter Brueggemann, in *Texts under Negotiation: The Bible and Postmodern Imagination* (Minneapolis: Fortress Press, 1993), 15, compares Green's work with David Bryant's *Faith and the Play of Imagination: On the Role of Imagination in Religion* (Macon, Ga.: Mercer University Press, 1989). Whereas Green proposes a more passive stance in imaginative encounter with Scripture, what he calls learning to "see as," Bryant offers a more active role in reading, arguing that we not only "see as" but also "take as" (compare Tracey's "hermeneutic of retrieval"). Such a reading means to lay claim on the text and to redefine the tradition, a task arguably central to canon formation and transmission. Green's approach is perhaps more receptive (deference to the text), whereas Bryant's is more constructive (deference to the reader). If these two approaches represent poles on a continuum, one might argue that Sanders' canonical imagination inclines more toward the former, my own toward the latter.

45. Sanders, "Canon (Hebrew Bible)," *ABD*, 1:843. In *God: A Biography*, Jack Miles manages to ignore historical-critical exegesis completely and in doing so tells the story of God as protagonist of the biblical story—an unabashed construct in which God's own self-concept and personality hinge on the whims and changes of the creatures created in God's image.

46. Brian Wicker, *The Story Shaped World: Fiction and Metaphysics* (Notre Dame: University of Notre Dame Press, 1975), 101. Meier Sternberg, *The Poetics of Biblical Narrative: Ideological Literature and the Drama of Reading* (Bloomington: Indiana University Press, 1987), suggests that a narrator unfolding a *historical* panorama must speak with the authority of omniscience. Whether by the novelistic tradition generally or under the ancient rules of storytelling specifically, the biblical narrator's world— whatever his or her stance vis-à-vis his or her world—boasts of an omnipotent agent (100, 153).

47. Hauerwas, *Truthfulness and Tragedy*, 31.

48. McClendon, *Ethics*, 45.

49. James W. McClendon, Jr., and James M. Smith, *Understanding Religious Convictions* (Notre Dame: University of Notre Dame Press, 1975), 118. Compare Sanders's claim in *Canon and Community*, 73, that to theologize is to read from three perspectives: honesty, humility, humor. This captures the notion advocated here by the principle of fallibility. My only argument with Sanders is that these are, in fact, ethical stances.

50. McClendon, *Ethics*, 353. This is not to suggest that such important factors as evidence, confessions, or claims based on scientific method are not critical when arguing one's truth claims. It is to suggest that such factors are secondary to the story-formed truthful character. On the formal arguments defending "character" as the principal category of all ethical definitions (based on Aristotle's notion of practiced wisdom and the apprenticeship model), see Stanley Hauerwas, *Community of Charac-*

ter: Toward a Constructive Christian Social Ethic (Notre Dame: University of Notre Dame Press, 1981), and Alasdair MacIntyre, *After Virtue,* 2d ed. (Notre Dame: University of Notre Dame Press, 1984).

51. McClendon, *Doctrine,* 28.

52. Foucault, *Power/Knowledge,* 1–36, 86–87.

53. Nicholas Lash, *Theology on the Way to Emmaus* (London: SCM Press, 1986), 10–17. Lash calls this iconoclastic stance an appropriate (Christian) fear of ideological self-deceit; to consent to God as GOD is to risk "the exposure of our own idolatries, self-serving beliefs and comfortable falsehoods."

54. Sanders, *God Has a Story Too,* 17.

55. Sanders, *From Sacred Story,* 99.

56. Foucault, *Power/Knowledge,* 141.

57. Robert P. Carroll, "Rebellion and Dissent in Ancient Israelite Society," *ZAW* 89 (1977): 176–204. For similar explanations of the rhetorical tour de force of the prophets, see John Barton, "History and Rhetoric in the Prophets," in *The Bible as Rhetoric: Studies in Biblical Persuasion and Credibility,* ed. Martin Warner (London: Routledge, 1990), 51–64, and J. L. Berquist, "Prophetic Legitimation in Jeremiah," *VT* 39 (1989): 129–139.

58. Gotthold Ephraim Lessing, *Lessing's Theological Writings,* trans. Henry Chadwick, A Library of Modern Religious Thought (Stanford: Stanford University Press, 1957), 53, 55.

59. Yoder, "On Not Being Ashamed of the Gospel," 285–300. Hereafter, references to this article will be cited parenthetically in the text. Whereas Yoder deliberates from a New Testament perspective, his comments are apropos in what follows in this context. To be sure, Yoder relies much more closely on the "assured results" of the historical-critical method than would a reader-response advocate using his insights as proposed here. See also Yoder, "'But Do We See Jesus?': The Particularity of Incarnation and the Universality of Truth," in *The Priestly Kingdom: Social Ethics as Gospel* (Notre Dame: University of Notre Dame Press, 1984), 46–62.

60. See Michael Fishbane's discussion based on E. Becker and O. Rank regarding the volatile nature of conflicting immortality systems, *Garments of Torah,* 130–131.

61. Yoder, *The Priestly Kingdom,* 47. The perceptive reader will note my use of both Gordon Kaufman, *In Face of Mystery* (earlier), and John Yoder in this work. The former is very much an advocate of seeking common-denominator language in public life; the latter, as we see here, very much opposed. Kaufman's belief in universality does conflict with Yoder's arguments for particularity of any universal claims. However, even those differences haven't stopped Kaufman from trying to argue for his particular normative construction of theology, or Yoder for his. I do not have to accept Kaufman's view of reality, or his belief in an empirically based universalism, or what his particular construction of theology finally looks like (which is too impersonal for me) to borrow his method of argumentation in a more modest attempt at persuading others to my own particular normative constructions which I hope will be accepted universally. Earlier, my use of Kaufman was limited to clarifying the ethical implications in Sanders's "monotheizing hermeneutic."

62. McClendon, *Doctrine,* 24.

63. See James W. McClendon, Jr., *Biography as Theology: How Life Stories Can Remake Today's Theology* (Nashville: Abingdon Press, 1974), James W. McClendon, Jr., and James M. Smith, *Understanding Religious Convictions* (Notre Dame: University of Notre Dame Press, 1975), and especially James W. McClendon, Jr., *Ethics,* vol. 1 of *Systematic Theology* (Nashville: Abingdon Press, 1991), 347–356.

64. This is an adaptation of Wittgenstein's concept of the "form of life," wherein what counts as good interpretation does not have with it the logic of a non-narrative validation. Gerald Bruns uses just this notion in describing the form of validation inherent in midrash. in "The Hermeneutics of Midrash," 203.

65. Hauerwas, *Truthfulness and Tragedy,* 31.

66. Summary statement by Gerald Bruns of Stanley Cavell in Cavell's *The Claim of Reason: Wittgenstein, Skepticism, Morality, and Tragedy* (New York: Oxford University Press, 1971), 3–36; see Bruns's reference, "The Hermeneutics of Midrash," 203.

67. Hauerwas, *The Community of Character,* 53. See also John H. Yoder, *Body Politics: Five Practices of the Christian Community before the Watching World* (Nashville: Discipleship Resources, 1989), esp. vi–xi, 72, and "The Christian Case for Democracy," in *The Priestly Kingdom,* 151–171.

68. Here one thinks of Charles Taylor's "mattering"; that what counts is what matters to people, what they choose to have matter, what they choose to have claim on their lives. See Charles Taylor, *Philosophical Papers,* vol. 1, *Human Agency and Language* (Cambridge: Harvard University Press, 1985), 97–114; see also Taylor, *Sources of the Self: The Making of the Modern Identity* (Cambridge: Harvard University Press, 1989), and the more recent *The Ethics of Authenticity* (Cambridge: Harvard University Press, 1992).

69. "If anyone can help me over it, let him do it, I beg him" (Lessing, *Lessing's Theological Writings,* 53, 55).

70. "Blindness" here is not a negative judgment per se. Early (nineteenth-century) claims for objectivity and neutrality were valid, given their context as seen now with hindsight. As Christopher Seitz has noted, "The whole gathering accumulation of possible religio-historical conclusions had yet to make its influence known. There was a rightful claim to neutrality that could emerge in the naive spirit of the day: the 'first naivete' of early historical-critical optimism." See Seitz, *Theology in Conflict: Reactions to Exile in the Book of Jeremiah* (New York: de Gruyter, 1989), 3.

71. Paul Armstrong, *Conflicting Readings: Variety and Validity in Interpretation* (Chapel Hill: University of North Carolina Press, 1990). Hereafter, references to this work will be cited parenthetically in the text.

72. Foucault, *Power/Knowledge,* 52. Armstrong classifies literary theorists who identify themselves closely with the politics of literature into three categories, all of which share the assumption that power is deeply implicated in the process of understanding. For summary and bibliography, see Armstrong, *Conflicting Readings,* 134, 181, nn. 1–3.

73. "This is what present convictions seem to be (on such and such evidence), this is what they appear to mean (for such and such reasons)" (McClendon, *Doctrine,* 24).

74. David Tracey, *Plurality and Ambiguity: Hermeneutics, Religion, and Hope* (San Francisco: Harper & Row, 1987), 90.

75. Ibid.

76. Berquist, "Prophetic Legitimation in Jeremiah," 129–139.

77. Fritjof Capra, *The Turning Point: Science, Society, and the Rising Culture* (Toronto: Bantam Books, 1982), 280–282.

78. Aaron Wildavsky, "Equity versus Hierarchy: A Speculation on the Survival of the Jewish People," in *The Nursing Father: Moses as a Political Leader* (University: University of Alabama Press, 1984), 217–233.

79. Ibid., 231.

80. Max Kadushin, *The Rabbinic Mind*, 3d ed. (New York: Bloch Publishing, 1972), x, 14–34.

81. W. V. Quine and J. S. Ullian, *The Web of Belief* (New York: Random House, 1979). A more accessible formulation of this model can be found near the conclusion of Quine's "Two Dogmas of Empiricism" in *From a Logical Point of View* (Cambridge Mass.: Harvard University Press, 1961). On centers and margins, see also Mary Douglas and Aaron Wildavsky's anthropological and sociological observations in *Risk and Culture* (Berkeley: University of California Press, 1982); Frank Kermode on literary centers and margins in "Institutional Control of Interpretation," in Kermode, *The Art of Telling* (Cambridge: Harvard University Press, 1983), 168–184; and Walter Brueggemann's use of the same for his comments on canonical interpretation in "Canonization and Contextualization," *Interpretation and Obedience: From Faithful Reading to Faithful Living* (Minneapolis: Fortress Press, 1991), 119–158.

82. For the full argument regarding this alternative, see Yoder, "The Hermeneutics of Peoplehood," in *The Priestly Kingdom,* 15–45, esp. 24–25.

83. Robert Carroll, "Rebellion and Dissent," 176–204. On rhetorical techniques of persuasion, see also Berquist, "Prophetic Legitimation in Jeremiah," 129–139.

84. Sanders, "Hermeneutics," *IDBSup,* 402–407, "Canonical Hermeneutics: True and False Prophecy," in *From Sacred Story,* 103, and *Torah and Canon,* 15–21.

In Old Testament studies, a number of scholars have suggested a similar bipolar understanding of Old Testament faith in order to move beyond the dominance of a single center. The variety of options, immediately suggests the pertinence of earlier arguments about the priority of reader over text and the constructive over the descriptive in much historical-critical work. Each would argue for an oscillating dynamic to be maintained between the two concepts, not resolving in either direction. Sanders's construction is here advocated for heuristic reasons, though I would not limit it to these two only, nor to the necessity of a bipolar over a multipolar model. Alternative options of bipolar constructs include Walter Brueggemann's several groups of two: his "structure of legitimation (hope)" and "embrace of pain (hurt)," in *Old Testament Theology: Essays on Structure, Theme, and Text* (Minneapolis: Fortress Press, 1992); "orientation and disorientation," in *The Message of Psalms,* Augsburg Old Testament Studies (Minneapolis: Augsburg Press, 1984); and "imagination" and "memory," in *David's Truth in Israel's Imagination and Memory* (Minneapolis: Fortress Press, 1985). Other bipolar models are Claus Westermann's "blessing and deliverance," in *What Does the Old Testament Say about God?* (Atlanta: John Knox Press, 1979) and *Elements of Old Testament Theology* (Atlanta: John Knox Press, 1982); Samuel Terrien's "aesthetic and ethical," in *The Elusive Presence,* Religious Perspectives. no. 26 (New York:

Harper & Row, 1978); and Paul D. Hanson's "cosmic and teleological," in *Dynamic Transcendence* (Philadelphia: Fortress Press, 1978).

85. Tracey, *Plurality and Ambiguity*, 114, calls for a not-too-dissimilar dialogue between a hermeneutics of "resistance" (prophetic critique?) and that of "hope" (constitutive support?). Compare Ricoeur's hermeneutics of suspicion as balanced by his more hopeful stance, what he calls the "second naïveté," the latter being a hermeneutical "wager" on the order of a "second Copernican revolution." See Paul Ricoeur, *The Symbolism of Evil*, trans. Emerson Buchanan (Boston: Beacon Press, 1967), 356–357.

86. On the advantage of external critique in community discernment, see Stephen Fowl and Gregory L. Jones, *Reading in Communion: Scripture and Ethics in Christian Life* (Grand Rapids: Eerdmans, 1991), 110–134.

87. See Brevard Childs, "The Old Testament as Scripture of the Church," *CTM* 43 (1972): 709–722, and Sheppard, "True and False Prophecy within Scripture," 262–282, esp. 276–277. On the suggested Persian proposal, see G. Widengren, "The Persian Period," in *Israelite and Judean History*, ed. J. H. Hayes and J. M. Miller (Philadelphia: Fortress Press, 1977), 514–523.

88. See Bruns, "The Hermeneutics of Midrash," 194, 196.

89. Sociological models have suggested parallels here to Israelite society during the period of the judges. Max Weber's descriptions of a "federation by oath" or a "regulated anarchy" comes to mind. More recently, Crusemand and Schafer have borrowed the phrase "segmentary society" from ethnology. The essential character of a "segmentary society" is the political equality of individual subgroups (clans, tribes) and the lack of a superior central authority. Temporary charismatic leaders provide stability, if only until new issues and concerns require new leaders. See R. Rendtorff's summary in *The Old Testament: An Introduction*, trans. John Bowden (Philadelphia: Fortress Press, 1986), 28. Also, Aaron Wildavksy's "moveable hierarchy" would fit such a model; see his "Equity versus Hierarchy," 231.

90. For what follows, I have related the insights of Yoder's "The Hermeneutics of Peoplehood," 28–41, with those of Sanders's "believing communities" in *Canon and Community*.

91. Yoder, "The Hermeneutics of Peoplehood," 29.

92. Joseph Blenkinsopp, *Prophecy and Canon: A Contribution to the Study of Jewish Origins* (Notre Dame: University of Notre Dame Press, 1977), 152.

93. Yoder, "The Hermeneutics of Peoplehood," 31.

94. Ibid.

95. Sanders, *Canon and Community*, 5.

96. What is here claimed in canonical terms has been stated by James McClendon as the beginning of ethical reflection for any church believing that the biblical story is the place to begin such deliberation. See McClendon, *Ethics*, 31, 32.

97. Hauerwas, *Community of Character*, 54.

98. For a full defense of "truth as manifestation," see Tracey (following Heidegger and Ricoeur), *Plurality and Ambiguity*, 28–30.

99. Yoder, "The Hermeneutics of Peoplehood," 41.

100. Robert P. Carroll, "A Non-cogent Argument in Jeremiah's Oracles," *ST* 30 (1976): 51.

Chapter 5

1. James A. Sanders, *From Sacred Story to Sacred Text* (Philadelphia: Fortress Press, 1987), x.

2. Claude F. Mariottini, "Joel 3:10 [H 4:10]: Beat Your Plowshares into Swords," *Pers* 14 (Summer 1987): 125–130.

3. See especially dissertations by students of Sanders which have begun to fill this void, including Merrill P. Miller, "Scripture and Parable: A Study of the Function of the Biblical Features in the Parable of the Wicked Husbandman and Their Place in the History of Tradition" (Ph.D. diss., Claremont Graduate School, 1974); Paul E. Dinter, "The Remnant of Israel and the Stone of Stumbling in Zion According to Paul (Romans 9–11)" (Ph.D. diss., Claremont Graduate School, 1979); William Miller, "Early Jewish and Christian Hermeneutic of Genesis 18:1–16 and 32:23–33" (Ph.D. diss., Claremont Graduate School, 1979); Mary H. Calloway, "Sing, Oh Barren One" (Ph.D. diss., Claremont Graduate School, 1979); Jane Schaberg, *The Father, the Son, and the Holy Spirit: The Triadic Phrase in Matthew 29:19b* (Chico, Calif.: Scholars Press, 1982); Sharon H. Ringe, "The Jubilee Proclamation in the Ministry and Teaching of Jesus: A Tradition-Critical Study in the Synoptic Gospels and Acts" (Ph.D. diss., Claremont Graduate School, 1980); Craig Evans, *To See and Not Perceive: Isaiah 6:9–10 in Early Jewish and Christian Interpretation, JSOTSup* 64 (Sheffield: JSOT Press, 1989); Marvin Sweeney, *Isaiah 1–4 and the Post-Exilic Understanding of the Isaianic Traditions,* BZAW no. 171 (Berlin: de Gruyter, 1983); Stephen Delamarter, "The Death of Josiah: Exegesis and Hermeneutics in Scripture and Tradition" (Ph.D. diss., Claremont Graduate School, 1990); David Carr, "Royal Ideology and the Technology of Faith: A Comparative Midrash Study of I Kings 3:2–15" (Ph.D. diss., Claremont Graduate School, 1988). See also Phyllis Trible, "Journey of a Metaphor," in *God and the Rhetoric of Sexuality* (Philadelphia: Fortress Press, 1978), 31–59, along with Michael Fishbane's *Biblical Interpretation in Ancient Israel* (Oxford: Clarendon Press, 1985).

4. G. Campbell Morgan, *The Minor Prophets* (N.J.: Fleming Revell, 1960); J. Ridderbos, *Isaiah,* trans. John Vriend, Bible Student's Commentary (Grand Rapids: Zondervan, 1985); E. Leslie, *Isaiah* (Nashville: Abingdon Press, 1963); G. Ernest Wright, *The Book of Isaiah,* Layman's Bible Commentary no. 11 (Richmond: John Knox Press, 1964).

5. Within this group, the opinions are even more divided. See especially the two following sections for a review of the historical-critical options.

6. Otto J. Baab, *The Theology of the Old Testament* (New York: Abingdon Press, 1949), 183; Douglas Stuart, *Hosea–Jonah,* WBC no. 31 (Waco, Tex.: Word Books, 1987), 269; G. Wade, *The Books of the Prophets Micah, Obadiah, Joel, and Jonah* (London: Methuen, 1925); J. D. W. Watts, *Isaiah 1–33,* WBC no. 24 (Waco, Tex.: Word Books, 1985), 28.

7. J. Hardee Kennedy, "Joel," in *The Broadman Commentary* (Nashville: Broadman Press, 1972), 78, calls it a "parody on Isa. 2:4." Hans Walter Wolff suggests the difference is ultimately explained by "irony" in *Joel and Amos: A Commentary on the Books of the Prophets Joel and Amos,* trans. Waldemar Janzen, S. Dean McBride, and

Charles Muenchow, Hermeneia (Philadelphia: Fortress Press, 1977), 14 and by "sarcasm" in "Swords into Plowshares: A Misuse of Biblical Prophecy?," *CTM* 12 (1985): 134.

8. John Calvin, *Commentaries on the Twelve Minor Prophets, 12: Joel, Amos, Obadiah,* trans. John Owen (reprint; Grand Rapids: Eerdmans, 1950), 127–128, explains the differences as being "figurative"; John Gough, *Minor Prophets* (Philadelphia: American Baptist Publication Society, 1935), 29–30, explains the difference by a "period of time" between the two traditions (that is, after the nations are annihilated, then they turn to God); David Hubbard, *Joel and Amos* (Downers Grove, Ill.: InterVarsity Press, 1989), suggests Joel is being "deliberately humorous"(!); Otto Kaiser, *Isaiah 1–12: A Commentary,* rev. ed., OTL (Philadelphia: Westminster Press, 1983), 55, explains the reversal in Joel as owing to the prophet's hatred of the Gentiles because of the suffering imposed on the Jews by them. He does not draw out hermeneutically the implications of such a statement. Claude F. Mariottini, "Joel 3:10," explains the difference historically.

9. Walter Brueggemann, "At the Mercy of Babylon: A Subversive Rereading of the Empire," *JBL* 110:1 (1991): 17. On the political dimension of all rhetoric, see Terry Eagleton, *Literary Theory: An Introduction* (Minneapolis: University of Minnesota Press, 1983), and Richard Harvey Brown, *Society as Text: Essays on Rhetoric, Reason, and Reality* (Chicago: Chicago University Press, 1987).

10. Ernest Becker, *The Denial of Death* (New York: Free Press, 1973); Otto Rank, *Truth and Reality: A Life History of the Human Will,* trans. Jessie Taft (New York: Knopf, 1936). See also Merold Westphal, *God, Guilt, and Death* (Bloomington: Indiana University Press, 1987), and John Donnelly, ed., *Language, Metaphysics, and Death* (New York: Fordham University Press, 1978), esp. 25–31, 69–87, 106–115, 216–227.

11. In his 1990 Presidential Address (n. 9, above), Brueggemann, following Schussler Fiorenza's own address to the society in which she observed that the guild's detached scienticism generally avoided all notion of public responsibility, challenged the society to take responsibility for "the spillover of the text into present social reality" (21); compare E. Schussler Fiorenza, "The Ethics of Interpretation: De-centering Biblical Scholarship," *JBL* 107 (1988): 3–17. This summons is inherent to the biblical canon as it has been described by M. Fishbane in his *remez* reading of Scripture, *Garments of Torah: Essays in Biblical Hermeneutics* (Bloomington: Indiana University Press, 1989), 116–118. In similar temper, the life and death responsibility intrinsic to the hermeneutical task is articulated well by Rolf Knierim in "The Task of Old Testament Theology: A Response to W. Harrelson, S. Towner, and R. E. Murphy," *HBT* 6:2 (December 1984).

12. Craig Evans and James A. Sanders, *Luke and Scripture* (Minneapolis: Fortress Press, 1993), 9.

13. Regina Schwartz argues that the Joseph story, for example, emerges out of a hermeneutic of "re-membering." Indeed, the whole Bible is similarly imperiled over and over. On this last point, she notes the lost book found amid the debris of the Temple (2 Kings) that called for a "re-membering hermeneutic" to emerge in "Joseph's Bones and the Resurrection of the Text: Remembering in the Bible," *PMLA* 103 (1988): 117.

14. Douglas Knight, *Rediscovering the Traditions of Israel: The Development of the Traditio-historical Research of the OT, with Special Consideration of Scandinavian Contributions* (Missoula, Mont.: Society of Biblical Literature Press), 202.

15. David J. Murray, "Gestalt Psychology," in *A History of Western Psychology* (Englewood Cliffs, N.J.: Prentice-Hall, 1983), 243–257.

16. Ibid., 243–244.

17. Wolfgang Iser, *The Act of Reading: A Theory of Aesthetic Response* (Baltimore: Johns Hopkins University Press, 1978), 119–120.

18. Wolfgang Iser, "The Reading Process: A Phenomenological Approach," *NLH* 3:2 (1972): 289.

19. Wolfgang Iser, *The Act of Reading*, 163.

20. Knight, *Rediscovering the Traditions*, 26–28.

21. Ibid., 28.

22. There are three general positions regarding the origin of the Zion tradition: (1) it is a continuation of traditions of the Jebusite city (H. Schmid, G. von Rad, J. Hayes, and many others); (2) it was created exclusively by the Davidic court (J. J. M. Roberts and R. Clements); and (3) it was a transfer of older (Shiloh-Ark) theology, already fused with Canaanite imagery, to a new locale and political context in Jerusalem (D. Eiler, drawing on O. Eissfeldt and M. Noth). For a brief survey of these options, see Ben C. Ollenburger, *Zion, the City of the Great King: A Theological Symbol of the Jerusalem Cult,* JSOTSup no. 41 (Sheffield: JSOT Press, 1987), 15–19.

23. Whereas Gerhard von Rad, "Die Stadt auf dem Berge," *EvT* 9 (1948/49): 439–447, and M. Noth, "Jerusalem und die israelitische Tradition," *OTS* 8 (1950): 28–46, provided the impetus for the discussion of the Zion tradition, it was von Rad's student E. Rohland who provided the specific designation "Zion tradition" and the list of features associated with it. See E. Rohland, "Die Bedeutung der Erwählungstraditionen Israels für die Eschatologie der alttestamentlichen Propheten" (diss. Heidelberg, 1956), 142; compare Ollenburger, *Zion,* 15, and the lists of J. J. M. Roberts, "The Davidic Origin of the Zion Tradition," *JBL* 92 (1973): 329–344, and R. E. Clements, *Isaiah and the Deliverance of Jerusalem,* JSOTSup no. 13 (Sheffield: JSOT Press, 1980), 72–89. The articles by G. von Rad and M. Noth can also be found in *Gesammelte Studien zum Alten Testament,* TBü no. 11 (Munich: Chr. Kaiser, 1958), 214–224 and 172–187, respectively.

24. Hans Wildberger adds this fifth motif to Rohland's four in his "Die Völkerwallfahrt zum Zion: Jes. II 1–5," *VT* 7 (1957): 62–81. This could be a combination of the pre-exilic motifs of pilgrimage to a shrine and that of the later pilgrimage of the nations to the king in Jerusalem (Ps. 72:8–11). Wildberger, basing his argument on Isaiah 2:2–4 (cf. Isa. 60–62 and Ps. 102), which he dates to the post-exilic period, suggests a later addition of this motif to the Zion complex. Compare Ollenburger, *Zion,* 18. See also Bertil Albrektson's overview of the Zion tradition, *Studies in the Text and Theology of the Book of Lamentations,* STL no. 21 (Lund: CWK Gleerup, 1963), 219–230, and R. J. Clifford, *The Cosmic Mountain in Canaan and the Old Testament,* HSM no. 4 (Cambridge Mass.: Harvard University Press, 1972), 131–160.

25. For a detailed discussion of the traditio-historical background and evaluation of the scholarly discussion related to the various theories about the birth and growth of the Zion tradition, see especially Ollenburger, *Zion,* 23–52.

26. Sigmund Mowinckel, *He That Cometh,* trans. B. W. Anderson (Oxford: Basil Blackwell, 1956). See also Mowinckel, "Jahves dag," *Norsk teologisk Tidskrif* 59 (1958): 1–56.

27. Gerhard von Rad, "The Origin of the Concept of the Day of Yahweh," *JSS* 4:2 (April 1959): 97–108.

28. F. C. Fensham, "A Possible Origin of the Concept of the 'Day of the Lord,'" *Biblical Essays* OTWSA 9 (1966): 90–97.

29. M. Weidd, "The Origin of the 'Day of the Lord'—Reconsidered," *HUCA* 37 (1966): 29–60.

30. Frank Moore Cross, Jr., *Canaanite Myth and Hebrew Epic: Essays in the History of the Religion of Israel* (Cambridge Mass.: Harvard University Press, 1973), argues from Israel's earliest poetry that the imagery of Yahweh as warrior and king was adopted very early from Canaanite mythology. See especially "The Divine Warrior," "The Song of the Sea and Canaanite Myth," and "Yahweh and Ba'l," in ibid., 91–194.

31. F. Schwally, *Der Heilige Krieg im alten Israel,* vol 1 (Leipzig: Deiterich, 1901), 59. Gerhard von Rad's *Der Heilige Krieg im alten Israel* (Göttingen: Vandenhoeck & Ruprecht, 1958), translated by Marva J. Dawn as *Holy War in Ancient Israel* (Grand Rapids: Eerdmans, 1991), quickly set the standard for all discussions of war in the Old Testament that followed. To place von Rad's classic in its historical context, see the excellent introduction by Ben Ollenburger to the English translation (1–33).

32. Schwally, *Der Heilige Krieg im alten Israel,* attributed this to "later Jewish historiography," which set the stage for the debate. See also Millard Lind, *Yahweh Is a Warrior: Theology of Warfare in Ancient Israel* (Scottdale, Pa.: Herald Press, 1980). Compare Patrick Miller, *The Divine Warrior in Early Israel* (Cambridge Mass.: Harvard University Press, 1973).

33. Hermann Gunkel, *Israelitisch Heldentum und Kriegesfrömmigkeit im Alten Testament* (Göttingen: Vandenhoeck & Ruprecht, 1916).

34. Ibid., 1, 25.

35. Lind, *Yahweh Is a Warrior.*

36. This is earliest date given by a now fleeting number of scholars for the book of Joel. See Wolff, *Joel and Amos,* 3.

37. I would argue for direct access. The question of authorship of the plowshare fragment is a thorny one. Among those who deny Isian authorship are K. Marti, *Das Buch Jesaja erklärt,* KHCAT no. 10 (Tübingen: Mohr, 1900), 27; G. B. Gray, *A Critical and Exegetical Commentary on the Book of Isaiah I through XXVII,* ICC (Edinburgh: T. & T. Clark, 1912), 43; Georg Fohrer, *Das Buch Jesaja,* ZBK (Zurich: Zwingli Verlag, 1960), 51; Johannes Lindblom, *Prophecy in Ancient Israel* (Philadelphia: Fortress Press, 1965), 390; and Ott Eissfeldt, *The Old Testament: An Introduction,* trans. Peter Ackroyd (San Francisco: Harper & Row, 1965), 318. A greater number of scholars, including more recent ones, attribute to Isaiah (early or late) this tradition, or at least find no reason not to: G. A. Smith, *The Book of Isaiah,* The Expositor's Bible, 2d ed. (London: Hodder & Stoughton, 1889) 1:25–27; B. Duhm, *Das Buch Jesaia* (Göttingen: Vandenhoeck & Ruprecht, 1922), 36; O. Proksch, *Jesaia I–XXXIX,* KAT (Leipzig: Deichert, 1930), 1:61–63; Oliver Rankin, *Israel's Wisdom Literature: Its Bearing on Theology and the History of Religion* (New York: Schocken

Books, 1969), 128; Fischer, *Das Buch Isaias übersetz und erklärt,* 2 vols., HSAT (Bonn: Hanstein, 1937–1939), 36; Edward Kissane, *The Book of Isaiah,* rev. ed. (Dublin: Browne & Nolan, 1960), 22; Gerhard von Rad, "The City on the Hill," in *The Problem of the Hexateuch,* 232–242 (originally published in German in *EvT* 8 [1948/49], 439–447); Wildberger, "Die Volkerwallfahrt zum Zion: Jes. II 1–5," 62–81, and *Isaiah 1–12* (Minneapolis: Fortress Press, 1991), 81–96 (original German, *Jesaja 1–12* [1972]); Hans Walter Wolff, "The Understanding of History in the Old Testament Prophets," *Essays on Old Testament Hermeneutics,* trans. K. R. Crim, ed. Claus Westermann (Richmond: John Knox Press, 1963) (original German in *EvT* 20 [1960]: 218–235); T. C. Vriezen, "Essentials of the Theology of Isaiah," in *An Outline of Old Testament Theology,* trans. S. Neuijen (Oxford: Basil Blackwell, 1958), 134, 144; J. Jensen, *The Use of tôrâ by Isaiah: His Debate with the Wisdom Tradition, CBQ* Monograph Series no. 3 (Washington, D.C.: Catholic Biblical Association of America, 1973), 84–85; Norman Gottwalt, *All the Kingdoms of the Earth: Israelite Prophecy and International Relations in the Ancient Near East* (New York: Harper & Row, 1964), 196; R. E. Clements, *Isaiah 1–39,* NCBC (Grand Rapids: Eerdmans, 1980); John H. Hayes and Stuart A. Irvine, *Isaiah: The Eighth-Century Prophet* (Nashville: Abingdon Press, 1987), 82–83; and John Oswalt, *The Book of Isaiah* (Grand Rapids: Eerdmans, 1986), 115. Clearly, any attempt to find a sure solution to the problem has proven elusive.

38. See Childs, *Introduction,* 316–325. For surveys of research on Isaiah 1–39, see J. Vermeylen, *Du prophète Isaïe a l'apocalyptique: Isaïe, i–xxxv, miroir d'un demimilleraire d'experience religieuse en Israel* (Paris: Loocoffre, 1977), 1–30. On Isaiah 56–66, see Otto Kaiser, *Introduction to the Old Testament: A Presentation of Its Results and Problems,* trans. John Sturdy (Minneapolis: Augsburg Press, 1975), 268–272.

39. For the various arguments for and against and a bibliography, see Sweeney, *Isaiah 1–4,* 135. The Masoretes also recognized a distinction between verses 2–4 and verse 5 in that they placed a *petuhah,* "open section," after verse 4, indicating a paragraph separation of greater importance than a "closed section," marked by a *setumah.*

40. Vermeylen, *Du Prophète Isaïe a l'apocalyptique,* 131. Verse 5 has been formed with verse 3 as its model: imperative verb, *waw*-consecutive, first person plural imperfect verbs. See Hans Wildberger, *Jesaja,* vol. 10/11 BKAZ (Netherlands: Neukirchener Verlag, 1972), 75–90, now available in English as *Isaiah 1–12,* trans. Thomas H. Trapp (Minneapolis: Fortress Press, 1991), 81–96; Kaiser, *Isaiah 1–12: A Commentary,* 24–36; Hayes and Irvine, *Isaiah: The Eighth-Century Prophet,* 82–83; and Adam S. Van der Woude, "Micah IV 1–5: An Instance of the Pseudo-Prophets Quoting Isaiah," *Symbolae Biblicae et Mesopotamicae Francisco Mario Theodoro de Liagre Boehl Dedicatae,* ed. M. A. Beek et al. (Leiden: Brill, 1973), 396–402.

41. Kaiser, *Isaiah 1–12: A Commentary,* 24. Wildberger, *Jesaja 1–12,* 78, labels it *Verheissungswort.*

42. Sweeney, *Isaiah 1–4,* 138.

43. Wildberger, *Jesaja 1–12,* 75, "Die Völkerwallfahrt zum Zion."

44. This study assumes the conclusions of David Carr regarding the redactional complexity of the book of Isaiah in "Reaching for Unity in Isaiah," *JSOT* 57 (1993):

61–80. As he rightly argues, no editor intervened deeply enough into the book to make it all conform to an overall conception: "As a result, the book of Isaiah displays the kind of fractured thematic and inter-textual unity that might be expected in a text whose authors/editors did not generally subsume the book's earlier parts into a larger whole" (78). In essence, Carr argues for the Book of Isaiah what is here argued for the canon as a whole: namely, that rather than subsuming or reorganizing the materials into their new redactional conception of the whole, the editors of Isaiah (and eventually the canon itself) allowed the early materials to stand over against the perspective implicit in their redactional additions. Thus, the Book of Isaiah, like the canon, suggests that there are limits to any search for structural or literary coherence in biblical texts (79) providing ample literary space for contradiction and intertextuality. As argued, this is to the Bible reader's epistemological advantage, and, perhaps, to the Bible's longevity.

45. For example, Marvin Sweeney believes this passage was not written until Jerusalem was reestablished as Yahweh's throne. His argument hinges on the close parallels between verse 31a of 2 Kings 19:31a and Isaiah 2:3b. He reasons backward from the argument that since "*most scholars* recognize that 2 Reg 19:29–31/Isa. 37:30–32 belongs to a legendary source . . . which dates to post-exilic times . . . *it must be concluded* that the text of Isa. 2:2–4 . . . *was known* in post-exilic times" (emphasis added). He then goes on to argue persuasively for a development from Deutero-Isaiah to Tritio-Isaiah and Zechariah, wherein Yahweh *sends* his Torah and justice to the nations (Isa. 51:4–6), to later texts in which the Torah goes forth but also *the nations come* to Zion seeking Yahweh (Isa. 56:6–8, 60:1–22; Hag. 2:7–9; Cech. 8:20–23(!), 2:14–16). Sweeney concludes that Isaiah 2:2–4 should be dated after Deutero-Isaiah, to the period of the return when Jerusalem was reestablished as Yahweh's home (*Isaiah 1–4,* 170–173).

Of course, it is an important hermeneutical step to argue from the possibility that a text "*was known*" by Zechariah and Deutero-Isaiah and that it therefore had to be written in the same period. This may or may not have been the case. It is equally possible to argue forward from the text having been written earlier (so Hayes et al.) and imperiled, as it were, after the Jerusalem debacle, regaining its functional usefulness in its current redaction and parallels in later prophets—all this after Cyrus's decree.

For purposes of this study, it is important to note again how a reader's initial assumptions can provoke historical reconstructions that exclude other possibilities. But, as we have suggested, the truth of this or that reconstruction is often as much a rhetorical coup d'etat dependent on the persuasive technique (that is, Sweeney's use of the phrase "most scholars recognize") of this or that reader as an objective historical "fact."

46. Alhough he would possibly defend only the Hezekian date of Isaiah 2:2–4, Seitz's observations otherwise support my suggestion here. See Christopher Seitz, "Isaiah 1–66: Making Sense of the Whole," in Seitz, ed., *Reading and Preaching the Book of Isaiah* (Philadelphia: Fortress Press, 1988), 121.

47. Peter R. Ackroyd and others have noted the existence of a major subsection in Isaiah 1–12 that functions as a synopsis of Isaiah's role with God's people from Uzziah

to Hezekiah. In these chapters, Isaiah is shown to be a prophet of judgment, though not entirely, for whom Zion theology was transformed and heightened. See Ackroyd, "Isaiah 1–12: The Presentation of a Prophet," in *Congress Volume: Gottingen 1977, VTSup* no. 29, ed. J. A. Emerton et al. (Leiden: Brill, 1978), 16–48.

Seitz has correctly pointed out, however, that within the cleansing judgments of the Syro-Ephraimite debacle (7–8) and the later (701) assault, the seeds of future hope and restoration are sown. He underscores the apparent direct contrast between the depiction of King Hezekiah and that of Ahaz by noting the formal parallels between chapters 36–37 and chapters 7–8: Hezekiah is the man of faith par excellence; Ahaz, his disobedient counterpart. See Seitz, "Isaiah, Book of (First Isaiah)," *ABD*, 3:482–483.

Hayes and Irvine, *Isaiah*, 382–383, argue that in actuality, Hezekiah showed less confidence in Isaiah's promises than had Ahaz (for example, paying Sennacherib tribute, 2 Kgs. 18:14–16). However, it seems in "popular tradition" that the outcome was nonetheless recalled as the result of divine deliverance. Of course, this conclusion depends on how one interprets the thorny insert regarding Hezekiah's capitulation to the Assyrians (2 Kgs. 18:14–16, "Account A"). For example, Seitz insists that the Isaiah narrative has priority over the account in Kings, interpreting the insert (Account A) as placed there by later Deuteronomistic hands to account for the fact that there was no absolute deliverance in 701 B.C.E., explained now by Hezekiah's sin and thus diminishing Hezekiah's earlier status as the greatest reformer (2 Kgs. 18:5) vis-à-vis the Deuteronomist's agenda to have Josiah be seen as the great reformer. See Seitz, "Isaiah, Book of (First Isaiah)," 483. Clearly, not only is the Deuteronomist's agenda noteworthy, but so also is the agenda of those reading and reconstructing the events around Hezekiah's reign. Whether later "popular tradition" made Hezekiah more noble than he actually was (Hayes), or later tradition diminished Hezekiah's popularity somewhat (Seitz), the prophetic plowshare oracle as understood by the historical Hezekiah or by the Isaianic tradition about Hezekiah might still be reconstructed in much the same fashion as proposed here.

48. For the historical context here described, see Hayes and Irvine, *Isaiah*, 42–46. Also see John Bright, *History of Israel*, 2d ed. (Philadelphia: Westminster Press, 1979), 267–277.

49. See Hayes and Irvine, *Isaiah*, 46–49, and Bright, *History of Israel*, 277–288.

50. Bright, *History of Israel*, 284; compare Brevard Childs, *Isaiah and the Assyrian Crisis* (London: SCM Press, 1967).

51. Here, I am recounting events based upon the Book of Isaiah, leaving aside the question of two attacks by Sennacherib, the earlier one in 701 B.C.E., the later one in ca. 688 B.C.E.; so Bright's reconstruction, *History of Israel*, 284–285.

52. Jensen, *The Use of tôrâ by Isaiah*, 89.

53. Millard Lind, "Perspectives on War and Peace in the Hebrew Scriptures," in *Monotheism, Power, Justice: Collected Old Testament Essays*, Text-Reader Series no. 3 (Elkhart, Ind.: Institute of Mennonite Studies, 1990), 175.

54. Jensen, *The Use of tôrâ by Isaiah*, 89f. On wisdom in Isaiah, see J. William Whedbee, *Isaiah and Wisdom* (Nashville: Abingdon Press, 1971).

55. J. Mauchline suggests that the two great deliverances that might provide the

setting for the vision of Isaiah 2:2–4, wherein the people of Judah were saved without the use of human military intervention, were the return of the exiled Jews by the decree of Cyrus and the deliverance of Jerusalem and the Temple from the Assyrians in 701 B.C.E.. Of course, for Mauchline, Isaiah would have written Isaiah 2:2–4 sometime after the miracle of 701 B.C.E., not as a prophetic challenge beforehand. See J. Mauchline, *Isaiah 1–39: Introduction and Commentary* (New York: Macmillan, 1962), 62f.

56. Hayes and Irvine, *Isaiah,* suggest Isaiah 2:2–4 was used as a prophetic challenge to the survivors of the massive earthquake in the days of Uzziah/Jereboam II. Isaiah attempted to cajole those who understood their survival as divine protection instead of seeing in the quake God's judgment into repentance by positing an ideal future in contrast to the pathetic now. Verse five then becomes the call to "walk in the way" thus described.

57. Seitz, "Isaiah, Book of (First Isaiah)," 483, suggests the paradigmatic influence of the contrast between Ahaz and Hezekiah for future generations of readers. I am relating his suggestion to the Josiah reformation as one possible step further along in the canonical process of this tradition-*Gestalt.*

58. Sanders, *Torah and Canon,* x.

59. Ibid., 31–53.

60. Blenkinsopp, *Prophecy and Canon,* 124.

61. Rolf Knierim, "The Vocation of Isaiah," *VT* 18:1 (1968): 47–68, suggests it was finally Isaiah's personal experience of the theophany in the Temple that provided the necessary motivation to actualize the old traditions. Similarly Abraham Heschel, *The Prophets: An Introduction* (New York: Harper & Row, 1962), ix, understands the prophet via his "consciousness." However, one criterion for including the prophets into the canon was their role as exhibits to the truth and defense of the Torah-Moses story (and its Deuteronomistic addendum = the Former Prophets); see Sanders, *Torah and Canon,* 54–90.

62. Mowinckel, "The 'Spirit' and the 'Word,'" 199–227.

63. Klaus Koch, *The Prophets: The Assyrian Period,* vol. 1, trans. Margaret Kohl (Philadelphia: Fortress Press, 1982), 150–153 (original German, *Die Propheten I: Assyrische Zeit* [Stuttgart: Verlag W. Kohlhammer GmbH, 1978]); compare Frederick Moriarity, "Word as Power in the Ancient Near East," in *A Light unto My Path: Old Testament Studies in Honor of Jacob M. Meyers,* ed. H. Bream, R. Heim, and C. Moore (Philadelphia: Temple University Press, 1974), 345–374.

64. Marvin Sweeney and others see this time as one of the major stages of formation of the Isaianic complex, most particularly the redactional layer he identifies in Isaiah 2–4. For what follows, see Sweeney, *Isaiah 1–4,* 192–202.

65. Ibid., 193, argues that the redaction of Isaiah 2–4, with its apparent contradictions of judgment and hope now juxtaposed, can be explained by "the two periods of history at whose crossroads this redaction stood." Looking back, it was now possible to see the cleansing effect that the Babylonian destruction had on the exiles. Looking forward, a time when the Jewish community would be reconstituted on Mount Zion could now be envisioned. Ironically, Hayes and Irvine, *Isaiah,* make practically this same argument from their pre-exilic reading: looking back to the earthquake and

forward to a reconstituted people in Zion (69–84). While a canonical reading has no problem with Sweeney's argument for such a redactional seam, it does not insist with him that Isaiah 2:2–4 be read over against so-called judgmental passages of Isaiah, as if to say Isaiah 2:2–4 could have ever been read only as a message of hope. Shown previously is how Isaiah 2:2–4 could very well have been read as a prophetic challenge (judgment?) against Ahaz and Hezekiah prior to this redaction. Of course, given its new vulnerable readership, a new hermeneutic was now employed. As will be shown later, Sweeney allows for a more nuanced reading of Isaiah 2:2–4 given a new reading context toward the end of the fifth century B.C.E.

66. For the full argument, see Sweeney, *Isaiah 1–4,* 102–133, 194–196.

67. On these rival factions, see Paul D. Hanson, *The Dawn of the Apocalyptic* (Philadelphia: Fortress Press, 1979), "Human Crisis," in *Old Testament Apocalyptic,* IBT (Nashville: Abingdon, 1987), 75–107, and "Apocalyptic Seers and Priests in Conflict, and the Development of the Visionary/Pragmatic Polarity," in *The Diversity of Scripture: A Theological Interpretation,* Overtures to Biblical Theology no. 11 (Philadelphia: Fortress Press, 1982), 37–62; and Morton Smith, *Palestinian Parties and Politics that Shaped the Old Testament* (London: SCM Press, 1971), 96–112.

68. Klaus Koch, "Ezra and the Origins of Judaism," *JSS* 19 (1974): 173–197.

69. Sweeney, *Isaiah 1–4,* 195.

70. Ibid., 195, 196.

71. Robert Carroll, *When Prophecy Failed: Cognitive Dissonance in the Prophetic Traditions of the Old Testament* (London: SCM Press, 1979) 150–156; L. Festinger, H. Riechen, and H. and S. Schachter, *When Prophecy Fails: A Social and Psychological Study of a Modern Group that Predicted the Destruction of the World* (New York: Harper & Row, 1956). The theory of cognitive dissonance suggests that the disappointment provided by the nonrealization of expectations results in explanations to overcome the dissonance felt as a result. Carroll, using the insights of Festinger et al. applies this theory to Third Isaiah; Sweeney argues for its use in the redaction (what I am calling the reading) of Isaiah 1–4.

72. Sweeney, *Isaiah 1–4,* 196.

73. Wolff, "Swords into Plowshares: Misuse of a Word of Prophecy?," 142.

74. Childs, *Introduction,* 431. Indeed, he notes this impasse in the strongest of terms, as "academic debris." See also K. Jeppesen, "New Aspects of Micah Research," *JSOT* 8 (1978): 3–32, and E. H. Scheffler, "Micah 4:1–5: An Impasse in Exegesis?," *OTE* 3 (1985): 46–61.

75. The differences between Isaiah 2:2–4, 5 and Micah 4:1–4, 5 are of two types: (1) several minor textual differences (e.g., word order) and (2) unlike Isaiah, Micah 4:1–3 continues with another verse: "And they shall sit, each under his vine and under his fig tree and there shall be no one to frighten [them] for the mouth of Yahweh Sebaot has spoken." Both conclude with somewhat different confessional statements (v. 5), the audience of whom will become important to the discussion that follows. See especially Wolff, *Micah,* 112–113.

76. All of the variations were debated from early on during the literary-critical phase of the study of prophecy. See the summary by John M. P. Smith in his *A Critical and Exegetical Commentary on Micah, Zephaniah, Nahum, Habakkuk, Obadiah, and*

Joel, ICC (New York: Scribner's, 1911), 83–89. A more recent survey of the options is succinctly outlined in E. Cannawurf, "The Authenticity of Micah 4:1–4," *VT* 13 (1963): 26–33. He favors the option of a later insertion made into both Micah and Isaiah. For representative defenses of the various options, see also Leslie Allen, *The Books of Joel, Obadiah, Jonah, and Micah,* NICOT (Grand Rapids: Eerdmans, 1976), 239–404, who argues for pre-exilic Isaiah as originator (243–244); D. Hillars, *Micah* (Philadelphia: Fortress Press, 1984), 4–8, 51–53, who sees this passage as pre-exilic (that is, by Micah, Isaiah, a contemporary, or someone earlier); and Hans Walter Wolff, *Micah: A Commentary,* trans. Gary Stansell (Minneapolis: Augsburg Press, 1990), 118 (original German, 1982), and J. L. Mays, *Micah,* OTL (Philadelphia: Westminster Press, 1976), 96, who argue for this being a "post-exilic psalm" (515 B.C.E.).

77. Van der Woude, "Micah in Dispute with the Pseudo-Prophets," 244–260, and "Micah IV 1–5: An Instance of the Pseudo-Prophets Quoting Isaiah," 396–402. Hereafter, citations will be noted parenthetically in the text.

78. Koch, *The Prophets,* 94; Heschel, *The Prophets,* 98.

79. Leslie Allen, citing A. F. Kirkpatrick (1918), *The Books of Joel,* 240.

80. E. Sellin, *Das Zwölfprophetenbuch*[2,3], KAT no. 12 (Leipzig, 1929), 332.

81. Micah 2:1–5, calamity; 2:6–11, calamity (opponents mentioned); 2:12–13, hope; 3, calamity; 4:1–5, hope; 4:6–8, hope; 4:9, hope; 4:10, calamity; 4:11–13, hope; 4:14–5:3, calamity; 5:4–5, hope.

82. Hans Walter Wolff, *Micah the Prophet,* trans. Ralph Gehrke (Philadelphia: Fortress Press, 1981), 85, (original German, *Mit Micha reden: Prophetie einst und jetzt* [1978]).

83. Van der Woude, "Micah in Dispute with the Pseudo-Prophets," 247, 249. H. Gunkel coined the term *Disputationswort,* which would be revised by others. See his "Die Propheten als Schriftsteller und Dichter," in H. Schmidt, *Die Größen Propheten,* SAT vol. 2, part 2, 2d ed., xxxiv–lxx. For an update on the use of terms and genre, see D. F. Murray, "The Rhetoric of Disputation: Re-examination of a Prophetic Genre," *JSOT* 38 (1987): 95–121.

84. Brevard Childs states in redactional language what Van der Woude is here describing as possible in a specific "original" context. Childs argues for "mutual influence among a common circle" of redactors/editors of the traditions of Isaiah and Micah in and around Jerusalem from seventh century to the early post-exilic period in *Introduction,* 434–436.

85 The phrase is nowhere used by Micah. See Van der Woude, "Micah IV 1–5" 401. For a survey of the usage and suggested meanings of "Yahweh of hosts," see James Crenshaw, "Yahweh Sᶜba'ot Sᶜmo: A Form Critical Analysis," *ZAW* 81 (1969): 167–175.

86. Wolff, *Micah,* 117, 76–79.

87. Willem W. Prinsloo, *The Theology of the Book of Joel,* BZAW no. 163 (Berlin: De Gruyter, 1985), 123, is a notable exception, seeing the book instead as a series of nine pericopes, each representing a *Steigerung* on its precursor.

88. However, there is no real consensus about the unity of the book. B. Duhm, "Anmerkungun zu den Zwölf Propheten," *ZAW* 31 (1911): 1–43, 184–187, sees the

earlier section as a collection of early prophetic poetry, the second section as that of a later prose hand of an apocalyptic preacher in a Maccabean synagogue. Arvid Kapelrud, *Joel Studies* (Uppsala: A. B. Lundquistska Bokhandeln, 1948), sees the book as a unity whose two sections are divided liturgically between a lament (including a ritual of repentance) and an oracle of absolution/vindication. Hans Walter Wolff, *Joel and Amos*, 6–12, also defends Joel's unity, though divided in a literary symmetry rather than by liturgical performance.

89. Theodore Hiebert, "The Book of Joel," *ABD*, 3:875; Hanson, *The Dawn of the Apocalyptic*, 123–134.

90. So Wolff, *Joel and Amos*, 74; compare Gerhard von Rad, *Old Testament Theology* vol. 2 (New York: Harper & Row, 1965), 124, n. 39.

91. Sweeney, *Isaiah 1–4*, 169.

92 Amos 1:2 = Joel 4:16 [Eng. 3:16]; 9:13 = 4:18 [Eng. 3:18]; Isaiah 13:6 = Joel 1:15; 13:10 = 2:10; 45:5, 6, 18, 21 = 2:27; 51:3 = 2:3; 52:1 = 4:17 [Eng. 3:17]; 63:3 = 4:13 [Eng. 3:13]; 66:18 = 4:2 [Eng. 3:2]; Jeremiah 30:3; 33:15; 50:4, 20 = Joel 4:1 [Eng. 3:1]; Zephaniah 1:7 = Joel 1:15; 1:14–15 = 2:2; 1:16 = 2:1; Ezekiel 30:2–3 = Joel 1:15; 32:7 = 2:10, 3:4 [Eng. 2:31]; 36:11 = 4:17 [Eng. 3:17]; 36:35 = 2:3; 39:29 = 3:1 [Eng. 2:28]; 47:1–12 = 4:18 [Eng. 3:18]; Nahum 2:11 [Eng. 2:10] = Joel 2:6; Jonah 3:9 = Joel 2:14; 4:2 = 2:13; Malachi 3:2 = Joel 2:11; 3:23 [Eng. 4:5] = 2:11, 3:4 [2:31]; Zechariah 14:2 = Joel 4:2 [Eng. 3:2]; 14:8 = 4:18 [Eng. 3:18]; Obadiah 10 = Joel 4:19 [Eng. 3:19]; 11 = 4:3 [Eng. 3:3]; 15 = 1:15, 4:4 [Eng. 3:4]; 17 = 3:5 [Eng. 2:32]. See Mariottini, "Joel 3:10 [H4:10]," 126, and Wolff, *Joel and Amos*, 76.

93. This assumes Joel to be post-exilic.

94. Prinsloo, *Theology of Joel*, 5.

95. Allen, *The Books of Joel*, 19–25; Mariottini, "Joel 3:10 [H 4:10]," 125; Wolff, *Joel and Amos*, 6.

96. According to Allen, *The Books of Joel*, 19, K. A. Credner, *Der Prophet Joel*, 40–52, offered the definitive ninth-century argument supported by Ewald, Pusey, Keil, and von Orelli.

97. Kapelrud, *Joel*, 190, argued for a later pre-exilic date, seeing Joel as a younger contemporary of Jeremiah, and Koch, *The Prophets*, 159–161, using as his primary criteria the expression "Day of Yahweh" (also in Amos and Obadiah and Isaiah and not in post-exilic prophets), assigns Joel to the late Assyrian period just as its power began to break up (612 B.C.E.).

98. Prinsloo, *Theology of Joel*, 126–127.

99. Von Rad, *The Message of the Prophets*, 259–263. The theme of eschatalogical pilgrimage of the nations to Zion is also found several times in the apocryphal literature: Tobit 13:9–73, 14:5–7; Enoch 90:28–33; Syb. Or. 3:703–731.

100. This was perhaps in the disappointing days sometime after the Temple was rebuilt and the optimistic prophecies of Ezekiel, Second Isaiah, and Zechariah were not yet in sight.

101. Hiebert, "The Book of Joel," 877.

102. Wolff, *Joel and Amos*, 6.

103. The five levels described were (1) intertextuality and reality, (2) intertextuality

and syntax, (3) intertextuality and context, (4) intertextuality and process, and (5) intertextuality and the reader.

104. One is especially aware of the apocalyptic scenarios of a war to end all wars, not least of which found their way into Qumran ("war of the sons of light against the sons of darkness") and even into the New Testament (Rev. 12, 19), though there, certainly the Word of the Lamb takes on a much more powerful role once again as the sole weapon of God.

105. Fishbane, *Garments of Torah,* 127.

106. Ibid., 131. "Concordant" in that all these views are contained in the Bible; "discord[ant]" because these are exclusivist views of sacrality.

107. Sanders, "Intertextuality and Dialogue," *Explorations* 7:2 (1993) 4.

108. This intertextual dialogue begins in the opening chapters of the biblical canon in the two disparate creation stories. The one story focuses on God's transcendence as Creator, who, not incidentally, creates with the Word (shades of Isaiah). The other story narrates a more intimate portrayal of God as Redeemer walking in the garden, tailoring clothing for the fallen Adam and Eve.

109 Fishbane, *Garments of Torah,* 131–132, has described the Hebrew Bible in these terms. The Bible is critical of the potential and dangers of human symbolic systems of any kind, and so "relativizes the idols of the human *textus* for the sake of the divine *textus*"; compare J. Sanders's "monotheizing hermeneutic."

Chapter 6

1. Paul B. Armstrong, *Conflicting Readings: Variety and Validity in Interpretation* (Chapel Hill: University of North Carolina Press, 1990), 151.

2. James A. Sanders, "Intertextuality and Dialogue," *Explorations* 7:2 (1993): 4, recounts the debate between James Kugel in "Biblical Studies and Jewish Studies," *Association for Jewish Studies Newsletter* 36 (Fall 1986): 22, and J. D. Levenson in "Theological Consensus or Historicist Evasion?: Jews and Christians in Biblical Studies," in *Hebrew Bible or Old Testament?: Studying the Bible in Judaism and Christianity,* ed. Roger Brooks and John J. Collins (Notre Dame: University of Notre Dame Press, 1990), 109–145.

3. Larry Stammer, "Meeting of World Religions Leads to Ethics Rules," *Los Angeles Times,* 5 September 1993, A1, A31.

4. Jürgen Moltmann, "Political Discipleship of Christians Today," in *Communities of Faith and Radical Discipleship: Jürgen Moltmann and Others,* ed. G. McLeod Bryan (Macon, Ga.: Mercer University Press, 1986), 31.

5. In this vein, whether one fully agrees with him or not, Stanley Fish has provocatively restated his earlier theses about the centrality of the community of interpretation in meaning production in *There's No Such Thing as Free Speech . . . And It's a Good Thing Too* (Oxford: Oxford University Press, 1994).

6. Jacques Ellul, *Anarchy and Christianity,* trans. Geoffrey W. Bromiley (Grand Rapids: Eerdmans, 1991), tries to correct this great misunderstanding by linking the Church to anarchy where anarchy is described as "the nonviolent repudiation of

authority." See also Vernard Eller, *Christian Anarchy: Jesus' Primacy over the Powers* (Grand Rapids: Eerdmans, 1987). Emmanuel Levinas, *Ethics and Infinity: Conversations with Philipp-Nemo* (Pittsburgh: Duquesne University Press, 1985), describes ethics appropriately as an "an-archy" (10).

7. Millard Lind, "Reflections on Biblical Hermeneutics," in *Kingdom, Cross, and Community,* ed. J. R. Burkholder and Cal Redekop (Scottdale, Pa.: Herald Press, 1976), 93.

8. Daniel Liechty, *Theology in Postliberal Perspective* (Philadelphia: Trinity Press International, 1990), ix.

9. Walter Klaassen, *Anabaptism: Neither Catholic nor Protestant* (Waterloo, Ont.: Conrad Grebel Press, 1973).

10. Liechty, *Theology in Postliberal Perspective,* 63.

11. Ethics, according to Levinas, *Ethics and Infinity,* occurs "prior" to essence and being, conditioning them. Ethics is pure function, that is, the "compassion of being" (10). The ethical *relation* is of paramount concern against what he calls an inferior "onto-theo-logy" (8). The task of ethics as a function is to unsettle all "essences." Thus, survival or personal identity are relative to the conditioning of ethics, which for Levinas means the performance of "lovingkindness" as determined by face-to-face encounters (the "irreducible relation") (2, 11).

12. Stammer "Meeting of World Religions Leads to Ethics Rules."

13. See the discussion between Trutz Rendtorff and Dorothee Soelle reported in *Der Spiegel* 37:41 (10 October 1983), wherein Rendtorff argues using Joel against the pacifist Soelle's quotation of Isaiah. Also see the interesting debate between H. W. Wolff and Wolfhart Pannenburg captured in Wolff's response in "Swords into Plowshares: A Misuse of Biblical Prophecy?," *CTM* 12 (1985): 133–143, and Pannenburg's "Schwerter zu Pflugscharen—Beduetung und Missbrauch eines Prophetensortes," in the official newsletter of the German labor movement, "Securing the Peace" (March 1983).

14. Here, I insist with Brevard Childs, *Biblical Theology of the Old and New Testaments: Theological Reflection on the Christian Bible* (Minneapolis: Fortress Press, 1993), on the centrality of Christ as the norm over against all other cultural criteria in arguing for a fully *biblical* theology (721). His desire that any such "construal of a symbol system in which the fictive world of the reader is invited to participate" must stand *subject to* "the entrance of God's word into our world of time and space" (721) lingers still, so it would seem, at Lessing's "ditch." In fact, such a construal need not be embarrassed by the "trap of transforming the theocentric center of scripture into anthropology" (723), since an anthropological theology is the best that we can ever hope for. Hence, his (and my own) community's "construal of a symbol system" wherein God is said to enter time and space in Christ can only be, perhaps to Childs's chagrin, moored in (an ecclesial) community. What remains is for him to argue for that construal against the alternatives. Indeed, that he does just that in the profound closing confession of his biblical theology (725–726), in no way argues against the truth that his confession is, in the last analysis, a "witness" to his own community or communities of interpretation.

15. C. Norman Kraus, *Jesus Christ Our Lord: Christology from a Disciple's Perspective*

(Scottdale, Pa.: Herald Press, 1987), 17. Kraus offers the best "systematic" theology from an Anabaptist perspective to date.

16. Liechty, *Theology in Postliberal Perspective,* 100.

17. Gerhard Lohfink, "'Schwerten zu Pflugscharen': Die Rezeption von Jes 2:1–5 par Mi 4:1–5 in der Alten Kirche und im Neuen Testament," *Theologische Quartaschrift* 166 (1968): 184–209.

18. C. Norman Kraus, *Jesus Christ Our Lord,* 17.

19. Von Rad, *The Message of the Prophets* (New York: Harper & Row, 1965), 231, 232.

20. It is of interest to note how often John's battle visions are fought using power emanating from the mouth (1:16, 2:12, 16, 11:5, 12, 19:13, 15, 21) against blasphemous utterings (13:5–30).

21. Bernhard W. Anderson, ed., *Creation in the Old Testament,* Issues in Religion and Theology no. 6 (Philadelphia: Fortress Press, 1984).

22. A careful reading of Genesis 11 placed in its present context (cf. Gen. 1:28, 9:1, 10:1–32) reveals at the very least the importance of language as a peculiarly consequential human activity. It also sets the stage for the *relecture* of the tradition regarding the possibility of new language community still to come (Acts 2). See Walter Brueggemann, *Genesis: A Bible Commentary for Preaching and Teaching,* Interpretation (Atlanta: John Knox Press, 1982), 97–104.

23. For a wonderful history of traditions on the concept of an "original language," see, Umberto Eco, *The Search for the Perfect Language,* trans. James Fentress (Oxford: Basil Blackwell), 1995.

24. Fishbane, *The Garments of Torah,* 131.

25. Poem by Barbara Metzler, 1982; read to my congregation Pasadena Mennonite Church, Pasadena, California, in 1987.

Bibliography

Abrams, M. H. "The Deconstructive Angel." *CI* 3:3 (Spring 1977): 425–438.

———. *A Glossary of Literary Terms*. 5th ed. New York: Holt, Rinehart and Winston, 1985.

———. *The Mirror and the Lamp: Romantic Theory and Critical Tradition*. New York: Oxford University Press, 1953.

———. "Modern Theories of Literature and Criticism." In *A Glossary of Literary Terms*. 5th ed. New York: Holt, Rinehart, and Winston, 1985.

Ackroyd, Peter R. "Isaiah 1–12: The Presentation of a Prophet." In *Congress Volume: Gottingen 1977, VTSUP* 29, ed. J. A. Emerton et al. Leiden: Brill, 1978.

———. "The Open Canon." *Colloquium: The Australian and New Zealand Theological Review* 3 (May 1970): 286.

Ackroyd, Peter R., and C. F. Evans, eds. *The Cambridge History of the Bible: From the Beginnings to Jerome*. Vol. 1. Cambridge: Cambridge University Press, 1970.

Adams, Hazard. "Canons: Literary Criteria/Power Criteria," *CI* 14 (Summer 1988): 748–764.

Albrektson, Bertil. *Studies in the Text and Theology of the Book of Lamentations*. STL no. 21. Lund: CWK Gleerup, 1963.

Allen, Leslie. *The Books of Joel, Obadiah, Jonah, and Micah*. NICOT. Grand Rapids: Eerdmans, 1976.

Alter, Robert. *The Art of Biblical Narrative*. New York: Basic Books, 1981.

———. "A Literary Approach to the Bible." *Commentary* 60 (December 1975): 70–77.

———. *The World of Biblical Literature*. New York: Basic Books, 1992.

Alter, Robert, and Frank Kermode, eds. *The Literary Guide to the Bible*. Cambridge, Mass.: Harvard University Press, 1987.

Althusser, Louis. "Ideology and Ideological State Apparatuses." In *Lenin and Philosophy*. New York: Monthly Review Press, 1971.

Altieri, Charles. *Canons and Consequences: The Ethical Force of Imaginative Ideals*. Evanston, Ill.: Northwestern University Press, 1990.

Anderson, Bernhard W. "Crisis in Biblical Theology." *TToday* 28 (1971): 321–327.

———, ed. *Creation in the Old Testament*. Issues in Religion and Theology no. 6. Philadelphia: Fortress Press, 1984.

Archer, Gleason. *Encyclopedia of Bible Difficulties*. Grand Rapids: Zondervan, 1982.

Armstrong, Paul B. *Conflicting Readings: Variety and Validity in Interpretation*. Chapel Hill: University of North Carolina Press, 1990.

———. "The Conflict of Interpretations and the Limits of Pluralism." *Profession*, Special Edition of *PMLA* 98 (1983): 349.

Aune, David E. *Prophecy in Early Christianity and the Ancient Mediterranean World*. Grand Rapids: Eerdmans, 1983.

Baab, Otto J. *The Theology of the Old Testament*. New York: Abingdon Press, 1949.

Bailie, Gil. *Violence Unveiled: Humanity at the Crossroads*. New York: Crossroad, 1995.

Baker, Houston A., Jr., ed. *Reading Black: Essays in the Criticism of African, Caribean, and Black American Literature*. Chicago: University of Chicago Press, 1976.

Bakhtin, M. M. "Discourse in the Novel." In *The Dialogic Imagination:Four Essays.*, trans. and ed. Michael Holquist. Austin: University of Texas Press, 1981.

Bal, Mieke. "The Bible as Literature: A Critical Escape." *Diacritics 16:4 (1986): 71–79*.

———. *Death and Dissymmetry: The Politics of Coherence in the Book of Judges*. Chicago: University of Chicago Press, 1988.

Baltzell, E. Digby, Amitai Etzioni, Lewis S. Feuer, Irving L. Horowitz, Dorothy Ross, Warren J. Samuels, Thomas Sowell, and Aaron Wildavsky. *Cracking the Cultural Consensus,* special edition of *Society* 29:1 (November/December 1991): 5–44.

Barr, James. *The Bible in the Modern World*. London: SCM Press, 1973.

———. "Childs' Introduction to the Old Testament as Scripture." *JSOT* 16 (1980): 12–23.

———. *Holy Scripture: Canon, Authority, Criticism*. Philadelphia: Westminster Press, 1983.

———. *Old and New in Interpretation*. New York: Harper & Row, 1966.

———. "Reading the Bible as Literature." *BJRL* 56 (1973): 10–33.

———. *The Scope and Authority of the Bible*. Philadelphia: Westminster Press, 1981.

———. *The Semantics of Biblical Language*. London: Oxford University Press, 1961.

Barthes, Roland. *Elements of Semiology*. Trans. Annette Lavers and Colin Smith. London: Cape, 1967.

———. *Image, Music, Text*. New York: Hill and Wang, 1977.

Barton, John. "Classifying Biblical Criticism." *JSOT* 29 (1984): 25–28.

———. "History and Rhetoric in the Prophets." In *The Bible as Rhetoric: Studies in Biblical Persuasion and Credibility,* ed. Martin Warner. London: Routledge, 1990.

———. *Reading the Old Testament: Method in Biblical Study*. London: Darton, Longman and Todd, 1984.

Becker, Ernest. *The Denial of Death*. New York: Free Press, 1973.

Beckwith, Roger. *The Old Testament Canon of the New Testament Church.* Grand Rapids: Eerdmans, 1985.

Benavides, Gustavo. "Religious Articulations of Power." In *Religion and Political Power,* ed. Gustavo Benavides and M. W. Daly. New York: State University of New York Press, 1989.

Bennett, William. *To Reclaim a Legacy: A Report on the Humanities in Higher Education.* Washington, D.C.: National Endowment for the Humanities, 1984.

Berquist, J. L. "Prophetic Legitimation in Jeremiah." *VT* 39 (1989): 129–139.

Bic, M. Review of *Prophetic Conflict: Its Effect upon Israelite Religion,* by James Crenshaw. In *ThLZ* 97 (1972): 653–656.

Bleich, David. "The Subjective Paradigm in Science, Psychology, and Criticism." *NLH* 7 (1976): 313–334.

Blenkinsopp, Joseph. *Prophecy and Canon: A Contribution to the Study of Jewish Origins.* Notre Dame: University of Notre Dame Press, 1977.

Bloch, Renée. "Midrash," *IDBSup 5,* cols. 1263–1280. "Midrash," trans. Mary Howard, in *Approaches to Ancient Judaism: Theory and Practice,* ed. William S. Green. Brown Judaic Studies no. 1. Missoula, Mont.: Scholars Press, 1978.

Bloom, Allan. *The Closing of the American Mind.* New York: Simon & Schuster, 1987.

Bloom, Harold. *The Western Canon: The Books and School of the Ages.* New York: Harcourt Brace, 1994.

Boyarin, Daniel. *Intertextuality and the Reading of Midrash.* Bloomington: Indiana University Press, 1990.

Bright, John. *The Authority of the Old Testament.* Nashville: Abingdon Press, 1967.

———. *History of Israel.* 2d ed. Philadelphia: Westminster Press, 1979.

———. *The Authority of the Old Testament.* Nashville: Abingdon Press, 1967.

Brown, Richard Harvey. *Society as Text: Essays on Rhetoric, Reason, and Reality.* Chicago: Chicago University Press, 1987.

Brown, Schuyler. "Reader Response: Demythologizing the Text." *NTS* 34 (1988): 232–237.

Brueggemann, Walter. "At the Mercy of Babylon: A Subversive Rereading of the Empire." *JBL* 110:1 (1991): 17.

———. "Canonization and Contextualization." In *Interpretation and Obedience: From Faithful Reading to Faithful Living.* Minneapolis: Fortress Press, 1991.

———. *David's Truth in Israel's Imagination and Memory.* Minneapolis: Fortress Press, 1985.

———. *Genesis: A Bible Commentary for Preaching and Teaching.* Interpretation. Atlanta: John Knox Press, 1982.

———. *The Message of Psalms.* Augsburg Old Testament Studies. Minneapolis: Augsburg Press, 1984.

———. *Old Testament Theology: Essays on Structure, Theme, and Text.* Minneapolis: Fortress Press, 1992.

———. Review of *Prophetic Conflict: Its Effect upon Israelite Religion,* by James Crenshaw. In *Int* (1973): 220–221.

———. *Texts under Negotiation: The Bible and Postmodern Imagination.* Minneapolis: Fortress Press, 1993.

Bruns, Gerald L. "Canon and Power in the Hebrew Scriptures." *CI* 10:3 (March 1984): 462–480.

———. "The Hermeneutics of Midrash." In *The Book and the Text: The Bible and Literary Theory,* ed. Regina Schwartz. Cambridge, Mass.: Basil Blackwell, 1990.

———. "Midrash and Allegory." In *The Literary Guide to the Bible,* ed. Frank Kermode and Robert Alter. Cambridge, Mass. Belnap Press of Harvard University Press, 1987.

Bryant, David. *Faith and the Play of Imagination: On the Role of Imagination in Religion.* Macon, GA: Mercer University Press, 1989.

Buber, M. "Falsche Propheten." *Die Wandlung* 2 (1947): 279.

Calloway, Mary H. "Sing, Oh Barren One." Ph.D. diss., Claremont Graduate School, 1979.

Calvin, John. *Commentaries on the Twelve Minor Prophets, 12: Joel, Amos, Obadiah.* Trans. John Owen. Reprint. Grand Rapids: Eerdmans, 1950.

Cannawurf, E. "The Authenticity of Micah 4:1–4." *VT* 13 (1963): 26–33.

Capra, Fritjof. *The Turning Point: Science, Society, and the Rising Culture.* Toronto: Bantam Books, 1982.

Carr, David. "Reaching for Unity in Isaiah." *JSOT* 57 (1993): 61–80.

———. "Royal Ideology and the Technology of Faith: A Comparative Midrash Study of I Kings 3: 2–15." Ph.D. diss., Claremont Graduate School, 1988.

Carroll, Robert P. *From Chaos to Covenant.* New York: Crossroad, 1981.

———. "A Non-cogent Argument in Jeremiah's Oracles." *ST* 30 (1976): 51.

———. "Rebellion and Dissent in Ancient Israelite Society." *ZAW* 89 (1977): 176–204.

———. *When Prophecy Failed: Cognitive Dissonance in the Prophetic Traditions of the Old Testament.* London: SCM Press, 1979.

Cavell, Stanley. *The Claim of Reason: Wittgenstein, Skepticism, Morality, and Tragedy.* New York: Oxford University Press, 1971.

Childs, Brevard S. *Biblical Theology in Crisis.* Philadelphia: Westminster Press, 1970.

———. *Biblical Theology of the Old and New Testaments: Theological Reflection on the Christian Bible.* Minneapolis: Fortress Press, 1993.

———. *The Book of Exodus.* London: SCM Press. 1974.

———. *Introduction to the Old Testament as Scripture.* Philadelphia: Fortress Press, 1979.

———. *Isaiah and the Assyrian Crisis.* London: SCM Press, 1967.

———. "The Old Testament as Scripture of the Church." *CTM* 43 (1972): 709–722.

———. *Old Testament Theology in a Canonical Context.* Philadelphia: Fortress Press, 1985.

———. "A Response [to James Mays, James Sanders, Bruce Birch, David Polk and Douglas Knight]." *HBT* 2 (1980): 204.

———. Review of *Torah and Canon. Int* 27:1 (January 1973): 88–91.

———. "The Old Testament as Scripture of the Church." *CTM* 43 (1972): 709–722.

Chomsky, Noam. *Language and Mind.* New York: Harcourt Brace Jovanovich, 1972.

Chopp, Rebecca. *The Praxis of Suffering.* Maryknoll, N.Y.: Orbis Books, 1986.

Clements, R. E. *Isaiah and the Deliverance of Jerusalem. JSOTSup* 13. Sheffield: JSOT Press, 1980.

———. *Isaiah 1–39*. NCBC. Grand Rapids: Eerdmans, 1980.

Clifford, R. J. *The Cosmic Mountain in Canaan and the Old Testament.* HSM no. 4. Cambridge Mass.: Harvard University Press, 1972.

Clines, David. *What Does Eve Do to Help? and Other Readerly Questions. JSOTSup* 94. Sheffield: JSOT Press, 1990.

Cohen, Martin. "The Prophets as Revolutionaries." *BAR* 5:3 (1979): 12–19.

Conrad, Edgar W. "Changing Context: The Bible and the Study of Religion." In *Perspectives on Language and Text: Essays in Honor of Francis I. Andersen's Sixtieth Birthday, July 28, 1985,* ed. E. W. Conrad and E. G. Newing. Winona Lake, Ind.: Eisenbrauns, 1987.

Coote, Robert B., and Mary P. Coote. *Power, Politics, and the Making of the Bible.* Minneapolis: Fortress Press, 1990.

Coratto, Severino. *Biblical Hermeneutics: Toward a Theory of Reading as the Production of Meaning.* Eng. ed. Marynoll, N.Y.: Orbis Books, 1987.

Crenshaw, James. *Old Testament Wisdom: An Introduction.* Atlanta: John Knox Press, 1981.

———. *Prophetic Conflict: Its Effect upon Israelite Religion.* Berlin: De Gruyter, 1971.

———. "Yahweh Sᵉba'ot Sᵉmo: A Form Critical Analysis." *ZAW* 81 (1969): 156–175.

Cross, Frank Moore, Jr. *Canaanite Myth and Hebrew Epic: Essays in the History of the Religion of Israel.* Cambridge, Mass.: Harvard University Press, 1973.

Davaney, Sheila Greeve, ed. *Theology at the End of Modernity: Essays in Honor of Gordon D. Kaufman.* Philadelphia: Trinity Press International, 1991.

Deist, F. E. *Witnesses to the Old Testament: Introducing Old Testament Textual Criticism.* Literature of the Old Testament no. 5. Pretoria: NG Kerkboekhandel, 1988.

Delamarter, Stephen. "Concepts in Canonical Criticism." Master's thesis, Claremont Graduate School, 1984.

———. "The Death of Josiah: Exegesis and Hermeneutics in Scripture and Tradition." Ph.D. diss., Claremont Graduate School, 1990.

de Man, Paul. *Toward an Aesthetic of Reception.* Theory and History of Literature no. 2. Trans. Timothy Bahti. Minneapolis: University of Minnesota Press, 1982.

Derrida, Jacques. "Abysses of Truth." In *Spurs: Nietzsche's Styles.* Trans. Barbara Harlow. Chicago: University of Chicago Press, 1978.

———. "Differance." In *Speech and Phenomena,* trans. David Allison. Evanston, Ill.: Northwestern University Press, 1973.

———. *Margins of Philosophy.* Trans. Alan Bass. Chicago: University of Chicago Press, 1982.

———. *Of Grammatology.* Trans. Gayatri Spirak. Baltimore: Johns Hopkins Press, 1976.

———. "Structure, Sign, and Play in the Discourse of the Human Sciences." In *The Structuralist Controversy: The Languages of Criticism and the Sciences of Man,* ed. Richard Macksey and Eugenio Donato. Baltimore: Johns Hopkins University Press, 1972.

de Saussure, Ferdinand. *Course in General Linguistics*. Trans. Wade Bashin, ed. Charles Bally and Albert Sechehaye. New York: McGraw-Hill, 1966.

Detweiler, Robert. "Speaking of Believing in Gen. 2–3." In *Semeia 41: Speech Act Theory and Biblical Criticism,* ed. Hugh C. White. Decatur, Ga.: Scholars Press, 1988.

Dinter, Paul E. "The Remnant of Israel and the Stone of Stumbling in Zion According to Paul (Romans 9–11)." Ph.D. diss., Claremont Graduate School, 1979.

Donnelly, John, ed. *Language, Metaphysics, and Death*. New York: Fordham University Press, 1978.

Douglas, Mary, and Aaron Wildavsky. *Risk and Culture*. Berkeley: University of California Press, 1982.

Dreyfus, F. Review of *Prophetic Conflict: Its Effect upon Israelite Religion,* by James Crenshaw. In *RB* 80 (1973): 443–444.

Duhm, B. "Anmerkungun zu den Zwölf Propheten." *ZAW* 31 (1911): 1–43, 184–187.

———. *Das Buch Jesaia*. Göttingen: Vandenhoeck & Ruprecht, 1922.

Dupre, John. *The Disorder of Things: Metaphysical Foundations of the Disunity of Science*. Cambridge, Mass.: Harvard University Press, 1993.

Eagleton, Terry, *Literary Theory: An Introduction*. Minneapolis: University of Minnesota Press, 1983.

Eco, Umberto. *The Search for the Perfect Language*. Trans. James Fentress. Oxford: Basil Blackwell, 1995.

Eissfeldt, Otto. *The Old Testament: An Introduction*. Trans. Peter Ackroyd. San Francisco: Harper & Row, 1965.

Eller, Vernard. *Christian Anarchy: Jesus' Primacy over the Powers*. Grand Rapids: Eerdmans, 1987.

Ellul, Jacques. *Anarchy and Christianity*. Trans. Geoffrey W. Bromiley. Grand Rapids: Eerdmans, 1991.

Evans, Craig. *To See and Not Perceive: Isaiah 6:9–10 in Early Jewish and Christian Interpretation*. *JSOTSup*. 64. Sheffield: JSOT Press, 1989.

Evans, Craig, and James A. Sanders. *Luke and Scripture*. Minneapolis: Fortress Press, 1993.

Exum, J. Cheryl, and David J. A. Clines. *The New Literary Criticism and the Hebrew Bible*. Valley Forge: Trinity Press International, 1993.

Farrel, Thomas. *Norms of Rhetorical Culture*. New Haven: Yale University Press, 1993.

Fensham, F. C. "A Possible Origin of the Concept of the 'Day of the Lord.'" *Biblical Essays* OTWSA9 (1966): 90–97.

Festinger, L., H. Riechen, and S. Schachter. *When Prophecy Fails: A Social and Psychological Study of a Modern Group that Predicted the Destruction of the World*. New York: Harper & Row, 1956.

Fielder, Leslie A., and Houston A. Baker, Jr., eds. *English Literature: Opening Up the Canon*. Baltimore: Johns Hopkins University Press, 1981.

Fiorenza, E. Schussler. "The Ethics of Interpretation: De-centering Biblical Scholarship." *JBL* 107 (1988): 3–17.

Fiorenza, Francis. "The Crisis of Scriptural Authority: Interpretation and Reception." *Int* 44:4 (October 1990): 353–368.

Fischer, J. *Das Buch Isaias übersetz und erklärt*. 2 vols. HSAT. Bonn: Hanstein, 1937–1939.

Fish, Stanley. "Consequences." *CI* 11 (1985): 433–458.

————. *Is There a Text in This Class? The Authority of Interpretative Communities*. Cambridge, Mass.: Harvard University Press, 1980.

————. *There's No Such Thing as Free Speech . . . And It's a Good Thing Too*. Oxford: Oxford University Press, 1994.

————. "Why No One's Afraid of Wolfgang Iser." *Diacritics* 11:1 (1981): 2–13.

Fishbane, Michael. *Biblical Interpretation in Ancient Israel*. Oxford: Clarendon Press, 1985.

————. *Garments of Torah: Essays in Biblical Hermeneutics*. Bloomington: Indiana University Press, 1989.

————. "Inner Biblical Exegesis: Types and Strategies of Interpretation in Ancient Israel." In *Midrash and Literature*, ed. Geoffrey Hartman and Sanford Budick. New Haven: Yale University Press, 1986.

————. "Saving Scripture and Our Mortal Souls." *Explorations* 7:2 (1993): 6.

Fohrer, Georg. *Das Buch Jesaja*. ZBK. Zurich: Zwingli Verlag, 1960.

————. Review of *Prophetic Conflict: Its Effect upon Israelite Religion*, by James Crenshaw. In *ZAW* 83 (1971): 419.

Foucault, Michael. *The Archaeology of Knowledge*. New York: Pantheon Books, 1972.

————. *Language, Counter-memory, Practice: Selected Essays and Interviews*. Ithaca, N.Y.: Cornell University Press, 1977.

————. *Power/Knowledge: Selected Interviews and Other Writings, 1972–1977*. Trans. and ed. Colin Gordon. New York: Pantheon Books, 1980.

Fowl, Stephen, and Gregory L. Jones. *Reading in Communion: Scripture and Ethics in Christian Life*. Grand Rapids: Eerdmans, 1991.

Frei, H. W. *The Eclipse of the Biblical Narrative*. New Haven: Yale University Press, 1974.

Frye, Northrop. *The Anatomy of Criticism: Four Essays*. New York: Atheneum, 1967.

————. *The Great Code: The Bible and Literature*. San Diego: Harcourt Brace Jovanovich, 1983.

Gabel, John B., Charles Wheeler, and Anthony York. *The Bible as Literature: An Introduction*. New York: Oxford University Press, 1996.

Gates, Henry. *Loose Canons: Notes on the Cultural Wars*. New York: Oxford University Press, 1992.

Geertz, Clifford. *The Interpretation of Cultures*. New York: Basic Books, 1973.

Gilkey, Langdon. *Naming the Whirlwind: The Renewal of God-Language*. Indianapolis: Bobbs-Merrill, 1969.

Girard, René. *Deceit, Desire, and the Novel: Self and Other in Literary Structure*. 2d ed. Trans. Yvonne Freccero. Baltimore: Johns Hopkins University Press, 1976.

————. *The Scapegoat*. Baltimore: Johns Hopkins University Press, 1986.

————. *A Theater of Envy*. New York: Oxford University Press, 1991.

———. *Things Hidden since the Foundation of the World*. Stanford: Stanford University Press, 1987.

———. *To Double Business Bound*. Baltimore: Johns Hopkins University Press, 1988.

———. *Violence and the Sacred*. Baltimore: John Hopkins University Press, 1977.

Gorak, Jan. *The Making of the Modern Canon: Genesis and Crisis of a Literary Idea*. Athlone Series on Canons. London: Athlone, 1991.

Gottwalt, Norman. *All the Kingdoms of the Earth: Israelite Prophecy and International Relations in the Ancient Near East*. New York: Harper & Row, 1964.

Gough, John. *Minor Prophets*. Philadelphia: American Baptist Publication Society, 1935.

Gray, G. B. *A Critical and Exegetical Commentary on the Book of Isaiah I through XXVII*. ICC. Edinburgh: T. & T. Clark, 1912.

Green, Garrett. *Imagining God: Theology and Religious Imagination*. San Francisco: Harper & Row, 1989.

Greenslade, A. L., ed. *The Cambridge History of the Bible: The West from the Reformation to the Present Day*. Vol. 3. Cambridge: Cambridge University Press, 1963.

Gunkel, Hermann. "Die Propheten als Schriftsteller und Dichter." In H. Schmidt, *Die Größen Propheten*, SAT, Vol. 2, part 2. 2d ed.

———. *Israelitisch Heldentum und Kriegesfrömmigkeit im Alten Testament*. Göttingen: Vandenhoeck & Ruprecht, 1916.

Gunn, David, and Danna Nolan Fewell. *Narrative in the Hebrew Bible*. New York: Oxford University Press, 1993.

Habel, Norman. *Literary Criticism of the Old Testament*. Philadelphia: Fortress, 1971.

Habermas, J. *Knowledge and Human Interest*. Boston: Beacon Press, 1968.

Hallo, William. "Assyriology and the Canon." *American Scholar* 59:1 (Winter 1990): 105–108.

Hanson, Paul D. "Apocalyptic Seers and Priests in Conflict and the Development of the Visionary/Pragmatic Polarity." In *The Diversity of Scripture: A Theological Interpretation*. OBT no 11. Philadelphia: Fortress Press, 1982.

———. *The Dawn of the Apocalyptic*. Philadelphia: Fortress Press, 1979.

———. *Dynamic Transcendence*. Philadelphia: Fortress Press, 1978.

———. "Human Crisis." In *Old Testament Apocalyptic*. IBT. Nashville: Abingdon, 1987.

Harrington, Michael. *The Politics at God's Funeral: The Spiritual Crisis of Western Civilization*. New York: Holt, Rinehart and Winston, 1983.

Hartman, Geoffrey, and Sanford Budick, eds. *Midrash and Literature*. New Haven: Yale University Press, 1986.

Hasel, Gerhard. *Old Testament Theology: Basic Issues in the Current Debate*. Grand Rapids: Eerdmans, 1972.

Hatch, Nathan O. "Sola Scriptura." In *The Bible in America: Essays in Cultural History*, ed. Nathan O. Hatch and Mark A. Noll. New York: Oxford University Press, 1982.

Hauerwas, Stanley. *A Community of Character: Toward a Constructive-Christian Social Ethic* Notre Dame: University of Notre Dame Press, 1981.

———. *The Peaceable Kingdom: A Primer in Christian Ethics*. Notre Dame: University of Notre Dame Press, 1983.

———. *Truthfulness and Tragedy: Further Investigations in Christian Ethics*. Notre Dame: University of Notre Dame Press, 1977.

———. *Unleashing the Scripture: Freeing the Bible from Captivity to America*. Nashville: Abingdon Press, 1993.

Havel, Vaclav. "From Arrogance to Humility: The Ambiguous Power of Words." *Media Development* 1 (1990): 44–46.

———, ed. *The Power of the Powerless: Citizens against the State in Central-Eastern Europe*. New York: M. E. Sharpe, 1985.

Hayes, John H., and Frederick Prussner. *Old Testament Theology: Its History and Development*. Atlanta: John Knox Press, 1985.

Hayes, John H., and Stuart A. Irvine. *Isaiah: The Eighth-Century Prophet*. Nashville: Abingdon Press, 1987.

Hayes, Richard. *Echoes of Scripture in the Letters of Paul*. New Haven: Yale University Press, 1989.

Heschel, Abraham. *The Prophets: An Introduction*. New York: Harper & Row, 1962.

Hillars, D. *Micah*. Philadelphia: Fortress Press, 1984.

Hirsch, E. D. *The Aims of Interpretation*. Chicago: University of Chicago Press, 1976.

———. *Cultural Literacy: What Every American Needs to Know*. Boston: Houghton Mifflin, 1987.

———. *Validity in Interpretation*. New Haven: Yale University Press, 1967.

Holland, Norman. *Poems in Persons: An Introduction to the Psychoanalysis of Literature*. New York: Norton, 1973.

Holscher, Gustav. *Die Profeten: Untersuchungen zuv Religongeschichte*. Leipzig: J. C. Hinrich's Buchhandlung, 1914.

Holub, Robert C. *Reception Theory: A Critical Introduction*. London: Methuen, 1984.

Hubbard, David. *Joel and Amos*. Downers Grove, Ill.: InterVarsity Press, 1989.

Hyland, Peter, ed. *Discharging the Canon: Cross-cultural Readings in Literature*. Singapore: Singapore University Press, 1986.

Iser, Wolfgang. *The Act of Reading: A Theory of Aesthetic Response*. Baltimore: Johns Hopkins University Press, 1978. German original, *Der Akt des Lesens: Theorie ästhetischer Wirking*. Munich: Wilhelm Fink, 1976.

———. *The Implied Reader: Patterns of Communication in Prose Fiction from Bunyan to Beckett*. 2d ed. Baltimore: Johns Hopkins University Press, 1975.

———. "The Reading Process: A Phenomenological Approach." *NLH* 3:2 (1972): 279–299.

———. "Talk Like Whales." *Diacritics* 11:3 (1981): 82–87.

Jacob, Ed. Review of *Prophetic Conflict: Its Effect Upon Israelite Religion*, by James Crenshaw. In *Bib* 54 (1973): 135–138.

Jasper, Karl. *Vom Ursprung und Zeil der Geschichte*. Munich: Piper Verlag, 1949.

Jauss, Hans Robert. "Literary History as a Challenge to Literary Theory." In *NLH* 2 (1970): 7–37. Reprinted in *Toward an Aesthetic of Reception*, Theory and History of Literature no. 2, trans. Timothy Bahti. Minneapolis: University of Minnesota Press, 1982.

———. "Paradigmawechsel in der Literaturwissenschaft." *Linguistische Berichte* 3 (1969): 44–56.

————. *Question and Answer: Forms of Dialogic Understanding*. Minneapolis: University of Minnesota Press, 1989.

Jefferson, Ann, and David Robey. *Modern Literary Theory: A Comparative Introduction*. Jamesbury, N. J.: Barnes & Noble Books, 1982.

Jensen, J. *The Use of tôrâ by Isaiah: His Debate with the Wisdom Tradition*. CBQ Monograph Series no. 3. Washington, D.C.: Catholic Biblical Association of America, 1973.

Jeppesen, K. "New Aspects of Micah Research." *JSOT* 8 (1978): 3–32.

Kadushin, Max. *The Rabbinic Mind*. 3d ed. New York: Bloch Publishing, 1972.

Kaiser, Otto. *Introduction to the Old Testament: A Presentation of Its Results and Problems*. Trans. John Sturdy. Minneapolis: Augsburg Press, 1975.

————. *Isaiah 1–12: A Commentary*, rev. ed. OTL. Philadelphia: Westminster Press, 1972.

Kapelrud, Arvid. *Joel Studies*. Uppsala: A. B. Lundquistska Bokhandeln, 1948.

Kaplan, Carey, and Ellen Cronan Rose, eds. *The Canon and the Common Reader*. Knoxville: University of Tennessee Press, 1990.

Kaufman, Gordon D. "The Christian World-Picture (I): The Monotheistic Categorical Scheme." In *In Face of Mystery: A Constructive Theology*. Cambridge, Mass.: Harvard University Press, 1993.

————. *The Theological Imagination: Constructing the Concept of God*. Philadelphia: Westminster Press, 1981.

Kealy, Sean P. "The Canon: An African Contribution." *BTB* 9:1 (January 1979): 13–26.

Kennedy, J. Hardee. "Joel." *The Broadman Commentary*. Nashville: Broadman Press, 1972.

Kermode, Frank. "The Argument about Canons." In *An Appetitie for Poetry*. Cambridge, Mass.: Harvard University Press, 1989.

————. "Institutional Control of Interpretation." In *The Art of Telling*. Cambridge: Harvard University Press, 1983.

————. *The Sense of an Ending: Studies in the Theory of Fiction*. New York: Oxford University Press, 1967.

————. *Shakespeare, Spenser, Donne: Renaissance Essays*. New York: Viking Press, 1971.

Kierkegaard, Søren. *Fear and Trembling*. Princeton: Princeton University Press, 1945.

Kim, Wonil. "Toward a Substance-Critical Task of Old Testament Theology." Ph.D. diss., Claremont Graduate School, 1996.

Kissane, Edward. *The Book of Isaiah*. Rev. ed. Dublin: Browne & Nolan, 1960.

Klaassen, Walter. *Anabaptism: Neither Catholic nor Protestant*. Waterloo, Ont.: Conrad Grebel Press, 1973.

Knierim, Rolf. "On the Task of Old Testament Theology: A Response to W. Harrelson, S. Towner, and R. E. Murphy." *HBT* 6:2 (December 1984): 91–128.

————. "The Task of Old Testament Theology." *HBT* 6:1 (June 1984): 25–57.

————. "The Vocation of Isaiah." *VT* 18:1 (1968): 47–68.

Knight, Douglas. *Rediscovering the Traditions of Israel: The Development of the Traditio-historical Research of the Old Testament, with Special Consideration of Scan-*

dinavian Contributions. Missoula, Mont.: Society of Biblical Literature Press, 1973.

Koch, Klaus. "Ezra and the Origins of Judaism." *JSS* 19 (1974): 173–197.

——. *The Growth of the Biblical Tradition*. New York: Scribner's, 1969.

——. *The Prophets: The Assyrian Period*. Vol. 1. Trans. Margaret Kohl. Philadelphia: Fortress Press, 1982. Original German edition, *Die Propheten I: Assyrische Zeit*. Stuttgart: Verlag W. Kohlhammer GmbH, 1978.

Kraus, C. Norman. *Jesus Christ Our Lord: Christology from a Disciple's Perspective*. Scottdale, Pa.: Herald Press, 1987.

Krentz, Edgar. *The Historical-Critical Method*. Old Testament Series: Guides to Biblical Scholarship. Philadelphia: Fortress Press, 1978.

Kristeva, Julia. *Semeiotike: Recherches pour une Semanalyse*. Paris: Editions du Seuil, 1969.

Kruput, Arnold. "Native American Literature and the Canon." In *Canons*, ed. Robert von Hallberg, special edition of *CI* 10:1 (September 1983): 145–172.

Kugel, James L. "On the Bible and Literary Criticism." *Prooftexts: A Journal of Jewish History* 1 (September 1981): 217–236.

Kuhn, Thomas S. *The Structure of Scientific Revolutions*. 2d ed. Chicago: University of Chicago Press, 1970.

Lacan, Jacques. *The Four Fundamental Concepts of Psychoanalysis*. New York: Norton, 1979.

Lampe, G. W. H., ed. *The Cambridge History of the Bible: The West from the Fathers to the Reformation*. Vol. 2. Cambridge: Cambridge University Press, 1975.

Landes, George M. "Biblical Exegesis in Crisis: What Is the Exegetical Task in a Theological Context?" *USQR* 26 (1971): 274–298.

Lash, Nicholas. *Theology on the Way to Emmaus*. London: SCM Press, 1986.

Lauter, Paul. *Canons and Contexts*. Oxford: Oxford University Press, 1991.

——. "Society and the Profession, 1958–1983." *PMLA* 99 (May 1984): 414–426.

Lentricchia, Frank. *After the New Criticism*. Chicago: University of Chicago Press, 1980.

Leslie, E. *Isaiah*. Nashville: Abingdon Press, 1963.

Lessing, Gotthold Ephraim. *Lessing's Theological Writings*. Trans. Henry Chadwick. A Library of Modern Religious Thought. Stanford: Stanford University Press, 1957.

Levering, Miriam, ed. *Rethinking Scripture: Essays from a Comparative Perpective*. Albany: State University of New York Press, 1989.

Levinas, Emmanuel. *Ethics and Infinity: Conversations with Philippe Nemo*. Trans. Richard A. Cohen. Pittsburgh: Duquesne University Press, 1985.

——. *Totality and Infinity: An Essay on Exteriority*. Duquesne Studies Philosophical Series no. 24. Trans. Alphonso Lingis. Pittsburgh: Duquesne University Press, 1969.

Lewis, I. M. *Ecstatic Religion*. Baltimore: Penguin Books, 1971.

Liechty, Daniel. *Theology in Postliberal Perspective*. Philadelphia: Trinity Press International, 1990.

Liew, Tat-Sing Benny. "Adjudication: Deciding to Decide." Paper presented at SBL meeting, 1992, TMs.

Limburg, James. "The Prophets in Recent Study, 1967–1977." *Int* 32 (1978): 56–68.

Lind, Millard. "Perspectives on War and Peace in the Hebrew Scriptures." In *Monotheism, Power, Justice: Collected Old Testament Essays*, Text-Reader Series no. 3. Elkhart, Ind.: Institute of Mennonite Studies, 1990.

———. "Reflections on Biblical Hermeneutics." In *Kingdom, Cross, and Community*, ed. J. R. Burkholder and Cal Redekop. Scottdale, Pa.: Herald Press, 1976.

———. *Yahweh Is a Warrior: Theology of Warfare in Ancient Israel*. Scottdale, Pa: Herald Press, 1980.

Lindblom, Johannes. *Prophecy in Ancient Israel*. Philadelphia: Fortress Press, 1965.

Lohfink, Gerhard. "'Schwerten zu Pflugscharen': Die Rezeption von Jes 2:1–5 par Mi 4:1–5 in der Alten Kirche und im Neuen Testament." *Theologische Quartaschrift* 166 (1968): 184–209.

Long, B. "Social Dimensions of Prophetic Conflict." *Semeia* 21 (1981): 31–53.

Long, V. Philips. *The Art of Biblical History*. Grand Rapids: Zondervan, 1994.

MacIntyre, Alasdair. *After Virtue*. 2d ed. Notre Dame: University of Notre Dame Press, 1984.

Manahan, Ronald. "A Theology of Pseudoprophets: A Study in Jeremiah." *GTJ* 1 (1980): 77–96.

Mariottini, Claude F. "Joel 3:10 [H 4:10]: Beat Your Plowshares into Swords." *Perspectives in Religious Studies* 14 (Summer 1987): 125–130.

Marti, K. *Das Buch Jesaja erklärt*. KHCAT no. 10. Tübingen: Mohr, 1900.

Martin, Helmut. *Cult and Canon: The Origins and Development of State Maoism*. New York: M. E. Sharpe, 1982.

Marty, Martin. *Context* 25:9 (1 May 1993): 3.

Mauchline, J. *Isaiah 1–39: Introduction and Commentary*. New York: Macmillan, 1962.

Mays, James L. "Historical and Canonical: Recent Discussions about the Old Testament and Christian Faith." In *Magnalia Dei, the Mighty Acts of God: Essays on the Bible and Archaeology in Memory of G. Ernest Wright*, ed. Frank Moore Cross, Jr., Werner E. Lemke, and Patrick D. Miller. Garden City, N.Y.: Doubleday, 1976.

———. *Micah*. OTL. Philadelphia: Westminster Press, 1976.

McClendon, James W., Jr. *Biography as Theology: How Life Stories Can Remake Today's Theology*. Nashville: Abingdon Press, 1974.

———. *Doctrine. Vol. 2 of Systematic Theology*. Nashville: Abingdon Press, 1994.

———. *Ethics.: Vol. 1 of Systematic Theology*. Nashville: Abingdon Press, 1991.

McClendon, James W., Jr., and James M. Smith. *Understanding Religious Convictions*. Notre Dame: University of Notre Dame Press, 1975.

McKnight, Edgar V. *The Bible and the Reader: An Introduction to Literary Criticism*. Philadelphia: Fortress Press, 1985.

———. *Post Modern Use of the Bible: The Emergence of Reader-Oriented Criticism*. Nashville: Abingdon Press, 1988.

Metzger, Bruce M. "History of the Word *Kanon*." Appendix 1 of *The Canon of the New Testament: Its Origins, Development, and Significance*. Oxford: Oxford University Press, 1987.

Miles, Jack. *God: A Biography*. New York: Knopf, 1995.

Miller, David. *The New Polytheism: Rebirth of the Gods and Goddesses*. New York: Harper & Row, 1974.

Miller, Merrill P. "Scripture and Parable: A Study of the Function of the Biblical Features in the Parable of the Wicked Husbandman and Their Place in the History of Tradition". Ph.D. diss., Claremont Graduate School, 1974.

Miller, Patrick. *The Divine Warrior in Early Israel*. Cambridge, Mass.: Harvard University Press, 1973.

Miller, William. "Early Jewish and Christian Hermeneutic of Genesis 18:1–16 and 32:23–33." Ph.D. diss., Claremont Graduate School, 1979.

Moltmann, Jürgen. "Political Discipleship of Christians Today." In *Communities of Faith and Radical Discipleship: Jürgen Moltmann and Others,* ed. G. McLeod Bryan. Macon, Ga.: Mercer University Press, 1986.

Moore, Stephen. *Literary Criticism and the Gospels: The Theoretical Challenge*. New Haven: Yale University Press, 1989.

Morgan, G. Campbell. *The Minor Prophets*. Westwood, N. J.: Fleming, Revell, 1960.

Morgan, Donn F. *Between Text and Community*. Minneapolis: Fortress Press, 1990.

Moriarity, Frederick. "Word as Power in the Ancient Near East." In *A Light unto My Path: Old Testament Studies in Honor of Jacob M. Meyers,* ed. H. Bream, R. Heim, and C. Moore. Philadelphia: Temple University Press, 1974.

Mowinckel, Sigmund. *He That Cometh*. Trans. B. W. Anderson. Oxford: Basil Blackwell, 1956.

———. "Jahves dag." *Norsk teologisk Tidskrif* 59 (1958): 1–56.

———. "The 'Spirit' and the 'Word' in the Pre-Exilic Reforming Prophets." *JBL* 53 (1934): 199–227.

Muilenburg, James. "Form Criticism and Beyond." *JBL* 88 (1969): 1–18.

Mulder, Jan Martin, ed. *Mikra*. Philadelphia: Fortress Press, 1988.

Murphy, Nancey. *Theology in the Age of Scientific Reasoning*. Ithaca, N.Y.: Cornell University Press, 1990.

Murphy, Nancey, and James W. McClendon, Jr. "Distinguishing Modern and Postmodern Theologies." *Modern Theology* 5:3 (April 1989): 191–214.

Murray, D. F. "The Rhetoric of Disputation: Re-examination of a Prophetic Genre." *JSOT* 38 (1987): 95–121.

Murray, David J. "Gestalt Psychology." *A History of Western Psychology*. Englewood Cliffs, N.J.: Prentice-Hall, 1983.

Neusner, Jacob. *Death and Birth of Judaism*. New York: Basic Books, 1987.

———. *Self-Fulfilling Prophecy: Exile and Return in the History of Judaism*. Boston: Beacon Press, 1987.

Neusner, Jacob, Ernest S. Frerichs, and A. J. Levine, eds. "Systemic Analysis of Holy Books in Christianity, Islam, Buddhism, Greco-Roman Religions, Ancient Israel, and Judaism." In *Religious Writings and Religious Systems,* vols. 1 and 2. Brown Studies of Religion. Atlanta: Scholars Press, 1989.

Niebuhr, H. R. *Radical Monotheism and Western Culture*. New York: Harper & Brothers, 1960.

Nietzsche, Friedrich. *The Will to Power*. Trans. R. J. Hollindale and W. Kaufmann, ed. Walter Kaufmann. New York: Random House, 1967.

Noth, M. "Jerusalem und die israelitische Tradition." *OTS* 8 (1950): 28–46. Reprinted in *Gesammelte Studien zum Alten Testament*. TBu no. 11. Munich: Chr Kaiser, 1958.

Ohmann, Richard. "The Shaping of a Canon: U.S. Fiction, 1960–1975." *CI* 10:1 (September 1983): 199–223.

Ollenburger, Ben C. "From Timeless Ideas to the Essence of Religion: Method in Old Testament Theology before 1930." In *The Flowering of Old Testament Theology*, ed. Gerhard F. Hasel, Ben C. Ollenburger, and Elmer A. Martens. Sources for Biblical and Theological Study no. 1. Winona Lake, Ind.: Eisenbrauns, 1992.

———. *Zion, the City of the Great King: A Theological Symbol of the Jerusalem Cult*. JSOTSup 41. Sheffield: JSOT Press, 1987.

Osswald, Eva. *Falsche Prophtie im Alten Testament*. Tubingen: J. C. B. Mohr (Paul Siebeck), 1962.

Oswalt, John. *The Book of Isaiah*. Grand Rapids: Eerdmans, 1986.

Pannenburg, Wolfhart. "Schwerter zu Pflugscharen—Beduetung and Miss brauch eines Prophetensortes." In *"Securing the Peace "* (March 1983).

Patte, Daniel. *Ethics of Biblical Interpretation: A Reevaluation*. Louisville: Westminster John Knox Press, 1995.

Perdue, Leo G. *The Collapse of History: Reconstructing Old Testament Theology*. OBT. Minneapolis: Fortress Press, 1994.

Petersen, David. *The Roles of Israel's Prophets*. Sheffield: JSOT Press, 1981.

Piaget, Jean. *Biology and Knowledge*. Trans. Beatrix Walsh. Chicago: University of Chicago Press, 1971.

Polzin, Robert. *Moses and the Deuteronomist: A Literary Study of the Deuteronomic History*. New York: Seabury Press, 1980.

Powell, Mark A. *The Bible and Modern Literary Criticism: A Critical Assessment and Annotated Bibliography*. New York: Greenwood Press, 1992.

———. *What Is Narrative Criticism?* Philadelphia: Fortress Press, 1990.

Prinsloo, Willem W. *The Theology of the Book of Joel*. BZAW no. 163. Berlin: De Gruyter, 1985.

Proksch, O. *Jesaia I–XXXIX*. KAT. Leipzig: Deichert, 1930.

Quell, G. *Wahre und falsche Propheten*. Gutersloh: Bertelsmann, 1952.

Quine, W. V. "Two Dogmas of Empiricism." In *From a Logical Point of View*. Cambridge, Mass.: Harvard University Press, 1961.

Quine, W. V., and J. S. Ullian. *The Web of Belief*. New York: Random House, 1979.

Ramlot, L. "Les faux prophetes." *DBSup* 8 (Fasc. 47, 1971): cols. 1044, 1047–1048.

Rank, Otto. *Truth and Reality: A Life History of the Human Will*. Trans. Jessie Taft. New York: Knopf, 1936.

Rankin, Oliver. *Israel's Wisdom Literature: Its Bearing on Theology and the History of Religion*. New York: Schocken Books, 1969.

Rast, Walter E. *Tradition History and the OldTestament*. Philadelphia: Fortress Press, 1972.

Reiling, J. "The Use of 'Pseudoprophetes' in LXX, Philo, and Josephus." *NT* 13 (1971): 147–156.

Rendtorff, Rolf. *Men of God*. Trans. Frank Clarke. London: SCM Press, 1968.

———. *The Old Testament: An Introduction*. Trans. John Bowden. Philadelphia: Fortress Press, 1986.

———. "Reflections on the Early History of Prophecy in Israel." Trans. Paul J. Achtemeier. *History and Hermeneutic: Journal for Theology and the Church* 4 (1967): 14–34. Original German, in *ZThK* 59 (1962): 145–167.

Rendtorff, Trutz, and Dorothee Soelle. Discussion reported in *Der Spiegel* 37:41 (10 October 1983).

Reventlow, Henning Graf. *Problems of Biblical Theology in the Twentieth Century*. Philadelphia: Fortress Press, 1986.

Ricoeur, Paul. *The Conflict of Interpretations: Essays in Hermeneutics*. Ed. Don Ihde. Evanston, Ill.: Northwestern University Press, 1974.

———. *Interpretation Theory: Discourse and the Surplus of Meaning*. Fort Worth: Texas Christian University Press, 1976.

———. *The Symbolism of Evil*. Trans. Emerson Buchanan. Boston: Beacon Press, 1967.

Ridderbos, J. *Isaiah*. Trans. John Vriend. Bible Student's Commentary. Grand Rapids: Zondervan, 1985.

Riding, Laura, and Robert Graves. *A Survey of Modernist Poetry*. London: Heinemann, 1929.

Ringe, Sharon H. "The Jubilee Proclamation in the Ministry and Teaching of Jesus: A Tradition-Critical Study in the Synoptic Gospels and Acts." Ph.D. diss., Claremont Graduate School, 1980.

Rivkin, Ellis. *The Shaping of Jewish History: A Radical New Interpretation*. New York: Scribner's 1971.

Roberts, J. J. M. "The Davidic Origin of the Zion Tradition." *JBL* 92 (1973): 329–344.

Robertson, David. *The Old Testament and the Literary Critic*. Philadelphia: Fortress Press, 1977.

Rohland, E. "Die Bedeutung der Erwählungstraditionen Israels fur die Eschatologie der alttestamentlichen Propheten." Diss., University of Heidelberg, 1956.

Rorty, Richard, ed. *The Linguistic Turn*. Chicago: University of Chicago Press, 1967.

Rosen, Stanley. *The Ancients and the Moderns*. New Haven: Yale University Press, 1989.

Ryle, H. E. *The Canon of the Old Testament*. 2d ed. London: Macmillan, 1909.

Said, Edward. "Opponents, Audiences, Constituencies, and Community." *CI* 9 (1982): 1–26.

———. *Orientalism*. New York: Pantheon Books, 1978.

Sanders, James A. "Adaptable for Life: The Nature and Function of Canon." In *Magnalia Dei, the Mighty Acts of God: Essays on the Bible and Archaeology in Memory of G. Ernest Wright,* ed. Frank Moore Cross, Werner E. Lemke, and Patrick D. Miller. Garden City, N.Y.: Doubleday , 1976. Reprinted in *From Sacred Story to Sacred Text*. Philadelphia: Fortress Press, 1987.

————. "Biblical Criticism and the Bible as Canon." *Union Seminary Quarterly Review* 32 (1977): 157–165. Reprinted in *From Sacred Story to Sacred Text*. Philadelphia: Fortress Press, 1987.

————. *Canon and Community: A Guide to Canonical Criticism*. Old Testament Series: Guides to Biblical Scholarship. Philadelphia: Fortress Press, 1984.

————. "Canon as Shape and Function." In *The Promise and Practice of Biblical Theology*, ed. John Reumann. Minneapolis: Fortress Press, 1991.

————. "Canonical Context and Canonical Criticism." *HBT* 2 (1980): 173–197.

————. "Cave 11 Surprises and the Question of Canon." In *The Canon and Masorah of the Hebrew Bible*, ed. Sid Z. Leiman. New York: KTAV, 1974. Also in *New Directions in Biblical Archaeology*, ed. David Noel Freedman and Jonas C. Greenfield. Garden City, N.Y.: Doubleday, 1969. Original published in *McCormick Quarterly Review* 21 (1968): 284–298.

————. "Communities and Canon." In *The Oxford Study Bible: REB with the Apocrypha*, ed. M. Jack Suggs, Katharine D. Sakenfeld, and James R. Mueller. New York: Oxford University Press, 1992.

————. "The Dead Sea Scrolls and Biblical Studies." In *"Sha'arei Talmon": Studies in the Bible, Qumran, and the Ancient Near East Presented to Shemaryahu Talmon*, ed. Michael fishbane and Emanuel Tov. Winona Lake Ind.: Eisenbrauns, 1992.

————. "Deuteronomy." In *The Books of the Bible*, ed. B. W. Anderson. New York: Scribner's, 1989.

————. *From Sacred Story to Sacred Text*. Philadelphia: Fortress Press, 1987.

————. *God Has a Story Too*. Philadelphia: Fortress Press, 1979.

————. "Hebrew Bible *and* Old Testament: Textual Criticism in Service of Biblical Studies." In *Hebrew Bible or Old Testament?: Studying the Bible in Judaism and Christianity*, ed. Roger Brooks and John J. Collins. Notre Dame: University of Notre Dame Press, 1990.

————. "Hermeneutics." In *The Concise Encyclopedia of Preaching*, ed. William H. Willimon and Richard Lischer. Louisville: Westminster/John Knox Press, 1995.

————. "Hermeneutics." In *IDBSup*, ed. Keith Crim. Nashville: Abingdon Press, 1976.

————. "Hermeneutics in True and False Prophecy." In *Canon and Authority: Essays in Old Testament Religion and Theology*, ed. George W. Coats and Burke O. Long. Philadelphia: Fortress Press, 1977.

————. "The Integrity of Biblical Pluralism." In *"Not in Heaven": Coherence and Complexity in Biblical Narrative*, ed. Jason P. Rosenblatt and Joseph C. Sitterson, Jr. Bloomington: Indiana University Press, 1991.

————. "Intertextuality and Dialogue." *Explorations* 7:2 (1993): 4–5.

————. Review of *Introduction to the Old Testament as Scripture* by Brevard Childs. In *HBT* 2 (1980): 187.

————. Review of *Garments of Torah: Essays in Biblical Hermeneutics*, by Michael Fishbane. In *Today* 47 (January 1991): 433–445.

————. "Stability and Fluidity in Text and Canon." In *Tradition of the Text: Studies Offered to D. Barthelemy*, ed. G. J. Norton and S. Pisano. Göttingen: Vandenhoeck & Ruprecht, 1991.

————. "Text and Canon: Concepts and Method." *JBL* 98 (1979): 5–29.

————. *Torah and Canon.* Philadelphia: Fortress Press, 1972.

Sandmel, Samuel, Albert Sundberg, Jr., and Roland E. Murphy. "A Symposium on the Canon of Scripture." In *Old Testament Issues,* ed. Samuel Sandmel. New York: Harper & Row, 1968.

Schaberg, Jane. *The Father, the Son, and the Holy Spirit: The Triadic Phrase in Matthew 29:19b.* Chico, Calif.: Scholars Press, 1982.

Scheffler, E. H. "Micah 4:1–5: An Impasse in Exegesis?" *OTE* 3 (1985): 46–61.

Schwally, F. *Der Heilige Krieg im alten Israel.* Vol.1. Leipzig: Deiterich, 1901.

Schwartz, Regina. "Joseph's Bones and the Resurrection of the Text: Remembering in the Bible." *MLA* 103 (1988): 117.

————, ed. *The Book and the Text: The Bible and Literary Theory.* Cambridge, Mass.: Basil Blackwell, 1990.

Seitz, Christopher. *Theology in Conflict: Reactions to Exile in the Book of Jeremiah.* New York De Gruyter, 1989.

————, ed. *Reading and Preaching the Book of Isaiah.* Philadelphia: Fortress Press, 1988.

Sellin, E. *Das Zwölfprophetenbuch²,³.* KAT no. 12. Leipzig: A. Deichertsche, 1929.

Sheppard, Gerald T. "True and False Prophecy within Scripture." In *Canon, Theology, and Old Testament Interpretation: Essays in Honor of Brevard S. Childs,* ed. Gene M. Tucker, David L. Petersen, and Robert R. Wilson. Philadelphia: Fortress Press, 1988.

Showalter, Elaine, ed. *The New Feminist Criticism: Essays on Women, Literature, and Theory.* New York: Pantheon Books, 1985.

Smart, James. *The Past, Present, and Future of Biblical Theology.* Philadelphia: Westminster Press, 1979.

Smith, Barbara Herrnstein. "Contingencies of Value." *CI* 10:1 (1983): 1–35.

Smith, G. A. *The Book of Isaiah.* The Expositor's Bible. 2d ed. London: Hodder & Stoughton, 1889.

Smith, John M. P. *A Critical and Exegetical Commentary on Micah, Zephaniah, Nahum, Habakkuk, Obadiah, and Joel.* ICC. New York: Scribner's, 1911.

Smith, Jonathan Z. *Imagining Religion: From Babylon to Jonestown.* Chicago: University of Chicago Press, 1982.

————. *Map Is Not Territory: Studies in the History of Religions.* Leiden: Brill, 1978.

Smith, Morton. *Palestinian Parties and Politics That Shaped the Old Testament.* 2d ed. London: SCM Press, 1987.

Smith, Wilfred Cantwell. "Scripture as Form and Concept: Their Emergence for the Western World." In *Rethinking Scripture: Essays from a Comparative Perspective,* ed. Miriam Levering. New York: State University of New York Press, 1989.

————. "The Study of Religion and the Study of the Bible." In *Rethinking Scripture: Essays from a Comparative Perspective,* ed. Miriam Levering. New York: State University of New York Press, 1989.

————. *What Is Scripture?: A Comparative Approach.* Minneapolis: Fortress Press, 1993.

Stammer, Larry. "Meeting of World Religions Leads to Ethics Rules." *Los Angeles Times,* 5 September 1993, A1, A31.

Steinmetz, David. "The Superiority of Pre-critical Exegesis." *TToday* 37:1 (April 1980): 27–38.

Stendahl, Krister. "Biblical Theology." In *The Interpreter's Dictionary of the Bible,* ed. George A. Buttrick. Nashville: Abingdon, 1962.

Sternberg, Meir. *The Poetics of Biblical Narrative: Ideological Literature and the Drama of Reading.* Bloomington: Indiana University Press, 1986.

Stuart, Douglas. *Hosea–Jonah.* WBC no. 31. Waco, Tex.: Word Books, 1987.

Suchocki, Marjorie. *The Fall to Violence: Original Sin in Relational Theology.* New York: Continuum, 1995.

Suleiman, Susan, and Inge Crosman, eds. *The Reader in the Text: Essays on Audience and Interpretation.* Princeton: Princeton University Press, 1980.

Swartley, Willard M. *Slavery, Sabbath, War, and Women: Case Issues in Biblical Interpretation.* Scottdale, Pa: Herald Press, 1982.

Sweeney, Marvin. *Isaiah 1–4 and the Post-Exilic Understanding of the Isaianic Traditions.* BZAW no. 171. Berlin : De Gruyter, 1988.

Taylor, Charles. *The Ethics of Authenticity.* Cambridge: Harvard University Press, 1992.

———. *Philosophical Papers, I: Human Agency and Language.* Cambridge: Harvard University Press, 1985.

———. *Sources of the Self: The Making of the Modern Identity.* Cambridge: Harvard University Press, 1989.

Taylor, Mark. *Deconstruction in Context: Literarily and Philosophically.* Chicago: University of Chicago Press, 1986.

Terrien, Samuel. *The Elusive Presence.* Religious Perspectives no. 26. New York: Harper & Row, 1978.

Thomas, Robert L., ed. *The NIV Harmony of the Gospels, with Explanations and Essays Using the Text of the NIV.* San Francisco: Harper & Row, 1988.

Tompkins, Jane P., ed. *Reader-Response Criticism: From Formalism to Post Structuralism.* Baltimore: Johns Hopkins University Press, 1980.

Toynbee, Arnold. *A Study of History.* 10 Vols. London: Oxford University Press, 1947.

Tracey, David. *Plurality and Ambiguity: Hermeneutics, Religion, and Hope.* San Francisco: Harper & Row, 1987.

Trible, Phyllis. "Journey of a Metaphor." In *God and the Rhetoric of Sexuality.* Philadelphia: Fortress Press, 1978.

Tucker, Gene M., David L. Petersen, and Robert R. Wilson. *Canon, Theology, and Old Testament Interpretation: Essays in Honor of Brevard S. Childs.* Philadelphia: Fortress Press, 1988.

Ulrich, Eugene. "Double Literary Editions of Biblical Narratives and Reflections on Determining the Form to Be Translated." *Pers* 15 (1988): 101–116.

Van der Woude, Adam S. "Micah IV 1–5: An Instance of the Pseudo-Prophets Quoting Isaiah." In *Symbolae Biblicae et Mesopotamicae Francisco Mario Theodoro de Liagre Boehl Dedicatae,* ed. M. A. Beek et al. Leiden: Brill, 1973.

———. "Micah in Dispute with the Pseudo-prophets." *VT* 19 (1969): 244–260.

Vermes, Geza. "The Bible and Midrash: Early Old Testament Exegesis." In *The Cambridge History of the Bible: From the Beginnings to Jerome,* ed. P. R. Ackroyd and C. F. Evans. Cambridge: Cambridge University Press, 1970.

Vermeylen, J. *Du prophète Isaïe a l'apocalyptique: Isaïe, i–xxxv, miroir d'un demimilleraire d'experience religieuse en Israel.* Paris: Loocoffre, 1977.

Von Hallberg, Robert, ed. *Canons.* Special edition of *CI* 10:1 (September 1983).

Von Rad, Gerhard. "The City on the Hill." In *The Problem of the Hexateuch: and other Essays,* trans. Trueman Dicken. New York: McGraw, 1966

———. :Die falschen Propheten." *ZAW* 51 (1933): 109–120.

———. *Der Heilige Krieg im alten Israel.* Göttingen: Vandenhoeck & Ruprecht, 1958. *Holy War in Ancient Israel.* Trans. Marva J. Dawn. Grand Rapids: Eerdmans, 1991.

———. *The Message of the Prophets.* New York: Harper & Row, 1965.

———. *Old Testament Theology.* Vol. 2. New York: Harper & Row, 1965.

———. "The Origin of the Concept of the Day of Yahweh." *JSS* 4:2 (April 1959): 97–108.

———. "Die Stadt auf dem Berge." *EvT* 9 (1948–49): 439–447. Reprinted in *Gesammelte Studien zum Alten Testament.* TBu no. 11. Munich: Chr. Kaiser, 1958.

Vriezen, T. C. "Essentials of the Theology of Isaiah." In *An Outline of Old Testament Theology,* trans. S. Neuijen. Oxford: Basil Blackwell, 1958.

Wade, G. *The Books of the Prophets Micah, Obadiah, Joel, and Jonah.* London: Methuen , 1925.

Wallace, Mark I. *The Second Naiveté: Barth, Ricoeur, and the New Yale Theology.* SABH No. 6. Macon, Ga.: Mercer University Press, 1990.

Watts, J. D. W. *Isaiah 1–33.* WBC No. 24. Waco, Tex.: Word Books, 1985.

Waugh, Patricia, ed. *Postmodernism: A Reader.* London: Edward Arnold of Hodder & Stoughton, 1992.

Weber, Max. *Wirtschaft und Gesellschaft.* 1922. Reprint. Tübingen: J. C. B. Mohr, 1975.

Weidd, M. "The Origin of the 'Day of the Lord'—Reconsidered." *HUCA* 37 (1966): 29–60.

Weil, Simone. "The Iliad, or the Poem of Force." In *Revisions: Changing Perspectives in Moral Philosophy,* ed. Stanley Hauerwas and Alasdair MacIntyre. Notre Dame: University of Notre Dame Press, 1983.

Westermann, Claus. *Basic Forms of Prophetic Speech.* Trans. Hugh C. White. Philadelphia: Westminster Press, 1967.

———. *Elements of Old Testament Theology.* Atlanta: John Knox Press, 1982.

———. *What Does the Old Testament Say about God?* Atlanta: John Knox Press, 1979.

Westphal, Merold. *God, Guilt, and Death.* Bloomington: Indiana University Press, 1987.

Whedbee, J. William. *Isaiah and Wisdom.* Nashville: Abingdon Press, 1971.

———. "Why Read the Bible in a Post-Modern World: Difficulties, Dilemmas, and Dialogues." Speech delivered in Claremont, California, 1993. TMs (photocopy).

White, Hayden. *Metahistory: The Historical Imagination in nineteenth Century Europe.* Baltimore: Johns Hopkins University Press, 1975.

Wicker, Brian. *The Story Shaped World: Fiction and Metaphysics*. Notre Dame: University of Notre Dame Press, 1975.

Widengren, G. *The Literary and Psychological Aspects of the Hebrew Prophets*. Uppsala: Lundequistska Bokhandeln, 1948.

———. "The Persian Period." In *Israelite and Judean History*, ed. J. H. Hayes and J. M. Miller. Philadelphia: Fortress Press, 1977.

Wiesel, Elie. *Messengers of God*. New York: Random House, 1976.

Wildavsky, Aaron. "Equity versus Hierarchy: A Speculation on the Survival of the Jewish People." In *The Nursing Father: Moses as a Political Leader*. University: University of Alabama Press, 1984.

Wildberger, Hans. *Isaiah 1–12*. Minneapolis: Fortress Press, 1991.

———. *Jesaja*. BZAK, vol. 10, no. 1. Netherlands: Neukirchener Verlag, 1972. *Isaiah 1–12*. Trans. Thomas H. Trapp. Minneapolis: Fortress Press, 1991.

———. "Die Völkerwallfahrt zum Zion: Jes. II 1–5." *VT* 7 (1957): 62–81.

Williams, J. G. Review of *Prophetic Conflict: Its Effect upon Israelite Religion*, by James Crenshaw. In *JBL* 91 (1972): 402–404.

Wilson, Robert R. *Prophecy and Society in Ancient Israel*. Philadelphia: Fortress Press, 1980.

Wimsatt, William, and Monroe Beardsley. "The Affective Fallacy and The Intentional Fallacy." In *The Verbal Icon: Studies in the Meaning of Poetry*. Lexington: Universit of Kentucky Press, 1954.

———. "The Intentional Fallacy." In *The Verbal Icon: Studies in the Meaning of Poetry*. Lexington: University of Kentucky Press, 1954.

Winders, James. *Gender, Theory, and the Canon*. Madison: University of Wisconsin Press, 1991.

Wittgenstein, Ludwig. *Philosophical Investigations*. 3d ed. Trans. G. E. M. Anscombe. New York: Macmillan, 1971.

Wolff, Hans Walter. *Joel and Amos: A Commentary on the Books of the Prophets Joel and Amos*. Trans. Waldemar Janzen, S. Dean McBride, and Charles Muenchow. Hermeneia. Philadelphia: Fortress Press, 1977. Original German, *Dodekapropheten 2 Joel und Amos*. BKAT, vol. 14, no. 2. Neukirchen-Vluyn: Neukirchen Verlag, 1969.

———. *Micah: A Commentary*. Trans. Gary Stansell. Minneapolis: Augsburg Press, 1990 Original German, *Micha* BKAT. Neukirchen-Vluyn: Neukirchen Verlag, 1982.

———. *Micah the Prophet*. Trans. Ralph Gehrke. Philadelphia: Fortress Press, 1981. German edition, *Mit Micha reden: Prophetie einst und jetzt*. Munich: Chr. Kaiser Verlag, 1978.

———. "Prophecy from the Eighth through the Fifth Century." Trans. Sibley Towner with Joy Heebink. *Int* 32 (1978): 17–30.

———. "Swords into Plowshares: A Misuse of Biblical Prophecy?" *CTM* 12 (1985): 134.

———. "The Understanding of History in the Old Testament Prophets." In *Essays on Old Testament Hermeneutics*, ed. Claus Westermann. Richmond: John Knox Press, 1963. Original German, *EvT* 20 (1960): 218–235.

Wright, G. Ernest. *The Book of Isaiah*. Layman's Bible Commentary no. 11. Richmond: John Knox Press, 1964.

———. *God Who Acts: Biblical Theology as Recital*. Chicago: Henry Regnery, 1952.

———. *The Old Testament and Theology*. San Francisco: Harper & Row, 1969.

Yoder, John H. "The Authority of the Canon." In *Essays on Biblical Interpretation: Anabaptist-Mennonite Perspectives,* ed. Willard M. Swartley. Text-Reader Series no. 1. Elkhart, Ind.: Instute of Mennonite Studies, 1984.

———. *Body Politics: Five Practices of the Christian Community Before the Watching World*. Nashville: Discipleship Resources, 1989.

———. "On Not Being Ashamed of the Gospel: Particularity, Pluralism, and Validation." *Faith and Philosophy* 9:3 (July 1992): 285–300.

———. *The Politics of Jesus*. Grand Rapids: Eerdmans, 1972.

———. *The Priestly Kingdom: Social Ethics as Gospel*. Notre Dame: University of Notre Dame Press, 1984.

Zimmerli, W. *The Law and the Prophets*. Trans. R. E. Clements. Oxford: Basil Blackwell, 1965.

———. "Der Wahrheitserweis Jahwes nach der Botschaft der beiden Exilspropheten." In *Tradition und Situation: Festschrift A. Weiser,* ed. E. Wurthwein and W. Kaiser. Göttingen: Vandenhoeck Ruprecht, 1963.

Index

Abrams, M. H., 37, 155 n.56, 157
   n.25
Ackroyd, Peter, 188 n.47
Acts, Book of, 145
Adams, Hazard, 71–73
adjudication, 84, 173 n.1
advocacy, principle of, 97–98, 109, 139
   to avoid totalizing discourse, 104
   in choosing between Joel and Isaiah,
      134, 147
   to conserve ethic of canon, 135
aesthetics
   antithetical, 72, 78
   autonomy of, 58
   historical, 157 n.25
   of reception, 31
   theological, 78
Ahaz, 119–124, 127, 189 n.47
Altieri, Charles, 72–73
Anabaptists, 15, 49, 143, 144
anarchy
   in all claims to truth, 137
   biblical canon as reservoir of, 142
   confession as alternative to, 105
   as nonviolent repudiation of author-
      ity, 142, 194 n.6
   as situation between canons, 56, 75,
      104, 182 n.89
   temporary restraint to, 106

Anderson, Bernard, 164 n.29
apographs, textual, 62
archaeology
   of knowledge, 44
   of text, 32
Armstrong, Paul B., 102–106
"as," as copula of imagination, 177
   n.44
   as canon, 102, 107
   as Scripture, 97, 102, 107, 145,
      147
audience reception, 113, 117, 120,
      126, 128–130
authority, 4
   of canon, 137
      adaptability as key to, 25
      communally determined, 6, 46, 60,
         75, 90
      derived from its performance, 7
      questions of, 52, 74
   of communal memory, 108
   crisis of, 16
   ethical performance as, 140
   of interpretive community, 39–40,
      42, 140, 142
   1960s watershed, 54–55
   of Scripture (Bible), 102, 140
   of text/words, 39, 79
autographs, textual, 62

Bailie, Gil, 79
Barr, James, 65–67, 78, 164 n.29, 165
     n.35
Barthes, Roland, 24
Barton, John, 158 n.25
Beardsley, Monroe, 159 n.39
Beauvoir, Simone de, 103
beit midrash, 106, 141
"better" saying (Proverbs), 44, 94
Bible, as divine, 68
biblical theology, 147, 181 n.84
     in crisis, 59
     movement, 86
Bleich, David, 42, 163 n.13
Blenkinsopp, Joseph, 69, 108
Bloch, Reneé, 22
Bloom, Harold
     and the anxiety of influence, 40
     on the autonomy of the reader, 41
     on canon as battlefield of power, 72
     and irreducible autonomy of the
          aesthetic, vii, 41, 53, 58, 68
     as literary subjectivist, 37
     and the Western canon, 58
Booth, Wayne C., 37
Boyarin, Daniel, 13, 21, 23
Brown, Schuyler, 47, 160 n.58
Brueggemann, Walter, 54, 64, 178
     n.44, 181 n.84, 184 n.11
Bruns, Gerald, 70, 106
Bryant, David, 178 n.44
Buber, Martin, 175 n.13

Calvin, John, 49
canon(s), 60, 165 nn.39–40
     closure of biblical, 61, 141, 166 n.48
     in conflict, 4, 80
     demise of, 59–64
     as democracy of words, 140
     ethic of, 93
     final form, 66, 89, 144
     force of, 88, 132, 135
     formation, 5, 6
          dialectical process of, 31
          ethical gravity in, 93
          intense periods of, 79, 139
          reversing standard account of, 7,
               70
     as function, 102

Dead Sea scrolls invoke shift to,
     17, 62
     effects on Jewish/Christian dia-
          logue, 138
     at end of modernity, 76
     and history, 45
     in literature, 63
     requires prophetic risk, 134, 141
     and identity formation, 65
     literary, 63, 165 n.39, 167 n.58
     as "mere" literature, 7, 79, 140
     of modernity, 56
     multiple biblical, 61, 166 n.48
     multiple classical, 52–53
     multiple ecclesial, 36
     ontology of, 64
     as paradigm
          ethical demand of, 8, 75
          language system and, 26
          as model for nonviolent practice,
               139, 145
          as unifying construct of reality, 16,
               21, 77–78
     and pluralism, 65, 67
     politics of, 93–95, 102–110
          in defining literary canons, 63, 167
               nn.57–58
          insists on principle of advocacy,
               134
          invites hearing of all readings, 119,
               144
     of a postmodern world, 56
     as shape/content, 17, 62–63, 102,
          134
     survival of, 68
     ur-, 59, 62
     as vehicle of survival, 122
     Western, vii, viii, 41, 58
canonical autonomy, 46
canonical conversation, 109
canonical criticism
     as a constructive discipline, 76
     emergence of, 15–16, 29, 34, 65,
          137
     as model for adjudicating truth
          claims, 110, 139
     response to Knierim's critique of, 93
canonical habit of mind, 33, 60, 168
     n.62

canonical hermeneutics, 16, 87–89
canonical process
  authoritative function of, 79, 144
  as literary history, 33
  as method, 16, 75
  prior to canonical closure, 23
  use of text, 26
canon-maker(s), modern, 66
Capra, Fritjof, 104
Carr, David, 188 n.44
Carroll, Robert P., 110, 191 n.71
Childs, Brevard
  Christocentric biblical theology, 195
    n.14
  on crisis in biblical theology, 15, 59,
    150 n.9, 164 n.29
  critique of historical-critical method,
    170 n.70
  against James Barr, 65–67, 156
    n.11
  on Micah, 17, 150 n.11
  on true and false prophecy, 87–91
  and Wolfgang Iser, 36
Chomsky, Noam, 39
Chronicles, Books of, 119
community
  believing, 142
  canonical status of, 49
  as canon-maker, 46, 80, 139
  of coherence, 108
  of discourse, 113
  of interpretation, 38–43
    canonical autonomy of, viii, 137
    as political entity, 102
    remembering as a means to judge
      prophecy, 109
    text and reader situated in, 26, 47
    over text in meaning production,
      49
    as transmitter of tradition, 139
  irreducibility of, 54
  of memory, 109, 139, 143
  over reader(s), 140
  reading, 42, 83, 105, 137, 141
  as relational ethos, 6
  over Scripture, 6, 46, 90, 140
  voluntary, 139
comparative midrash, 22, 33, 114, 168
    n.62, 183 n.3

concretization, act of, 36–37
confessional claims
  as alternative to anarchy, 105
  and author's believing community,
    142, 144
  in biblical theology (Childs), 195
    n.14
  as "ground" of every construct, 67,
    75, 83, 90
  not being ashamed of, 99, 136
Constantinian worldview. *See* epis-
    temology: establishment
constitutive support, hermeneutic of,
    73, 87
  in canon politics, 108
  or hermeneutic of commitment, 78
  or hermeneutic of trust, 105
  post-exilic reading of Isaiah, 124,
    125
  pre-exilic reading of Zion tradition,
    117, 131
construction
  literary act of, 16, 36
  of meaning, 43
contradiction
  in Bible, 13
  epistemological advantage of, 103
  as nature of reality, 16, 25
conventions, reading, 40
Coote, Mary, 69–71
Coote, Robert, 69–71
1 Corinthians, "rule of Paul," 48–49
Crenshaw, James, 86
Crews, F. C., 37

Day of Yahweh, 7, 115–116, 128
Dead Sea scrolls (Qumran), 17, 61–62,
    166 nn.42, 48, 194 n.104
deconstruction
  of canon's own canonicity, 76
  as literary school, 6
de Man, Paul, 37
Derrida, Jacques, 19, 21, 23, 26, 37,
    171 n.92
de Saussure, F. *See* Saussure, Ferdinand
    de
determinate text. *See* text, stable
deuteronomist(ic), 125, 175 n.12
Deuteronomy, 6, 122

diachronic (historical) reading(s)
   to account for ethical force of text, 8
   in canonical criticism, 44
   and contingent rules of discourse, 45
   Dead Sea scrolls as model of, 61
   and literary history, 32–33
   meaning derived in context of, 26
   necessary for fully contextual exe-
      gesis, 111
   of plowshare passages, 112, 118–
      132, 140
Dilthey, Wilhelm, 24
discourse
   language as, 26, 54
   rules of, 43–45
Duhm, B., 127
dynamic analogy, 88–89, 91–92, 134,
   140

Eagleton, Terry, 164 n.27
Ecclesiastes, 95
eisegesis, 37, 113
Ellul, Jacques, 194 n.6
Enlightenment, standard story of, 96
Ephesians, Book of, 145
epistemology
   conflictual, 103
   contestable, 139
   establishment, 100, 145
   foundational, 54
   idealist-deductive, 95
   nonfoundational, 5, 163 n.13
   positivist-inductive, 95
ethics
   of mythos, 95
   narrative-based, 94
   over ontology, 93
   as way of life, 7, 93, 108, 137–
      138
exegesis
   vs. eisegesis, 37, 48
   fully contextual, 33, 101, 111
   inner-biblical, 22
   newly defined, 25, 35
   objective, 113
exile, 46, 77, 79, 139, 140
Exodus, Book of, 50, 97, 116, 128
Ezekiel, 128–129, 145
Ezra/Nehemiah, 124, 129

"facts," constructed, 55
fallibility, principle of, 97, 109, 135,
   178 n.49
false prophecy, 85. *See also* true and
      false prophecy, criteria of
   Joel 4:1–17 as, 141
Fiorenza, E. Schussler, 184 n.11
Fiorenza, Francis, 56–57
First Commandment (Exodus 20:3),
   50
Fish, Stanley, 37–43, 71–72, 143, 169
   n.66
Fishbane, Michael, 184 n.11, 194
   n.109
   on evaluating fragment texts, 132
   idealistic ideologies, 78
   inner-biblical exegesis, 22
   pilgrimage to mythic center, 146
   on theological kernel, 173 n.111
Foucault, Michel
   on determinism, 71–72
   on history, 44–45
   on "local knowledge," 162 n.12
   as radical historicist, 171 n.92
   relating knowledge and power, 103
   on rules of discourse, 43
   on truth, 45, 98
Frei, Hans, 150 n.9, 156 n.6, 177 n.43
Frye, Northrop, 21
function, textual, 26

Gadamer, Hans-Georg, 21, 31
Gates, Henry, 68
Genesis
   chapters 1 and 2, 6, 146, 194 n.108
   chapter 11, 196 n.22
   chapter 22, 78
Gestalt
   reading process, 35
   tradition, 114–116, 140, 142
Girard, René, 18, 79, 150 n.24
God
   as Creator, 133, 194 n.108
   as Redeemer, 133, 194 n.108
   Yahweh as warrior, 129, 133
God, the One
   canon and, 7, 76–78, 146
   as compressed history of the gods,
      97–98

as ethic of love, 138
pluralism ultimately restrained by, 88, 103, 107–108, 139
Gorak, Jan, 5, 67, 76, 161 n.3, 165 n.40, 170 n.76
Green, Garrett, 177 n.44
Gunkel, Hermann, 86, 116–117

Habel, Norman, 155 n.4
Hananiah, 85, 92
Hanson, Paul D., 182 n.84
Hatch, Nathan, 49
Hauerwas, Stanley, 49, 96, 172 n.104, 178 n.50
Havel, Vaclav, 4, 71
Hayes, John H., 189 n.47, 190 n.56
Hebrews, Book of, 146
Heidegger, Martin, 18, 21, 24
hermeneutic(s)
    Christocentric, 144
    of commitment/trust. *See* constitutive support, hermeneutic of
    community, 27. *See also* community: of interpretation
    constructive, 57
    continuum, 32–33, 133–134
    crisis of, 56
    hermeneutical circle, 56, 95
    of suspicion. *See* prophetic critique, hermeneutic of
    totalizing, 7, 77–78, 94, 98, 103, 172 n.109
    triangle
        in two dimensions, 56, 87, 151 n.13
        in three dimensions, 57, 88, 101, 111, 151 n.13
        unrecorded, 33, 44
Heschel, Abraham, 190 n.61
Hezekiah, 119–124, 127, 189 n.47
hierarchy, 70, 76–77, 104
Hirsch, E. D., 31, 37, 155 n.56, 174 n.1
historicism (historicist), 34, 66, 69, 78, 171 n.92
history
    compressed, 132
    literary, 31, 32, 114
    (re)constructed, 113, 123

Holland, Norman, 160 n.58
Holy War, 115–116, 128
horizon(s)
    of expectation, 32, 34, 44
    fusion of, 25, 31, 33

imagination
    ethical force of, 69, 71, 73, 78, 141, 177 n.44
    prophetic, 108, 142
in contra dictus, viii, 5, 20, 25, 42, 137, 146. *See also* contradiction
inspiration, 47, 68
Integrity of Reality, 77, 103, 144
intention, authorial, 43
intertextuality
    and (con)text, 20–21
    of midrash, 23
    and process, 21–23
    and reader, 24–25
    and reality, 18
    and syntax, 18–20
Irvine, Stuart, 189 n.47, 190 n.56
Isaiah, Book of
    on the efficacy of Yahweh's word (chaps. 40, 45), 145, 147
    plowshare oracle (2:2–4, 5), viii, 13, 147
        diachronic readings of, 118–125, 131
        methodology for reading, 111–112
        poem based on, 147
        synchronic reading of, 132–135
        textual differences with Micah, 191 n.75
        Yahweh as final arbiter, 9
Isaiah, the prophet, 85, 117, 145
Iser, Wolfgang, 34–38, 114

Jamnia, Council of, 61
Jauss, Hans R., 23, 30–34, 56–57, 114, 157 nn.12, 25
Jeremiah, 47, 85, 91–92
    competing for recognition, 104, 145
    as criterion for judging prophets, 91
Joel, Book of, plowshare oracle (4:9–17), 13, 135, 147
    diachronic readings of, 127–131
    as "false" prophecy, 141–142

Joel, Book of, plowshare oracle
(*continued*)
methodology for reading, 111–112
synchronic reading of, 132
Joel, the prophet, 117
John, Book of, 146
Joshua, Book of, 46, 79, 116, 140
Josiah, 122
Judaism, post-exilic, 125
Judges, Book of, 116, 128

Kadushin, Max, 104
kairos, 127
Kaufman, Gordon, 162 n.8, 172
n.109, 179 n.61
Kermode, Frank, 65, 67–68, 169
n.67
Kim, Wonil, 176 n.30
Kings, Books of, 85, 119–120, 129
Knierim, Rolf, 40, 93–95, 184 n.11,
190 n.61
Knight, Douglas, 114
knowledge, "local," 162 n.12
Koch, Klaus, 86, 123
Kraus, C. Norman, 195 n.15
Kristeva, Julia, 18
Kugel, James, 40, 138
Kuhn, Thomas, 55, 157 n.25, 162
n.10

Landes, George M., 164 n.29
language
function of (word as deed), 123,
138
nonreferential, 20
referential, 34, 54
system, unified and different, 21
Lash, Nicholas, 98
Lentricchia, Frank, 159 n.53
Lessing, G., 99, 102
Levenson, John, 138
Levering, Miriam, 169 n.63
Levinas, Emmanuel, 93, 103, 172
n.109, 195 n.11
Levi-Strauss, Claude, 21
Lewis, I. M., 91
Lind, Millard, 116–117, 121
linguistic competency, 39
linguistic turn, 17, 21

literary criticism, 42
classification of critical theories, 157
n.25
crises in, 57–58
Luke, Book of, 145
Luther, Martin, 49

magisterium of Roman Catholic
Church, 48
Man, Paul de. *See* de Man, Paul
Martin, Helmut, 169 n.63
Masoretic tradition (text), 61, 90
Matthew, Book of, 143
Mauchline, J., 189 n.55
McClendon, James
defining postmodern theologies, 162
n.9
on narrative-based truth, 95, 101,
178 n.50
on narrative ethics, 172 n.104
on persuasion as seeking assent,
103
on the principle of fallibility, 97
McKnight, Edgar, 30
meaning
community-determined, 6, 36, 47
constructed, 144
determinate, 25
inherent in text, 5, 32, 34–35, 39–40
as transitory cultural construct, 26
metahistory, 123
method, comparative, 113
Micah, Book of, plowshare oracle (4:1–
5), viii, 13
diachronic readings of, 125–127,
130–132
methodology for reading, 111–112
revolutionary coda (v. 5), 118, 146
synchronic reading of, 132–134
textual differences from Isaiah, 191
n.75
Micah, the prophet, 85, 117
Miles, Jack, 177 n.43, 178 n.45
modernity, 5, 6, 161 n.7
end of, 53, 68, 75–76, 162 n.8
foundational logocentrism of, 146
monotheizing hermeneutic (process),
76–78
as paradigm for postmodern living, 6

relative to ethical considerations, 138,
143–144, 172 n.104, 173
n.111, 179 n.61
as theocentric acceptance of pluralism, 33
as totalizing hermeneutic, 98
as a transsubjective horizon, 34
unifying function of, 67, 88
moralizing, 98, 172 n.104
Muilenburg, James, 29, 155 n.4
Murphy, Nancey, 54, 162 n.9
Murphy, Roland E., 166 n.48
mythos, 7, 93–94, 138

negotiation
communal, 73–74, 79–80
of conflicting texts, 48
of conflicting truth claims, 48
of web of convictions, 106
ethics of, 138
Neusner, Jacob, 50, 168 n.63
neutrality, claims of, 95
New Criticism, 20, 29, 35, 66
Nietzsche, Friedrich, 4, 73, 83, 110
nonviolence
and ethic of canon, ix, 7–8
as negotiating stance, 79, 106, 139,
142
as reading strategy, 102
norm, transcendent, 137
norma normans. *See* canon: as function
norma normata. *See* canon: as shape/
content
Numbers, Book of, 21

objective claims
in exegetical method, 40
to knowledge and "facts," 55
as learned constructions, 42
limited by horizons of expectation,
32–34
origins as key to, 31
orthodoxy of historical critics, 14,
66
reading strategies made vulnerable
by, 38–39
textual determinacy and, 40, 47
of universality and neutrality, 26, 39,
95, 99

Ollenburger, Ben C., 185 nn.22, 25
original intention, meaning found in,
20, 31
"original" readings, 113, 118

Parliament of World Religions, 138,
144
particularity
of all truth claims, 98–100, 144, 179
n.61
better politics of, 110
debate as check to radical, 107, 139
scandal of, 93, 99
Patte, Daniel, 47
peace, universal coexistence, 133
persuasion
canons defended by, 75
Joel protected by ethic of, 142
martyrdom as supreme act of, 143
metacommentary as, 188 n.45
methodological assumption of author, 136
as negotiating stance of biblical
canon, 7, 98, 146–147
Plato's political philosophy of, 80
as political defense of all truth claims,
103, 146
as rhetorical method of prophet, 99,
115, 134, 145
scientific paradigms require, 55
scriptural authority depends on, 50
as task of (literary) criticism, 42–43,
92–93
1 Peter, 50
Peterson, David, 91
Piaget, Jean, 42
Plato, 3, 9, 80, 161 n.7
plowshare passages, 112, 115. *See also*
Isaiah, Book of: plowshare oracle; Joel, Book of, plowshare
oracle; Micah, Book of, plowshare oracle
reading summary, 131
summary of diachronic readings of,
130–132
synchronic reading of, 132–133
pluralism
balancing radical, 107, 139
cultural and social, 74

pluralism (*continued*)
  in language, 5
  textual, 37
politics of canon. *See* canon: politics of
polytheism, 75, 77, 98
postmodernity
  biblical canon as life paradigm in, 6
  crises on horizon of, 53–59, 74
  exegesis through lens of, 48
  heuristic benefit and limits to desig-
    nation, 161 n.7
  historical markers of, viii, 162 n.9
  horizon of canonical criticism, 17,
    137
  requires new canons, vii, 5
  rhetorical nonfoundationalism in,
    146
Powell, Mark A., 155 nn.4, 57
power, 69
  aesthetic, 69
  hermeneutic, 103
  historical, 69
  and knowledge, 55
  literary force and, 7, 17
  power-authority sequence, 47
  power contrary to, 70–72
  rhetorical, 112, 123
  self-imposed limits to, 73
  use of, 4, 69, 139
  will to, 69–70, 73
Prinsloo, Willem, 128
prophet(s), 85
  as agent of direction, 108, 134
  authority of, 123
  as second part of canon, 79
prophetic conflict, 137
prophetic critique, hermeneutic of
  canonical criticism and, 87
  as challenge to Ahaz, Hezekiah, and
    some post-exilic readers, 121,
    125
  groups advocating change, 105
  and hermeneutic of suspicion, 73, 78
  against Joel by author, 147
  summary of diachronic readings, 131
Proverbs. *See* "better" saying
Psalms, 40
  Zion tradition, 115, 121
pseudoprophetes, 85

"public" criterion, 101
"public" meaning, 100

Quell, Gottfried, 85
Quine, Willard V., 55, 104
Qumran. *See* Dead Sea scrolls

rationality of narrative form, 96
reader, informed (competent), 39
reader response, viii, 23, 29–30, 34,
    44, 156 n.7
reading(s)
  act of, 35, 43
  conflicting, 83
  normative, 100
  pre-critical, 89
  post-exilic, of Isaiah, 122–125
  pre-exilic, of Isaiah, 119–122
realpolitik, 119, 121, 123, 127, 139
Revelation, Book of, 144, 146–147,
    196 n.20
rhetorical criticism, 29, 155 n.4
Ricoeur, Paul, 24, 26, 174 n.1
Robertson, David, 155 n.4
Roman Catholic Church, 49
Rosen, Stanley, 161 n.7
Ryle, H. E., 60–61

sacred violence, 79, 141
Samuel, Books of, 115–116
Sanders, James A.
  "antithetical persuasion" and, 72
  compared to Childs, 150 nn.9–11
  counters Barr's critique, 165 n.35
  epistemology of, 95–96
  and F. Fiorenza on the hermeneutic
    triangle, 56
  Fish as corrective to Iser and, 38, 47
  and Foucault, 44–45
  founder of canonical criticism, 4, 15–
    16, 156 n.9
  and the historicist/aesthetic debate,
    65, 67–68
  and intertextuality, 13, 23
  and Iser, 36–38
  and Jauss's literary historiography,
    32–34, 38
  and Kermode as *via media*, 65, 67–
    68

monotheizing process of, 76
ontology of, 103
and the principle of fallibility, 178 n.49
theologizing hermeneutic, viii, 172 n.104
and true and false prophecy, 87–91
on use of term "canon," 53
Sandmel, Samuel, 166 n.48
Saussure, Ferdinand de, 18, 21, 23, 25
Schleiermacher, Friedrich, 21, 24
Schwartz, Regina, 63
science, disunity of, 54, 163 n.13
Scripture(s), 50, 172 n.107
canon of, 144
Christian, 144
comparative, 168–169 n.63
Seitz, Christopher, 180 n.70, 189 n.47, 190 n.57
self-correcting system(s)
of Bible as canon, 7, 33–34, 134, 142
God's power qualified in, 78, 98
in Jauss's literary history, 32, 34
juxtaposition of conflicting stories as, 106
text-reader relation as, 35
Sheppard, Gerald, 14, 87, 91–93
Simons, Menno, 143
Smart, James, 163 n.29
Smith, Barbara H., 174 n.1
Smith, Jonathan Z., 5, 169 n.63
Smith, Wilfred C., 50, 63, 170 n.72, 172 n.107
sociology of knowledge, 55
sola scriptura, 15–16, 49
Spirit of Yahweh (God), 85, 123
Stendahl, Krister, 30
story
Bible (biblical canon) as, 28, 46, 69–97, 139, 155 n.1, 177 n.43
establishment, 102
ethical force of, 7, 95, 97, 132, 143
as knowledge, 95
rationality of, 107, 138
Torah as, 79
structuralism, 19, 29
subjectivists in literary circle, 37
subjectivity, 31, 38–39, 42

Suchocki, Marjorie, 152 n.24
Sundberg, Albert, 166 n.48
Sweeny, Marvin, 124, 188 n.45, 190 nn.64–65
synchronic (literary) readings
balance to diachronic readings, 32–33, 45
evidenced at Qumran, 61
hermeneutic benefit of, 8, 111
intertextuality as context in, 20–21
meaning derived from, 26
methodological commitment, 112
of plowshare passages, 132–133
systems "tree," 104

text(s)
adaptable (indeterminate), 36–38
criticism, 36, 62
divine status of, 47, 50, 68
final form, 29–30
formal features of, 39–40
function of, 107
of terror, 141
text, stable (determinate)
as explanatory construct, viii, 6
and inherent textual meaning, vii, 40
intertextual nature defies, 26
and New Critical formalisms, 39
relatively speaking, 38
situated by communal norms, 103, 137
and text-as-artifact, 36–37
theologizing, 98, 172 n.104, 178 n.49
Torah
-Christ story, 99, 107
first part of canon, 79
oral, 48
-word, 115, 121, 123, 132, 147
totalitarian claims. *See* hermeneutic: totalizing
Tracey, David, 18, 26, 103
transsubjective horizon, 34
transtribal validation, 94, 100
true and false prophecy, criteria of
canonical hermeneutics provides, 87–88
character as supreme, 143
church's dogma determined, 15

true and false prophecy, criteria of
    (*continued*)
    and deciding between canonical
        prophets, 112
    function of community, 137
    historical-critical impasse, 15
    questions about, 8, 136
    and readers' context, 7, 107
    standard search for, 84–87
    story-formed, 101, 107
true and false prophecy, standard story
    of research, 7, 84–85
truth
    communally situated, 147
    narrative-dependent, 95, 99, 101,
        107
    in rhetorical discourse, 94
truth, politics of, 102–106
    of author, 142
    claim and counterclaim in prophecy,
        113
    of readers reading, 113
    strategies of community discourse,
        92, 98, 141

universality, claims of
    denied by canonical criticism, 137
    and objectivity, 26, 39
    and particularity, 99–102, 110, 179
        n.61
    of prophet, 92
    research in true and false prophecy as
        test of, 83–84
    textual restraints as means to, 26,
        39
    universality beyond one's own, 94

van der Woude, Adam S., 86, 125–
    127
Vermes, Geza, 22
von Rad, Gerhard, 85–86, 116, 175
    n.12, 176 n.19

vox populi. See audience recep-
    tion

war. *See also* Holy War
    rhetoric of, 3, 4
    universal, 133, 140
web, belief system as, 105
Weber, Max, 69, 182 n.89
Wellhausen, Julius, 85
Westermann, Claus, 181 n.84
Wiesel, Elie, 28
Wildavsky, Aaron, 104
Wilson, Robert, 91
Wimsatt, William, 159 n.39
Wink, Walter, 150 n.9
Wittgenstein, Ludwig, 18, 21
word(s)
    power of, 3, 145
    as rhetorical weapons, 3–4, 7, 80,
        147
Word(s) of Yahweh (God)
    claims of, heighten canonical conflict,
        140
    as criterion of true prophecy, 85
    history constructed by, 123
    and Isaiah's inclusive rhetoric, 141–
        142, 147
    as semiotic unifying construct, 145–
        146
    as weapon (sword), 3, 146
Wright, G. E., 164 n.29

Yoder, John H., 49, 99, 172 n.104,
    179 nn.59, 61

Zechariah, Book of, 128, 130
Zion tradition
    cluster of motifs defining, 115
    relative use (by Joel/Isaiah) of, 121,
        129–132, 141
    Sitz im Leben, 115–116, 120
Zwingli, Huldrych, 49